William Francis Butler

A Life 1838–1910

To the Memory of my Father

William Francis Butler
A Life 1838–1910

MARTIN RYAN

THE LILLIPUT PRESS
DUBLIN

First published 2003 by
THE LILLIPUT PRESS LTD
62–63 Sitric Road, Arbour Hill,
Dublin 7, Ireland
www.lilliputpress.ie

A CIP record for this title is available
from The British Library.

ISBN 1 84351 015 4

The Lilliput Press receives financial assistance from
An Chomhairle Ealaíon / The Arts Council of Ireland.

Set in 10.5 on 14 Hoefler Text by Marsha Swan
Printed in Ireland by ßetaprint of Dublin

CONTENTS

Preface and Acknowledgments vii

1 Roots 1

2 Gone for a Soldier 8

3 Canada and the Red River 19

4 Searching for a Road 35

5 The White Man's Grave 50

6 Southern Africa 66

7 'Your Life Is Still Before You' 80

8 The Egyptian Campaign and its Aftermath 93

9 The Gordon Relief Expedition 105

10 On the Sudan Frontier 121

11 The Campbell Divorce Case 133

12 Retrenchment and Renewal 150

13 The New South Africa 168

14 'The Central Storm Spot of the World' 178

15 New Horizons 192

16 Home 204

Epilogue 217

Notes and References 221

Sources 232

Select Bibliography 233

William Francis Butler: A Chronology 238

Index 240

ILLUSTRATIONS

Half-tones between pages 132 and 133

Map 1 Butler's Canadian Travels 1870-73   34
Map 2 The Asante Campaign 1873-74   65
Map 3 Wadi Halfa to Khartoum   132

PREFACE AND ACKNOWLEDGMENTS

When I was a boy I read avidly, and key scenes from classic adventure stories still tug at my imagination: Jim Hawkins crouching in the apple barrel on the deck of the *Hispaniola*; Tom Sawyer walking up the church aisle to confound the congregation mourning his apparent drowning; Robinson Crusoe finding a single footprint in the sand. However, nothing in fiction from those years had the impact of my first meeting with Red Cloud, the Oglala Sioux, as he rode into the novel of which he is the eponymous hero to greet the two young Irishmen who would become his companions in adventure on the American prairies. 'I am the last of my people', he told them – and me – 'the last of the Mandan branch of the Sioux race.' Since I first encountered *Red Cloud*, almost half a century ago, the figure of 'The Solitary Sioux', to use the subtitle of the novel, has stayed with me, at first simply as a boy's hero, later as a symbol of freedom and loss.

My copy of *Red Cloud* was a tattered school edition left lying about the house by an older brother, its red cover torn and defaced, its pages dog-eared. Its provenance was of no interest to me as a boy. It was not until my twenties, when I came across an Irish translation of the novel, *Neall Dearg*, on a second-hand bookstall, that I became curious about the Victorian adventurer, author and military man, Sir William Francis Butler, whose work had become a school text in the Irish Free State, but about whom in the 1960s information was scarce and interest almost non-existent.

Butler died at his Tipperary home in 1910. In the decades that followed, the world he represented disappeared. In 1951 Sir Shane Leslie, in his *Salutation to Five*, said of Butler: 'His memory has received bitter scorn and derision. Let this essay prove the beginning of a vindication.' Leslie, however, was too late. Butler had already been out of the frame of cultural and political reference for almost half a century.

In 1967 Edward McCourt's biography, *Remember Butler*, was published in London. McCourt, a professor of English at the University of Saskatchewan, wrote warmly of Butler, though he treated him as a curiosity, something of an Irish Don Quixote – fanciful and over-idealistic.

The plea in the title of McCourt's biography, *Remember Butler*, was not heard in Ireland. In the aftermath of the fiftieth anniversary celebrations of 1916, Butler was a remote, irrelevant figure on the losing side of History: a Catholic and a senior British army officer whose career had been made in small imperial wars; a supporter of Home Rule who had believed that Ireland's interests were best served by staying within the British empire. Over the latter part of the twentieth century, outside Tipperary historical circles, Butler has suffered near-oblivion. He deserves better.

Butler's life encompassed such varied events as two treks across the Canadian prairies, in 1870–1 and 1873; the abortive attempt by Gladstone's government to rescue Gordon from Khartoum in 1884–5; the sensational 1886 London divorce scandal of Lady Colin Campbell in which Butler was cited as a co-respondent; his command of the imperial forces in South Africa in 1898–9, when he refused to play the Jingo card before the outbreak of war; his attempt to run as a Home Rule candidate in a Dublin by-election in 1904; his selection as a Liberal candidate for East Leeds in the 1906 general election; his involvement as a senator with the new National University of Ireland in 1908.

As an army officer Butler was a member of the influential 'Wolseley Ring', one of the two coteries that between them dominated the British military hierarchy during the last quarter of the nineteenth century. The Ring was led by that 'very model of a modern major-general' – Garnet Wolseley from Goldenbridge in Dublin.

An energetic man with an enquiring mind, forceful, opinionated and articulate, Butler had considerable intellectual gifts. His Canadian report of 1871 led to the foundation of the North-West Mounted Police. The 1905 Butler Report on the £6.5 million scandal of army supplies following the South African War caused public outrage in England.

Butler's pen was not only deployed in report writing. He was a descriptive and narrative writer of notable style. His fourteen books included accounts of his military campaigns, and biographies of Generals

Charles Gordon, Charles Napier and George Pomeroy Colley. He wrote two books on his Canadian travels, one of which, *The Great Lone Land*, became a classic of nineteenth-century travel literature.

One of Butler's most notable characteristics was his sensitivity to the values of cultures outside the European mainstream. Whether in Africa, Asia or America, he observed and learnt from cultures other than his own, sometimes slowly and with some pain. In particular, the Plains Indians of the American West had a lasting influence on him. His own love of space and solitude was deepened and enhanced by his experience and study of the First Nations of Canada, and he recognized and celebrated the strong spiritual dimension in Indian culture.

Socially confident, a formidable conversationalist and a witty raconteur, Butler had friends and acquaintances in diverse and influential circles. These included Victor Hugo, the Empress Eugenie Napoleon, Henry Morton Stanley, Lady Colin Campbell, Charles Stewart Parnell, Olive Schreiner, John Redmond, Alice Stopford Green, and Winston Churchill. Butler married the English artist Elizabeth Thompson, the foremost mid-Victorian battle-painter. She introduced him to the resurgent world of Roman Catholicism in England and this in turn brought him actively in his later years into the Catholic Truth Society.

Butler's family background, that of Ireland's landed gentry, gave him in pre-democratic Ireland a birthright that was one of social and political leadership. His family's tenacity in holding on to land and religion through the preceding generations had inculcated strong feelings of self worth in his forebears. Butler's own character – strong-minded, energetic, self-confident – was allied with intelligence and articulacy. These traits, combined with his background and complemented by a strong sense of moral responsibility for the less advantaged, made for a singular approach to the world. To borrow from Thomas Drummond: for Butler, leadership had its duties as well as its rights. As his daughter Eileen wrote, Butler 'in his public life invariably championed the under-dog'. This also set him at odds with the jingoistic imperialism that pervaded establishment circles during the final years of his army career.

An eminent Irish Victorian, with strong European links and sympathies, Butler did not fare well in twentieth-century Ireland. With this biography I give him to the reader at a time when Irish nationalism is more easily reconcilable with wider allegiances.

ACKNOWLDEGMENTS

Nobody writes a biography without the help of others.

I am particularly indebted to two friends, Adrian Kenny and Joe Walsh. Adrian Kenny nudged me towards this project for years. Joe Walsh's informed enthusiasm for Sir William Francis Butler helped me appreciate the importance of local context in Butler's story.

Four of Butler's descendants, Charles Butler, Rupert Butler, Viscount Gormanston and Anthony Preston, were most encouraging and helpful.

Elizabeth Hawkins, a grand-niece of Lady Elizabeth Butler, was a welcoming host during my inspection of the Meynell Archive.

Thanks are due to Dr Dennis J. Duffy of the University of Toronto and to Dr Jim Jackson of Trinity College, Dublin. I am most grateful to Dr Michael Laffan of University College Dublin, who suggested lines of approach that proved most valuable. Lord Dunboyne was a fount of advice, comment and suggestions on medieval Munster and the general history of Butler dynasties.

Jenny Spencer-Smith, Head of the Department of Fine and Decorative Art at the National Army Museum, Chelsea, was a fruitful source of information on Lady Elizabeth Butler and on the Wolseley Ring. I also wish to thank Commandant Pat O'Brien for his advice on military matters.

To Jack Burns and William Prendergast, a debt owed for their photographic assistance. Thanks also to Tara Hipwell, who compiled the maps.

Those who sustained me during the research and writing, include Tim Lehane of RTE, who in 1988 produced my radio feature *Please Remember Me*, Marcus Bourke of the *Tipperary Historical Journal*, Dr Máire Ní Mhurchú, Pheilim O'Reilly, and the late Mike Reed.

Others to whom I am indebted for include Dr Paul Bidwell, Liam Carroll, Peter Costello, Kieran Dempsey, Dr Patrick Fagan, Claire Mullan, Anraí Ó Braonáin, Arthur O'Donnell, Pauline Power, Rev. Stephen Redmond SJ, and Jonathan Williams. Dom Philip Jebb, archivist at Downside Abbey, was extremely helpful during my stay.

In Tipperary, John and Rose Prendergast of Ballyslatteen House have always been most welcoming since, in the spring of 1988, I first called on them unannounced, as a stranger; while Sean and Teresa Russell of Bansha Castle have been very hospitable hosts on my several visits.

Thanks to the staff at The Lilliput Press for their help and friendliness. I was fortunate to have Antony Farrell as a publisher. As pre-publication pressures crowded in on me he was clear-sighted, unfussed and – most importantly – available. Aoife Carrigy was a vigilant editor with a keen eye for stylistic lapses, and Dhammika Wijetunge a scrupulous proofreader.

For permission to quote from manuscripts and records in their possession, I thank the following:

The Rector, Clongowes Wood College, County Kildare; The Abbot, Downside Abbey, Somerset; The Librarian, Hove Central Library, Hove, Sussex; The Directors of the National Archives of Ireland, the National Library of Ireland and the Public Records Office, Kew. Also, Brian Whitlock Blundell; Catherine Eden, Hermia Eden and Elizabeth Hawkins; and Viscount Gormanston.

For their continuing assistance and courtesy, I am grateful to the staffs of the National Library, Dublin; the Boole Library, University College Cork; the libraries of Trinity College and of University College Dublin.

For permission to use Lady Elizabeth Butler's *Evicted* I am indebted to The Department of Irish Folklore, University College Dublin.

The painting of Lady Colin Campbell is by kind permission of the National Portrait Gallery, London; the photograph of the Dublin Commissioners by kind permission of the University Archivist, University College Cork. The owners of private photographs of William Butler and of Elizabeth Butler are individually acknowledged; those of Butler's birthplace and final home are courtesy of John and Rose Prendergast, and of John and Teresa Russell, respectively.

My involvement with William Francis Butler has impinged upon my family, who in their various ways contributed to the finished work: my daughters Cathy and Lucy; and my sons Emmet and Cathal. To my wife, Mary, I owe a double debt: she bore with inexhaustible patience the extended intrusions made by William Butler on her time; more importantly, she read the original draft with a nuanced feeling for the written word and a sensitivity to solecism.

Financial assistance towards publication is gratefully acknowledged from the following: Cahir Social and Historical Society, Viscount Gormanston and John Magnier.

Martin Ryan
Dublin, March 2003

Chapter One

ROOTS

One day I was taken by my father to the scene of an eviction ... The sheriff, a strong force of police, and above all the crowbar brigade – a body composed of the lowest and most debauched ruffians – were present. At a signal from the sheriff the work began. The miserable inmates of the cabins were dragged out upon the road; the thatched roofs were torn down and the earthen walls battered in by crowbars (practice had made those scoundrels adepts at their trade); the screaming women, the half-naked children, the paralysed grandmother, and the tottering grandfather were hauled out. It was a sight I have never forgotten. I was twelve years old at the time but I think if a loaded gun had been put in my hands I would have fired into that crowd of villains as they plied their horrible trade by the ruined church of Tampul-da-voun.[1]

Thus in his autobiography does William Francis Butler describe how as a boy in 1851 he witnessed the mass eviction of twelve cottier families from their homes. This experience was one of the seminal events of his life, and not simply because it exposed an impressionable boy to the harrowing sight of suffering. The key feature of this event, which sank into William Butler's psyche, was something he never acknowledged publicly: the evicting landlord at Templedavoun was his own father, a Catholic nationalist. All evidence around this eviction points to the fact that the families whom the boy saw thrown on the roadside were tenants or sub-tenants of his father. Yet Butler hides this fact in the opening pages of his autobiography, where, dealing at length with the Great Famine and the eviction scene of his childhood, he goes to contorted lengths to exonerate his landlord father from blame.[2]

What profoundly affected the twelve-year-old boy was the shock of realizing that the material well-being of his own family, landed gentry, was at the cost of such anguish, degradation and suffering of others. He learnt early one of the world's hard facts: that life is ordered inequitably, and that to those that have shall be given. The eviction significantly shaped his view of the world and of his place within it. As an adult he would consistently speak out against oppression and would invariably argue for the weaker party in the imperial issues of his time. This trait can be seen as a sublimation of filial anger, but the eviction scene from Butler's boyhood also provides a motif that will appear constantly through his life. Butler was part of the established order, yet he is somewhat outside that order – critical of its conduct and deeply angered by it.

William Francis Butler was born on 31 October 1838 at Ballyslatteen, County Tipperary, in the valley of the river Suir, north of the town of Cahir. Seven days later he was baptized into the Roman Catholic faith at the parish church of New Inn. The Butlers had been substantial local landowners for generations, and the ancestral family seat was just across the Suir at Ballycarron. In his autobiography, Butler claimed descent from James Butler, the 9th Earl of Ormond. The 9th Earl would have been an illustrious ancestor. Lord High Treasurer of Ireland, he was poisoned in London in 1546. Butler, however, was descended not from Ormond but from a cadet branch of the Butlers, the Lords Dunboyne. His paternal line has been traced to James, 9th Lord Dunboyne, who died in 1508.[3]

Theobald Walter was the founder of the Butler family in Ireland. He was among those Norman adventurers who settled in the country in the latter part of the twelfth century as subjects of the Plantagenet King Henry II. Theobald held the state office of Chief Butler of Ireland and from the title of this office came the family surname. Over the generations the Butlers, together with other Norman families, were drawn in varying degrees into the Old Gaelic world of the majority. During the Reformation, with its accompanying religious wars, the confusions of royal policies split the Butlers, as it did other long-established dynasties. In 1536 Henry VIII was declared to have replaced the pope as head of the Church in Ireland and in 1541 he was declared King of Ireland. Over the following decades extensive settlements were undertaken. The new planters, from England and Scotland, held their lands directly from the Crown. They kept themselves apart from the old order in Ireland, and they were Protestant. The power and prestige of the old Anglo-Norman families began to evaporate and they were drawn closer to their Gaelic compatriots, as much by their concern for their lands as by shared religious beliefs. In the seventeenth century England's royalist–parliamentarian conflict spread to Ireland and engulfed the Butlers in fratricidal feuds and shifting religious allegiances.

The savage upheavals of the seventeenth century gave way to the rule of a new ascendancy and to a series of Penal Laws. The new ascendancy was exclusively Protestant. It had its own parliament in Dublin and its power was buttressed by a series of discriminatory enactments which barred Catholics from parliament and public service, revoked their voting rights, prohibited Catholic religious observance and education and, in general, attempted to destroy the foundations of the old society by curtailing rights to land and property. However, these laws were applied selectively. Long-established, Catholic landed families had a claim on the London court going back centuries that the parliament in Dublin had no wish to put to the test. Several devices were available, such as raising a selected member of an extended family as a Protestant who would assume nominal ownership of family lands and lease those lands to his Catholic relatives. However, such stratagems could never be proof against family rivalry and feud. If, for example, any son of a Catholic family abjured his faith, he forthwith assumed his father's land and property. William Butler remarked that 'the lives of some of my progenitors at Ballycarron must have been somewhat Damoclesian'.

The Butlers of Ballycarron were part of a liberal elite of eighteenth-century Ireland whose interests and connections were as much with continental Europe as with England. With the repeal of the Penal Laws their security and public status was much enhanced. William Butler's father, Richard, was born at Ballycarron in 1792. He attended a grammar school in Tipperary town before going to Lancashire to board at the private Catholic school of Ulverston, run by a distant Irish kinsman, a Dr Everard who had been a co-adjutor bishop of Bordeaux before the French Revolution. He returned as a young man to Ballycarron where his eldest brother had succeeded to the estate. The Butlers had 'the habit of seeking wives near at hand' and Richard took this custom to an extreme by proposing marriage to the governess of his brother's children, Ellen Dillon from Donnybrook in Dublin. The couple were married in Dublin in 1831 and came to live at Ballyslatteen House, a comfortable gentleman's residence close to the Suir which still stands. Here William was born. He was his parents' seventh child, and would be the fifth to survive infancy. He had four older siblings: Richard, born in 1833, Mary in 1834, John in 1835, and Thomas in 1837. His mother bore six more children, four of whom died as infants; two girls – Alice, born in 1840, and Frances, born in 1843 – would survive. William's earliest memories were happy:

> Everything was ours – the green foreground where the spotted rabbits nibbled and nuzzled together; beyond these, long glimpses of green grass seen between lime and beech trees; then a glistening river, with shimmering shallows and bending sallows; beyond that more green fields; and then a long blue mountain range, which grew bolder and loftier as it stretched westward, where it ended in two peaked summits, behind which the sun came down only to come up again next morning at the east end of the range – our sole unquestioned property still. Such are my earliest recollections of the home of the little sallow – Ballyslateen [*sic*].[4]

Those bold and lofty mountains were the Galtees, a compact range of old red sandstone rising sharply from the fertile limestone plains of the Suir valley. The countryside about Ballyslatteen was rich in antiquities. Three miles upriver to the north was the ruined thirteenth-century Augustinian abbey of Athassel. Ten miles by road to the south was the historic town of Cahir, with its medieval castle dramatically sited on a rocky islet in the river Suir. The castle, stronghold of the Cahir Butlers – another cadet branch of the Butler dynasty – had fallen under Tudor siege, and in 1650 Cromwell had taken it. Upriver from Cahir, an hour's walk from Ballyslatteen, was the motte of Knockgraffon, seat of the Eoghanacht, ancient kings of Munster, before the principal royal residence was moved to Cashel. The Rock of Cashel, a striking ninety-foot limestone salient topped with spectacular ruins, stood six direct miles north-east of Ballyslatteen. Enhancing the impact of this environment was a local society with a strong oral tradition that telescoped the years and gave an immediacy to history.

Richard Butler had several landholdings. According to the Griffith valuation of 1841, he was the lessor of seven properties totalling 94 acres in the civil parish of Clonbullogue. Around Ballyslatteen he owned 52 acres and he rented land himself. He held his Ballyslatteen estate on a lease. It totalled 144 acres at this time and the rateable valuation of his house was £20, a sum well in excess of most property values in Tipperary. Most of the

Ballyslatteen estate appears to have been given over to pasture. To put those landholdings in context: most farms in the province of Munster were between 5 and 10 acres, and anything over 30 acres was a good-sized farm which allowed its occupiers to live in some comfort, in contrast to the mass of the population. Richard Butler added steadily to his holdings during the mid-1840s, but his landed interests did not translate into great wealth and he had continually to juggle finances to maintain a gentrified lifestyle for his family.

Ellen Butler was not physically robust, and her health was drained by continual pregnancies and the demands of a young family. In 1842 William was sent to Artane in Dublin, to Ellen's sister and her husband, 'the kindest relatives that child could have'. He stayed in Dublin for some three years, during which he had an historic encounter. In 1801 the United Kingdom of Great Britain and Ireland had come into being and, as a result, Ireland had lost its local parliament. The Repeal Movement, led by Daniel O'Connell and strongly backed by the Catholic middle classes, campaigned for the restoration of the Dublin parliament. 1843, when repeal agitation was at its height, was the year of O'Connell's 'monster meetings'. Over the following summer the sixty-nine year-old O'Connell, having been found guilty of conspiracy, was detained in Richmond Gaol – now Griffith College – on Dublin's South Circular Road. Conditions were most comfortable, and he was allowed almost unlimited access to visitors. William was brought to meet the Liberator. His recollections of the visit were of great gates and doors, an apple orchard, and a big man, who 'moved forward and, taking me in his arms, lifted me above his head, while he shouted in a great strong voice, "Hurrah for Tipperary"'.

In March 1846 William returned home by post-chaise (it would be over three years before the railway would link Tipperary and Dublin). On the last stretch of the road to Ballyslatteen, his elder sister Mary listed off the names of the cottiers whose cabins bordered the road. This litany was a dirge for the end of a traditional peasant society facing the calamity of a second successive failure of the potato harvest, a failure that was to unleash the Great Famine of the late 1840s. The Famine transformed Ireland. Out of a total population of some eight million, approximately one million emigrated, and a million more died from disease and starvation.

William was sheltered from much of the Famine horror. In 1847 he was sent to the College of St Stanislaus in Tullabeg, a Jesuit-run preparatory boarding-school in King's County (modern County Offaly), with two of his elder brothers, John and Thomas. The registration of his enrolment reads:

'William Butler came, September 12th 1847, 9 years old 31st October. No Latin, no French; no English grammar, can spell, but poorly, as also with reading; simple addition and subtraction; not 1st Communion nor Confirmation.' The reference to '1st Communion' is a reminder of how different this significant aspect of Catholic practice was to what it would later become. The ritual of First Holy Communion, now undergone at seven or eight years of age, was not then the ornate ceremonial rite of passage into which it would develop, and was not usually undergone before the age of ten or eleven. The Tullabeg prospectus advertised a system of instruction and discipline:

> ... particularly intended for children of tender years ... Morning and evening prayer, with daily Mass and frequent instructions on the principles and observance of religion are the ordinary means employed to form the tender mind to virtue and piety ... In the time allotted to sleep, which is nine hours – in their food which is wholesome and nutritious – and in the frequent transitions from application to amusement, which, even when they are most engaged with study, occur six times in the day – every reasonable attention is paid to the preservation of their health: and the effect of this attention, combined with the salubrity of the air, is evinced by the fact that medical assistance or advice is very rarely required.[6]

The adult Butler, however, was to have no fond memories of Tullabeg or 'the salubrity of its air':

> It was situated in the midst of a great region of bogland as its name implies – Tullabeg, the little bog – in contradistinction, I suppose, to the great many big bogs which surrounded it. My recollections of this school are not happy ones. I was nine years old and thin and delicate, and the cold of the winter, in that elevated marshland which lies to the north of the Slieve Bloom Hills and almost in the centre of the island, seemed to strike into the heart and soul of a frame such as mine.[7]

Schools like Tullabeg placed an emphasis on team sports and group competitiveness. This was something Butler was never to set much value by for himself, growing up instead to enjoy shooting, riding and fishing.

In July 1848 Ellen Butler died, leaving her husband with the care of seven children. Richard, the eldest, was fifteen; Frances, the youngest, five; William nine. Two of his brothers fell very ill for a time: social status was no barrier to the contagion and disease that were sweeping the country. The effects of the Famine were at their worst, though Richard Butler was insulated from extremes. He was never in any danger of losing his home or lands, but his fortunes hit their lowest ebb as smaller tenants succumbed to the calamity of famine. The three Butler boys were withdrawn from Tullabeg: the annual fees, thirty guineas per boy per school year, were too high to meet. It was at this time that William witnessed the mass eviction at Templedavoun. He began to grow up quickly. Drawn into work on his father's estate, he developed a keen sense of thrift which would inform his entire life.

The post-Famine years brought about an increase in prosperity for Richard Butler, as for others of similar standing. The virtual elimination of the cottier class meant more land for pasture and higher rents from the small farmers who had survived. The Butler sons resumed their formal education, though John's life was cut short when he succumbed to illness in 1853. William returned to Dublin to attend a private school at 16-17 Harcourt Street. This was the Academy of St Laurence O'Toole, named after the patron saint of Dublin. It was run by a Reverend Dr Quinn, and the staff were mainly clerics, many of whom later 'attained celebrity as bishops in the colonial ecclesiastical world'. Here William received a standard denominational education, studying secular subjects including Logic, Greek, Latin and Mensuration. English literature strongly appealed to him: he read Shakespeare and Sir Walter Scott, and had an ear for verse, particularly enjoying the poetry of Tennyson.

During his time at the school, the city provided several diversions. In March 1854 Britain and France went to war against Russia in the Crimea and thousands of troops were called to action. As the various regiments of the Dublin garrison came through the city for embarkation, William and his fellow pupils joined the crowds that lined the streets: 'Daily we used to accompany some regiment of horse or foot cheering them as they marched.' The massed ranks, the colours, the drums, the pipes, the tramp of the infantry, the clatter of the cavalry: all this quickened the pulse of the fifteen-year-old youth.

Among those who came through the streets before sailing for the port of Balaclava was a twenty-year old lieutenant in the 90th Lancers, Garnet Wolseley from Goldenbridge House, County Dublin. More than anybody else, Wolseley was to be the instrument of Butler's rise in the imperial army of Queen Victoria.

Chapter Two

GONE FOR A SOLDIER

It was the Royal Navy that was the main instrument of British might during the nineteenth century. The army, by contrast, was a secondary force. Its main function was to garrison the colonies, India in particular. It was a volunteer army and was noticeable for its lack of middle-class orientation. The gentry and nobility held officers' commissions, while the rural labourer and, to a lesser extent, the slum-dweller, made up the mass of the rank and file, of whom in mid-century some thirty percent were Irish. The key unit in the army was the regiment. Officers bought their commissions under the Purchase system which denied advancement to men of talent unable to afford the sums involved. The lowest commissioned rank, that of ensign, cost £450 in an unfashionable foot regiment. A lieutenant-colonelcy in a fashionable regiment cost £4500. These were official figures, often grossly exceeded in a seller's market. In addition, moves up the promotional ladder were made one step at a time with a sale to an officer directly below and a purchase from an officer directly above. Young men unable to afford Purchase, and whose kin had held commissions, could be gazetted as ensigns, but without cash they could go no higher except in cases of outstanding service.

Two events during Butler's youth shattered military complacency. The first was the Crimean War of 1854–6, the conduct of which showed that incompetence and venality were rife in the army. The second event was the Indian Mutiny of 1857. India was vital to British pre-eminence as a great power. The mutiny shattered the illusion of a docile subcontinent and, once suppressed (with barbarities on both sides), gave further impetus to army expansion and reform.

It was to the army that Butler, having finished his schooling, looked for a career. As a child, he had heard stirring fireside tales of the Peninsular and Napoleonic Wars from Tipperary veterans who had spent years on the Continent soldiering with Wellington. His father, in Butler's words, 'was not keen that his son should enter a profession in which the disadvantage of the absence of money could only be overcome by the surrender of one's religion', but the son was certain that in an expanding army he would find what he wanted: travel, adventure, camaraderie and command. It helped that one of his Ballycarron cousins, Henry Butler, returned from the Crimean War as a decorated veteran. After 'a short interval of aimless expectation' at home in Ballyslatteen, the energetic and forceful young man prevailed on his father to let him join the army. Purchase was out of the question; it was too expensive. The young Butler was interviewed by a distant Protestant kinsman – Richard Doherty, a military veteran – who recommended him for a commission. In July 1858 the young man travelled to London, to Burlington House, Piccadilly, where he sat a routine examination, and on 17 September 1858 he was gazetted as an ensign in the 69th Regiment of Foot.

Foot regiments were the lowest regiments on a social register whose acme was the Horse Guards. The 69th was concentrated in Burma, but two of its companies were at Fermoy Barracks, County Cork, some thirty-five miles from Ballyslatteen. Butler went there in November 1858, just after his twentieth birthday. In the young man who presented himself at Fermoy, there was little trace of the thin small boy who had wintered at Tullabeg eleven years previously. Butler was now tall, six feet two inches in height, and sturdy. A contemporary photograph of him in the dress uniform of an ensign shows him open-featured, dark-haired and clean-shaven. He sits somewhat aloof, while his strong handsome face has a self-assurance which is accentuated by the formality of his attire with its shako and ceremonial sword.

At Fermoy, Butler found himself part of an officers' circle that included long-haired, bewhiskered, moustached veterans of the Crimea. Over leisurely dinners he joined in mess chat and arguments, making something of a name for himself as an opinionated and sharp-witted conversationalist, with a penchant for punning. His formal training consisted of several months' drilling after which 'I was ... declared a fit and proper person to command a company'. He took an enthusiastic part in athletics, winning the 250-yard hurdle for Fermoy in the 1860 regional military sports. In his free time he went riding and wildfowl shooting, and fished for salmon and trout along the Blackwater and its tributaries. He was hungry for service abroad and endured a frustrating wait until, in July 1860, he finally embarked at Queenstown (now Cobh) to join his regiment in Burma. He was one of two hundred soldiers squeezed aboard a three-masted sailing ship, the *Coldstream*, which was then towed out of harbour and released into a choppy sea. The journey was 'a crawl over the ocean'. The voyage to India in those days of sail, before the opening of the Suez Canal, could take four to five months; ships travelled far into the South Atlantic to catch the winds that would blow them across the southern seas well below the Cape of Good Hope and up into the Indian Ocean. It was early November when the *Coldstream* came in sight of Madras, 'a low coast beaten by a white surf, fringes of palm trees, some white houses, and a range of hills'.

Butler entered the closed world of the British army officer in peacetime: polo and pigsticking, billiards and whist. Intellectual pastimes were not highly regarded. European women were scarce; while senior officers frequently had their wives on station, junior officers were starved of socially acceptable female company, and in theory at least, went without substitutes for it, unlike other ranks who frequented brothels. If a social and material gulf existed between officers and other ranks, between British officers and Indian troops a cultural and racial chasm yawned. There was little attempt by the rulers to understand the ruled, who were referred to in common parlance as 'niggers'. The legacy of the Mutiny was distrust and suspicion, each culture chosing to see only the worst features of the other. Ensign Butler largely conformed to type:

> In the fullness of his animal life the British Subaltern in a marching regiment is not overmuch given to philosophic enquiry. He drops easily into the belief that he represents the highest form of civilisation, and that he has only to snipe-shoot or pig-stick his way through the world, while at the same time in some mysterious manner he is bearing aloft the banner of British freedom and Western culture ... I will not pretend that I was different from my fellows in this respect.'

However, Butler looked further ahead, as the following extract from his diary shows. It has a quality of reflection and prescience unusual for a man in his early twenties:

... the edifice we are uprearing in India has its foundation resting upon sand. We give the native of India our laws and our scientific discoveries; he sees that they are good and he adopts them and uses them as some counterbalance to the misfortune of our presence in his land ... We pull down the barriers within which his mind has hitherto moved, but the flood of his enquiry being set flowing, we cannot stay or confine it to our own limits. I can see signs that this great structure we are building will be a ruin before it is completed. I can find no instance in history of a nation which has long possessed an old and completed civilisation of its own being able to fuse it, imperfect though it may be, into a newer and foreign one.[2]

Arriving in Madras in November 1860, Butler had a short period of acclimatization before crossing the Bay of Bengal to join his regiment in Burma. The 69th was quartered at Toungoo, 200 miles and a relaxed twenty-day journey up the Sittang River in a flotilla of small graceful boats. This was Butler's first close contact with people of a different culture. The riverside villages charmed him: 'It would be impossible not to like the Burmese people – good natured, nice mannered, pleasant.'

Toungoo, surrounded by forest, was one of the remotest army posts in Burma. The 69th had been there for over three years and the strain and debilitation were showing. Butler was urged by old hands to make the most of the dry season before the monsoon rains turned the land into a quagmire. He made full use of this opportunity to seek out the unfamiliar and exotic; he rode often into the forest, inspected Buddhist ruins, and arranged a hunt complete with elephants in an unsuccessful attempt to bag a tiger. The monsoon, when it arrived, lived down to expectations. Insects bred in myriads, and snakes, washed out of their natural habitats, were common on the brick walkways of the cantonment. At night 'everyone went to mess with lanterns carried in front'.

In January 1862 the 69th was ordered to return to India. During his time in Burma, Butler had impressed his superiors with his energy and organizational skills. For the move to Madras, he was assigned as staff officer, 'adjutant, paymaster and quartermaster' for five companies, over 450 men. To cross the Bay of Bengal, Butler's wing embarked on two vessels, one a steamer, the other a sailing ship. Three days into the voyage they were hit by a storm, heralded by 'the rumbles of an incessant thunder'. Butler was on the *Tubalcain*, 'an old and cranky craft', being towed by the steamer. As the edge of the storm struck the *Tubalcain,* a wave swept the mate overboard. The storm was the forerunner of a hurricane and as the sea grew in violence the captain of the steamer, concerned for the safety of his own craft, released the towing hawser and abandoned the *Tubalcain* without a mate and with a captain who, losing his nerve, had shut himself in his cabin, leaving the ship in the hands of the second officer. The full force of the hurricane hit the *Tubalcain* after night fell. Butler's presentation of the cataclysm is graphic:

> No one can ever describe such a scene accurately. There are things in it which when put into words are bound to appear exaggerations. There is no sea and no sky and no air. They have all become one vast, black, solid, gigantic animal ... there is no sea running as in an ordinary storm; beneath this awful wind the sea crouches for a time like a lashed hound, and that is exactly what it is. It cannot get up and run before that vast wall of wind. It lies down at first and the wind mows it like grass, shaves it off in swathes of white foam which are caught up into the rushing wind itself, so that no eye can open against it, and no face can face its saltiness. But the roar is the thing that lives longest in the memory; it seems to swallow even the thunder as though that too, like the sea, had been brayed into it.[3]

It was the second officer, lashed to the mizzen mast, who got the ship through. The hurricane abated at dawn and the battered *Tubalcain* lurched towards Madras. When it arrived there, four days behind the steamer, it was to find that it and all aboard had been officially declared lost at sea.

Fort St George, in the heat and humidity of Madras, was 'a very hotbed of disease'. Officers and men were continually going down with fever and cholera, and fatalities were common. Each night the main sewer of the native quarter was discharged into the sea close to the fort, and 'a horrible black mess was carried slowly down the shingle' in front of the troop quarters. Butler had some relief from Madras by being assigned to oversee musketry practice at an inland depot, but the routine was boring. India was quiet. Mess gossip snatched avidly at any news of the world beyond the subcontinent. In America there was a civil war. Most mess views were pro-confederacy, reflecting attitudes in England. America was two oceans away and news was sketchy and infrequent. Only once in Butler's recollection were the repercussions of this conflict acutely felt. The army in Madras had its ice shipped to it from Boston and on one occasion the ice ship failed to arrrive as scheduled. The thought of this Yankee vessel having been sunk off the American coast by a confederate warship was enough to prompt a jocular switching of allegience among Butler and his colleagues until, with the eventual arrival of the ice ship, 'the Federal cause went down again to zero like the temperatures in our tumblers'.

For his long leave in 1863, Butler, with two companions, crossed India by train to the Malabar Coast, a region rich in backwaters and lagoons. The three men hired local boats and crews to carry them south through vibrant combinations of sun, sand and lush foliage; and Butler noted the grace of the local women with their 'rich golden skins and black, silky tresses'. As the small party continued south the eldest member, middle-aged and missing cantonment comforts, turned back. Butler and his remaining companion, Lieutenant Jim Mansfield from County Kildare, kept on. Travelling on land and sea, by bullock cart and native coaster, they rounded Cape Comorin at the southernmost tip of India and made their way back up the east coast to Madras. Reaching Madras in early July, Butler found that the 69th had shaken off its torpor despite the humidity of the monsoon: the regiment had received news that it would be going home the following February.

During his remaining time in India, Butler's growing interest in the past took him in his off-duty time to Vellore. Ninety miles west of Madras, Vellore Fort is one of the great defensive constructions of India. In 1806 it had been the scene of a sepoy mutiny. The British soldiers holding the fort were men of the 69th, and many were killed in their beds. Butler inspected the last resting place of those of his regiment who had died, 'a square mound of brick and mortar, without date or inscription, and broken with rents through which wild plants grew luxuriantly'. He determined to have a memorial erected at Vellore, and on his return to Madras, with the zest for which he was now well noted, he raised sufficient funds from his comrades to have the project implemented before the 69th left India.

While in the East, Butler had done no campaigning and had had no chance to prove himself in the field and earn a lieutenancy. In November 1863 he purchased his lieutenancy from John Whitford, a Dubliner who was leaving the 69th and who was happy to sell on his commission. It would have cost Butler in the region of £700, a large sum for one of his modest means. However, he had been thrifty, and was also able to call on his family for help. In his autobiography Butler makes no reference to his lieutenancy or how he got it. It was the one rank of his career which he bought. He had sat a qualifying examination before being gazetted as an ensign and all his upward moves in the army were based on merit, with this one exception. Writing an autobiography from the viewpoint of his closing years, Butler would have seen this purchase as an embarrassment, tainted with the old practices of the unreformed army.

In February 1864 the 69th embarked from Madras. Butler's abiding memory of his thirty-nine months in the East was a sense of its vibrancy:

> ... the dominating note of the land is life. This great fervid sun, these sweeps of rain, this rich soil, these limpid waters, have all combined to call forth in forest, plain, island, lake and shore an all-pervading sense of human, animal, bird, fish and insect existence ... you cannot get away from this fact of life; it jostles you in the towns, it roars at you in the forest, it flies and hums about you in the air, it swims around you in the waters.[4]

The 69th sailed home in two clipper ships, the *Trafalgar* and the *Lord Warden*. The clippers were an elegant coda to the age of sail. Sleek, beautifully proportioned, carrying up to thirty sails, these vessels came alive in the ocean. The two wings of the 69th raced each other from India to England and came up the English channel together in May with the freshness of early summer wafting from the land. They docked at Portsmouth.

There had been one scheduled stopover *en route*, which allowed Butler to indulge what was to become a lifelong interest. Before dawn on 15 April 1864 he was on the deck of the *Lord Warden*, his eyes straining into the darkness while the ship rode at anchor. As the sky became tinged with light Butler began to make out great brooding cliffs rising from the ocean before him. This was St Helena, one of the remotest islands in the world, forty-seven square miles of volcanic rock thrusting sharply from a desolate sea. It was easy to fancy that such a place had to have come into being for an exceptional purpose. This was the promethean pillar to which Napoloen Bonaparte had been tied from October 1815 until his death in May 1821, and where his remains had lain for nineteen years until their removal for ceremonial entombment in Paris.

Butler's fascination with Napoleon was partisan and largely uncritical. In old age he would explain this by reference to his own 'mental citadel':

> A young man entering the Army, particularly if he should be blessed, or cursed, with that indefinable thing called ambition, should early in his life begin to build himself a mental citadel into which, when fortune goes counter to him, as in ninety-nine cases out of a hundred it will go, he can retire. It is in the lives of bygone great soldiers that he will find the material from which this citadel, this safe place against 'the slings and arrows',

can be built. I am not speaking at random. I have often in life found doubts disappear, clouds lighten, and relaxing energies tighten again for the struggle by turning to a chapter in the wonderful memoirs in which the captive of St. Helena has told in undying language the story of his early campaigns. And you need never be afraid of placing your heroes too high in this mental citadel, nor your villains too low.[5]

Butler was to visit St Helena on three occasions. On this first visit, what appealed to the romantic in him was the symbolism of this giant of history, captive in the loneliest of prisons where he had been cast by pygmies. From the start of Napoleon's final exile, he became the subject of a stream of pamphlets and books in all the major languages of Europe. English works on him tended to be hostile, to emphasize his despotism, his ruthlessness and will to power, and his delusions of grandeur. The fact that France was Britain's traditional continental enemy helped shape these judgments. However, from the time of his death there had been a trickle of writing in English sympathetic to Napoleon, writing that concentrated on his last years. An Irishman, Barry O'Meara, had been first to be published. O'Meara was the naval surgeon assigned to St Helena as Napoleon's personal physician. He became convinced that he was being subtly pressured by the governor of the island to connive at Napoleon's death. He protested, was recalled to England, went public with his suspicions, and was dismissed from the service. In 1822 he published *Napoleon in Exile: or, A Voice from St. Helena*, a sympathetic two-volume account of the emperor's last years. It was frequently reprinted, and Butler bought his own copy early in his military career.

St Helena has a healthy climate, tempered by the trade winds. Inland from the rocky coast there is substantial greenery before the formidable heights of the crags. In his account of his first visit, Butler emphasized the island's bleak aspects. When the *Lord Warden* docked, he rode steeply from the harbour into an 'environment of charred desolation', to Longwood, Napoleon's final home. Here Napoleon had died, on 5 May 1821, at the age of fifty-one. Set on a plateau of dark basalt, the austerity of Longwood's location gave Butler an 'all-pervading sense of an inner prison, surrounded by even more impassable boundaries of lava, chasm, and rock wall than the ocean and the outer sea face of the island had already provided'. He enquired if anyone on the island remembered the years of Napoleon's captivity. He was directed to an old man, a retired British soldier who had been posted to the island fifty years earlier and had never left it, marrying into the small local community and settling down. The old man turned out to be Irish: 'Did ye ever hear tell o' Sligo?' he asked Butler. He remembered Napoleon and conjured an image of Napoloen's captivity that rivetted the young lieutenant. Speaking of the sentries who never left the environs of Longwood, he remarked that 'by night they were drawn in, and they closed up around the house'.

> I mounted and rode away, thinking over the words 'closed up around the house.' All these vast precipices, from the edges of which the passerby recoils in instinctive horror; these gloomy rampart rocks; all these camps of soldiers – one there at Deadwood, one hundred yards in front of the farmhouse; another at Hutt's Gate, where the sawback ridge begins which just suffices in its width at the top to carry the road on to Longwood between the prodigious rents in the earth plunging down one thousand feet in depth, below the narrow roadway; these were not wards and guards and barriers sufficient, placed though they were with thousands of leagues between them and the nearest land, but the line of sentries must *close up* at sunset around the walls of the miserable house itself.[6]

This strong descriptive passage is effective because of what it omits as well as what it says. Butler ignores all rationale for the night sentries being deployed as they were. St Helena was an important provision stop for ships of many nations traversing the southern oceans and, in the eyes of Napoleon's captors, an attempted rescue of their prisoner under cover of darkness was always a possibility.

Following his arrival at Portsmouth in May 1864, Butler's postings were in the south of England. He was stationed at Gosport for a short time before getting home to the Suir Valley on leave. There he regaled his family with stories of his experiences. Then it was back to staid garrison life, first at Hythe on the Hampshire coast, and later at Aldershot. Under the shock of the Crimean War, Aldershot had been converted from a training ground where troops lived under canvas while they underwent drill, musket practice, and manoeuvres, into a permanent camp. Its permanency did not equate with any degree of comfort. Butler found it 'a great expanse of sand' with 'wretched huts in which we were housed'. He fretted at the outmoded drills and at the close-order manoeuvres which eschewed mock-battle conditions. He also shared the scorn of his regimental colleagues for the Aldershot staff officers and their cossetted lifestyles.

But Aldershot had some compensations: foremost of thses was its library, donated by the recently deceased Prince Consort. Butler, hungry for mental stimulation, began to research the material for what would be his first published work, *A Narrative of the Historical Events Connected with the Sixty-Ninth Regiment*, a project that would occupy him intermittently for some five years before coming to fruition in 1870 as a slim volume destined for the specialist shelf. He also read voraciously and, for the first prolonged period in his life, gorged himself with books, 'reading of the wars on land and sea and of the men who fought them'.

During the early summer of 1865, Butler set off on a solitary walking tour of the cockpit of Europe to view the battlefields of the Low Countries. What most struck him at all the sites he visited was their smallness of scale. Each of these battlefields was readable from a single centre, 'a thing never to be possible again' because of developments in firepower. Quatre Bras in particular held him. Here on 16 June 1815, two days before the battle of Waterloo, the cavalry of Marshal Ney had slaughtered the men of the 69th. Their Dutch commanding officer on the day had refused to allow them to form a defensive square against the French onslaught and had ordered them to stand against the enemy in an extended line which the French horsemen then cut to pieces with their sabres. The high point of Butler's leisured and introspective journey was the Field of Waterloo itself. He traced the movements of both sides, transposing dry textbook references to the ground of battle.

Belgium was a stimulating interlude and, back at Aldershot, Butler found the routine wearisome. He again spent much of his free time reading. His visit to Europe had whetted his appetite for France and matters French. He was able to indulge this interest further when, in the summer of 1866, two companies of the 69th were unexpectedly posted to the Channel Islands and he found himself sailing for Guernsey. He would be stationed in the capital, St Peter Port, the home-in-exile of Victor Hugo.

The greatest of the French Romantic writers, Hugo had been born in 1802. His exile in Guernsey was political. He was a lifelong supporter of the ideals of the French Revolution and was strongly in favour of constitutional government. In 1851 Hugo was among the republicans who took to the streets in an unsuccessful attempt to stop the *coup d'etat* of Louis Bonaparte, Napoleon's nephew. With thousands of others, Hugo was banished from France and watched impotently as Louis established the Second Empire with himself at its head as Napoleon III. Hugo had been living in Guernsey for almost ten years when Butler was posted there and was the island's most illustrious resident.

Butler had recently read *Les Miserables* and the central concern of the novel, fraternity, engaged him strongly. He determined to meet the great man. He began taking French lessons from a penurious *emigré*, Hannet de Kesler, who, in the autumn of 1866, effected an introduction beween the young lieutenant and Hugo. Hugo then invited Butler, on a number of occasions, to join the loquacious company frequently asked to eat at his table. Hugo dominated these soirées where he played the role of homely philosopher, usually conversing in his mellifluous French and occasionally lapsing into formal English. Butler's journal from that time records his host as one who 'spoke a great deal'. Butler contributed his own share to discussions and prompted Hugo to say, 'I also am an Irishman. I love Ireland because she is to me a Poland and a Hungary, because she suffers.' On another occasion Hugo jokingly warned the company off Butler: '... take care of him, he is *l'enfant terrible*'. And once, after studying his face for some time: 'If ever I was to be tried, I would wish to have you for a judge.'

Hugo's passion for politics and his fiery liberalism fascinated Butler. He was outspoken on all manner of social and religious issues, and was implacably opposed to the pope, Pius IX. Butler, by contrast, having grown up as an Irish Catholic, and continuing to practise his religion, viewed the pope as the vicar of Christ on an earth beset by the forces of godless secularism. Here in Guernsey, Butler was exposed to contemporary continental thought, and to words used as powerful instruments of persuasion and sentiment, untrammelled by caution or procedural formality.

There was a further aspect to Hugo that must have intrigued Butler: his ménage. When Butler met him in Hauteville House, 38 Hauteville Street, Hugo was without his wife and sons, who were in Brussels. Down the street at number 20 lived Juliette Drouet, who had been Hugo's mistress for thirty-two years. She held frequent salons there for Hugo and, worked out in the soft green of her front lawn, was a floral pattern tracing the letters VH. This was Butler's introduction to continental sexual mores, far less restrictive than those of Ireland and less hypocritical than those of the British military officer serving abroad.

Butler spent less than a year in Guernsey, but it was a critical period in his intellectual development. It exposed him at a time of great impressionability to opinions and attitudes that flexed his mind, and it helped to clarify his views of the world at this time of high tide for the Century of Progress.

Chapter Three

CANADA AND THE RED RIVER

Butler was strongly attracted to France, where the emerging shapes of the new world were to be clearly seen. He was, however, no radical: the contemporary social order had some serious defects, but the way to effect change was to work for it within existing systems, something illustrated by the circumstances of his next posting. In March 1867 the 69th was abruptly sent to Ireland, to the Curragh military camp, twenty-five miles from Dublin. The Fenian Rising had just taken place.

The Fenians, heavily influenced by continental developments, were a secret society devoted to the overthrow of British rule in Ireland and to the creation of a separatist democratic republic. The rising was poorly executed and quickly suppressed – mainly by local constabulary. The role of the army was minimal. The rising was confined to a few areas; Tipperary was one place where Fenians actually came out. Rebels mustered in the Galtees, that 'long blue mountain range' of Butler's childhood, only to be dispersed by sleet and snow. Fenianism in Ireland was a minority movement. It had almost no adherents among the landowners and professional classes and was condemned from pulpits as a movement 'foolish in the extreme'. The majority nationalist view was that Irish grievances could be redressed by working within the existing constitutional system, seeking political and social change through the imperial parliament in London.

With Ireland quiet over the summer of 1867, the 69th was ordered to Canada in August. For Butler, approaching his twenty-ninth birthday, this was the posting that was to shape his future. Moreover, Canada was to exert an emotional hold over him that he would never shake free of, a hold that would afford him dreams and solace throughout his life.

Until just over a month before the 69th sailed for Canada, British North America had been a collection of self-governing colonies which, except for British Columbia on the Pacific coast, were clustered round the Saint Lawrence Seaway in the east. Between these enclaves lay the width of the continent. In July 1867 the colonies, with the exceptions of British Columbia and Newfoundland, federated as the Dominion of Canada.

Butler and the 69th had seen no action in Ireland. Paradoxically, it was Canada that offered the possibility of engagement with Fenians. In the United States the Fenian Brotherhood had exploited the sense of grievance which so many Irish immigrants had against Britain. Following the American Civil War there had been three Fenian incursions into Canada in 1866. The second of these, when a thousand men crossed the Niagara River into Ontario, led to the battle of Ridgeway where the Fenians routed the Canadian militia.

From the first, Butler was overwhelmed by America, spacious and majestic, and 'so full of the virility of a youthful people'. He was posted to the small, placid town of Brantford, between Lakes Erie and Ontario. Faced with the prospect of yet another stint of routine garrison duties, he determined to fulfil a long held dream. As a boy he had read James Fenimore Cooper's tales of the American wilderness and of the adventures of the white hunter Leatherstocking and his companion Chingachgook, the last of the Mohicans. Cooper's *The Prairie* had carried him in his imagination to the Great Plains. Now 'the mystic word *prairie* [was] at last a veritable reality. Since my early boyhood that word had meant to me everything that was possible in the breathing, seeing and grasping of freedom."

He secured two months' leave of absence and, with three companions, among whom was Jim Mansfield (his travelling companion in India), crossed into the United States and headed by the Union Pacific Railway for Omaha, Nebraska. He went via Niagara Falls which even then was commercialized: 'the tourists were doing the falls and the touts were doing the tourists'. *En route* to Omaha, his party kept encountering Union officers riding the railway to and from postings. To their delight they were drawn into a warm fellowship very different to the reserve and hauteur of their own military environment.

Nebraska had become the 37th state of the union the previous March, and Omaha still had all the dangerous vitality of a frontier town:

... a very lively place; railway navvies, gold-diggers, speculators abounded. Shooting went on pretty briskly in the gambling rooms and drinking saloons, of which there appeared to be an unlimited number. Every man policed himself with a sort of murderous solemnity which was most impressive.[2]

Omaha was the last town of any consequence on the railway which, at the rate of four miles a day, was still being laid across the continent. Two hundred miles farther west Butler's party reached Fort Kearney on the river Platte. Their recklessly hospitable military hosts, for whom whisky was a breakfast staple, introduced them to the prairie and the buffalo. Butler's first hunt began with a scene that mesmerized him:

the sight that struck us with astonishment was not the vastness of the scene, but the immensity of the animal life that covered it. From a spot three or four hundred yards from where we stood, far off to a remote horizon where sky and prairie came together on a line that was visible to us only by the small black specks of life that were on it, a vast herd of grazing buffaloes stretched away to the south.[3]

From his buffalo kills that day Butler took the customary two items, the tails as trophies, the tongues as table delicacies. His hunting continued over the next weeks, but there was something tawdry in the ease with which those mighty animals could be stampeded and shot. Butler's upset was compounded by a remark made to him by a high-ranking military officer he met: *kill every buffalo you can, every buffalo dead is an Indian gone*. Towards the end of his stay at Fort Kearney he was returning alone from a day's hunting when he came on three buffalo moving sedately towards the river Platte. One of the animals was a magnificent bull which careered away. Pursuit was irresistible. Firing from the saddle, Butler hit his quarry twice, in the flank and in the shoulder. The wounded animal slowed and turned to face his tormentor:

... his rage was calm and stately, he pawed the ground, and blew with short angry snorts the sand in clouds from the plain; moving thus slowly towards me he looked the incarnation of strength and angry pride. But his doom was sealed. I remember so vividly all the wild surroundings of the scene – the great silent waste, the two buffalo watching from a hilltop the fight of their leader, the noble beast himself stricken but defiant, and beyond, the thousand glories of the prairie sunset. It was only to last an instant for the giant bull, still with low bent head and angry snorts, advancing slowly towards his puny enemy, sank quietly to the plain and stretched his limbs in death ... never since that hour have I sought to take the life of one of these noble animals.[4]

After Nebraska, Butler was back in Brantford in time for the fall. He had had a taste of an untrammelled life and had been touched by the frontier spirit of a world where action was everything. Now as the fogs and dampness of the winter seeped into Brantford he found garrison life boring and confined. He had just turned thirty. After nine years of service he was still only a lieutenant, had never been on field service, had never seen military action. His frustration is well expressed in the concluding sentence of his history of *The Sixty-Ninth Regiment*, now a completed work in manuscript: 'My work has been ... done with a feeling of interest, which vanishes into nothing before the dull, hopeless level of long peaceful years.'

Butler could not afford to buy himself a captaincy. His thoughts began running towards joining those adventurers who were changing the West. However, routine service was broken in the spring of 1868 when he was assigned as 'look-out' officer from Brantford. Each month he made a 1500-mile lone circuit of the remote army look-out posts scattered along the lakeshores and in the woods of southern Ontario. His predecessor in this post was a man one year his junior, Lieutenant Redvers Buller of the 60th Rifles, an old Etonian and the son of a Devonshire MP. The two men had first met at Brantford during one of Buller's patrols. It was to be the start of a friendship that would last for forty years.

It was during his time as look-out officer that Butler had the lure of civilian life cast skilfully before him. One night at an inn in Watford he met a civilian called Horatio Nelson Case. Case was 'a down-Easter, sharp, determined, of restless eye, straight upper lip and firm-set lower jaw'. He was a speculator. Surely Butler could see that land he was patrolling had great economic potential? The right partnership – Butler's cash, Case's expertise – could take rich pickings. The two men exchanged addresses and a month later Case wrote to Butler with a scheme to exploit oil. They should purchase 200 acres of land near the aptly named town of Petrolia in southern Ontario. Could Butler raise $800?

Butler was interested, though cautious. He travelled out to inspect the area where only ten years before the first commercial oil well on the North American continent had been opened. The Case scheme seemed to have potential. Provisionally, Butler drew in a fellow officer to go halves in the investment. He then put the matter on hold.

By the time his look-out duties came to an end in the fall of 1868, the 69th had been posted to Montreal, the raucous commercial capital of Canada. There Butler made a formal request to work in the following spring on the military survey being conducted along the border with the United States. In connection with his application, he was asked to present himself to the Deputy Quartermaster of Her Majesty's Forces in Canada, thirty-five year-old Colonel Garnet Wolseley from Dublin.

Wolseley was the third generation of his immediate family to be born in Ireland and his Irish connections went back to the Williamite wars. In seventeenth-century Ireland, the Wolseleys were part of the new social order, the Protestant ascendancy, divided from the majority by the twin gulfs of religion and politics. The new ascendancy emphatically did not view itself as Irish. For Wolseley, 'the rainy and squally island' of Ireland held a curious people 'with noses so cut away that you can see where their brains should be ... They are a strange, illogical, inaccurate race, with the most amiable qualities, garnished with the dirt and squalor which they seem to love as dearly as their religion.'[5]

Wolseley's father, an ex-military man with an undistinguished career, died when Wolseley was still a boy and he was raised in genteel poverty by a doting mother. He joined the army at nineteen as an ensign without Purchase, as had Butler. However, his career was spectacularly different. From the first, Wolseley's postings took him into the field: in Burma he was wounded in the thigh, in the Crimea he was blinded in one eye. He saw action in the suppression of the Indian Mutiny and served in China.

Wolseley was a reformer, passionate about the need to modernize the army and disdainful of the blinkered thinking of his superiors. He watched out for talented officers to bring on: such talent, properly led, would act as a leaven to army standards. In 1868, when he first met Butler, he was writing *The Soldier's Pocketbook for Field Service*, which was later to be bought out by the War Office in London and issued as an official publication.

Wolseley stressed three qualities as being essential for an officer: '... first daring courage, second quick ability, and third a healthy powerful physique'. When he first interviewed Butler, it was more than the latter's physique that impressed him:

> I was much struck by the bright clearness of his intelligence and with his all round intellectual superiority to the general run of our officers. I en-

quired about him from those who knew him well, and ascertained that he was not only by far the cleverest man in his battalion, but was well known generally for his energy and various talents.[6]

Wolseley had recently returned from Ireland where he had married a Louisa Erskine from County Cork. He was familiar with the valley of the Blackwater having ridden with the Duhallow Hunt. Since Butler had spent over eighteen months at Fermoy, the two men shared a knowledge of this part of Ireland, something that registered strongly with the newly wed Wolseley.

However, for the present, Butler's application led nowhere; there was already a full complement of surveyors for the next season's work. He endured Montreal over the winter. Restless, he revisited Ontario in the new year to follow up Horatio Case's proposal. He went to Petrolia again, observed the continuing development of the oil industry and decided to join Case's venture. His military colleague, an Ensign Wodehouse, agreed to invest $400. It remained for Butler to raise his half share and chance his future in America:

> This America was a great mind stretcher. All these lakes, these immense prairies, these deep forests, these rivers of which the single lengths are greater than the width of the ocean between Canada and Europe; all the throbbing of the life that one saw everywhere, on the road and river, in the cities, on the plains; this great march that was ever going on – all seemed to call with irresistible voice to throw one's lot into the movement. It all seemed the exact opposite of the profession to which at this time I had given ten years of my life. There one seemed to be going round in a circle; here the line of march was straight to the west ... I determined to cross the Atlantic; raise the $400 necessary to begin a partnership with Horatio Nelson Case; and even if we failed to strike oil, to strike out some line in life other than that military one which, so far, seemed to lead to nothing.[7]

Army officers could take leave of absence on half-pay, enough for a junior officer without independent means to get by on. In September 1869 Butler took leave and came back to Ireland where his father, now seventy-seven, was dying. Butler cajoled the money for his oil venture from various relatives and sent it on to Canada. There was now nothing to do but wait. On the military front, his prospects were bleak. Thirty-one years old, he was acutely aware of time passing and was facing what was commonly accepted as the worst of professional disasters: 'being purchased over by junior subalterns for the rank of captain'.

Butler was temporarily distracted from his situation when in December he was asked to escort one of his former captains, now going senile, to Paris on a sightseeing trip. The two men reached the city on New Year's Eve, 'in the meridian hour of her glory' under the Second Empire.

After his visit to Paris, Butler returned to Tipperary where his father, who struggled through the winter, died in the early spring. Butler helped lay him to rest among his ancestors at Killardrigh, the reputed burial place of a legendary High King who had drowned in the Suir. If that legend was true, wrote Butler, then the burial of his own father in March 1870 was the burial of 'a second king among men'.

Butler's elder brother Thomas inherited Ballyslatteen.[8] Butler's own prospects lay outside Ireland. What gave him his break was trouble in Canada: resistance to the new Dominion by the Métis settlers of the Red River Valley. His first intimations of this came from Irish newspaper reports around the time of his father's death, in Butler's words, 'a small speck of revolt rising so far away'. Butler's use of the word *revolt* here is typical of establishment thinking of the time. Strictly, the Métis were not in revolt since they had not become part of the Dominion. The Métis were of mixed European and Indian blood: most of them had part-French ancestry. They were hunters, trappers, and small farmers. Fort Garry, at the confluence of the Assiniboine and Red rivers, was their main settlement. Fort Garry had originally been a Hudson's Bay Company (HBC) trading post, beside which had developed the village of Winnipeg. The Métis led independent lives, left mainly to their own devices by the HBC, for which many of them worked as agents or trappers. During the 1860s the traditional life of the Métis had come under threat. As the HBC prepared to sell its vast lands – Rupert's land and the North-Western Territory – to the British Crown, English-speaking settlers, mainly from Ontario, began to move increasingly into the lower Red River Valley. The establishment in 1867 of the Dominion of Canada exposed the fragility of the semi-autonomy of the Métis. In November 1869 the HBC sold its lands as the Northwest Territories to Great Britain, which in turn prepared to hand them over to Canada to enlarge the Dominion.

Without waiting for a formal transfer of the Northwest Territories, the federal government in Ottawa sent land surveyors to the Red River settlements. The Métis were already angry at having, in Butler's words, 'themselves and their possessions signed away without one word of consent or one word of approval'. On 8 December 1869 they proclaimed a provisional government, and three weeks later elected the twenty-five-year-old ex-seminarian Louis Riel[9] as its president.

Riel had one particularly strong card in dealing with the federal government in Ottawa. This was the Red River itself, which rose in the United States and flowed north through Minnesota, before crossing the international boundary on the 49th parallel at Pembina on its journey to Lake Winnipeg. In Minnesota it was felt that the entire river should be a United States waterway. This prospect was viewed with alarm in Ottawa and London. Riel would have to be persuaded or coerced into joining the new Canada. In a position of some strength, he was, however, out of his depth, unable to make a decisive move or to negotiate to his best advantage. In January 1870 he agreed that the Métis would join the Dominion as the new Province of Manitoba. However, the new English-speaking settlers agitated against being ruled by a Francophile Métis government. There were isolated outrages, and in March Riel took a fateful step when, without benefit of trial, he had one of the leading agitators shot.

In tandem with diplomatic moves in Ottawa to address Métis grievances, London was preparing the imperial forces in Canada for a military expedition to the Red River. The fastest route to Fort Garry was via the United States, but such a route was out of the question. A British-led force would have to confine itself to British territory. This would involve a long and gruelling passage, 550 miles of forests, ravines, lakes and rivers, from the western shore of Lake Superior to the Red River estuary at Lake Winnipeg. It would be a difficult and unorthodox expedition. The man chosen to lead it was Garnet Wolseley.

Firm reports of the proposed expedition appeared while Butler was still in Ireland. Via the recently laid transatlantic telegraph cable he wired the briefest of messages: 'To Colonel Wolseley. Winnipeg Expedition. Please remember me. Butler. 69th.'[10] He then crossed to London and booked passage across the Atlantic. Arriving in Canada, Butler went directly to meet Wolseley in Toronto. It was late May. Preparations for the expedition were well advanced. It would be a task force of 1200 soldiers, 500 British army regulars and 700 Canadian militia. Wolseley had already chosen his staff officers. He had been inundated with applications and had selected men of promise. He had received Butler's cable and had found a post for him:

> Up to that time the only information we had received from the Red River
> territory had come from unreliable sources ... I explained [to Butler] that I

wanted an able soldier that I could trust implicitly to go via the United States to the Red River settlement to judge for himself as to the conditions of affairs there ... This roving commission that required so many rare qualities was one after his own heart, and he was just the man to carry it out admirably."

Butler's assignment would have to be cleared by Ottawa: a British officer travelling through the United States on his way to a spying mission in a disputed territory was a delicate matter. At this juncture, with strong hopes of his mission being approved, Butler's cup ran over. On 24 May 1870 a stream of telegrams poured into military headquarters at Montreal. Armed men had been seen on the United States side of the frontier fifty miles south of Montreal. Their destination seemed to be Canada. The Fenians were again on the march.

The 69th, stationed in Quebec, were ordered immediately to the frontier, and Butler was instructed to rejoin them. When the 69th steamed into Montreal *en route* to the border village of Huntingdon, near Lake St Francis, the ebullient Butler, leading a powerful chestnut saddle horse to carry him into the backwoods of the frontier, was on the railway platform to meet them. Huntingdon was remote, little more than a village on a byroad, and the task of the 69th was to assist the local militia.

The morning after their arrival Butler led a small patrol along the dirt road towards the border. Reaching the international boundary, which was marked by a square stone set at the roadside, he waited for a time and then watched in disbelief as some two hundred men appeared in the distance marching four abreast towards him, morning sunlight glinting on their rifles. He pulled back beyond a wooded bend well on the Canadian side of the frontier. When he next ventured a reconnoitre he found the Fenians had not stopped at the border. Still in marching order, they were now within three hundred yards of him. This time they were close enough for action. Butler, in his red tunic, tall in the saddle, presented an irresistible target. As he wheeled his horse and galloped back round the bend, rifles cracked behind him. By the time Company 10 of the 69th – Butler's old company – and the militia had come up, the Fenians had barricaded the road and dispersed most of their men into hop-fields on either side of it. At the first volley from the 69th, the barricade was abandoned. The Fenians vanished into the fields and, hidden from the fire of the militia, retreated across the waterway which marked the international boundary. The 'Battle' of Trout River, 26 May 1870, the final Fenian incursion into

Canada, was over. Butler made no attempt to inflate its importance. Some years later in London he was

> in a haircutter's shop near the Haymarket. After the manner of his profession the barber was extremely communicative. He had had a brother in the 69th regiment, but he had suffered so much in Canada in the war there that he was never any good again. 'What war was it?', I asked. 'The War of Trout River', he answered; and then the details followed; – the men had no food, they lay for days and days in the forest, until they had to eat their blankets. I laughed so much that he suspended his operations to stare at my reflection in the glass. There are many ways of writing history.[12]

After Trout River, the 69th returned to Quebec where Butler's appointment as intelligence officer to the Red River Expedition was confirmed. Via Chicago and St Paul, he reached Fort Abercrombie on the Red River in mid-July. He was now 200 miles upriver from Fort Garry. There was no news of the expedition which had gone into the woods west of Lake Superior a month previously. Information on the situation in the Red River Valley was vague, though it was known that Riel had agents along the border who kept him informed of all strangers arriving at the frontier post of Pembina. Fortuitously, Butler's arrival at Fort Abercrombie was well-timed. A hundred miles to the north, a battered paddle steamer, the *International*, would shortly be making the trip down to Fort Garry. He spent a hard two days trail-riding to board the steamer. The *International* was decrepit, but its meandering progress towards the border was helped by the current. Somewhere *en route* Butler befriended a dog, a black pointer, which he kept by him with a view to getting in some wildfowl shooting. When they reached the frontier post of Pembina, he found

> ... a sense of dirt and debauchery which seemed to pervade the place. Some of the leading citizens came forth with hands stuck so deep in breeches' pockets, that the shoulders seemed to have formed an offensive and defensive alliance with the arms, never again to permit the hands to emerge into daylight unless it should be in the vicinity of the ankles.[13]

Steaming on into nominal British territory, Butler noticed two horsemen galloping away from Pembina in the direction of Fort Garry. The arrival of the steamer there would not be unannounced, and Butler had drawn attention to himself by the pier at Pembina when he inquired if there was any mail for him. In his cabin he went through his baggage and took from it some maps and official papers, a colt six-shooter and a carbine. He stuffed a supply of ammunition into his pockets. He passed the rest of his baggage over to the captain for safekeeping and, as the high summer evening closed in, waited while the steamer covered the last miles to Fort Garry.

One of his fellow passengers, an Englishman called Dreever, had earlier attracted his attention in conversation by being strongly anti-Riel. He took this man into his confidence, explaining that he was determined to avoid being detained when the *International* berthed. Safety was to be found twenty miles downriver from Fort Garry at the English-speaking settlement of Stone Fort. Butler was prepared to fight his way there if necessary.

His companion suggested a less risky course. It would be dark when they reached Fort Garry. The fort itself stood on the left bank of the Assiniboine River above its confluence with the Red. The steamer would swing sharply into the Assiniboine to reach its berth and as it swung it would brush that river's left bank. Both men would leap ashore and be in Winnipeg before the steamer had moored. As they approached their destination, Butler and Dreever took up their positions by the bow of the steamer. Butler's rifle was concealed under his black capote. The pointer stood quietly beside him.

The boat began to turn into the narrow Assiniboine. A short distance in front, the lights of Fort Garry appeared, and Butler could see figures moving. Both men jumped for shore and scrambled up the steep bank, Butler encumbered with rifle and dog:

> In a short time we had reached the vicinity of a few straggling houses whose white walls showed distinctly through the darkness; this, he told me, was the village of Winnipeg. Here was his residence and here we were to separate ... As I emerged from the farther side of the village I saw, standing on the centre of the road, a solitary figure. Approaching nearer to him, I found that he occupied a narrow wooden bridge which opened out upon the prairie. To pause or hesitate would only be to excite suspicion in the mind of this man, sentinel or guard as he might be. So, at a sharp pace I advanced towards him. He never moved; and without word or sign I passed him at arm's length. But here the dog, which I had unfastened when parting from my companion, strayed away, and, being loth to lose him, I stopped at the farther end of the bridge to call him back.[14]

It was a precarious position, and after a couple of self-conscious whistles Butler walked on without the dog which, obviously on home territory, was travelling no farther. Butler set off at a fast pace towards Stone Fort. Meanwhile, back at Fort Garry, Riel himself, on the information brought by the Pembina horsemen, had come to the pier to confront the British stranger. He was enraged at Butler's disappearance. He impounded the steamer, had Dreever hauled from his home in Winnipeg and put in custody, and sent half-a-dozen mounted men after Butler. They did not find him. Butler later heard that he had been represented as a man 'of colossal proportions ... [carrying] arms of novel and terrible construction and, more mysterious still, followed by a gigantic dog'. This explained why 'the pursuit, vigorously though it commenced, should have waned faint as it left behind the neighbourhood and habitations of men'.[15]

Butler reached the safety of Stone Fort where there was disappointing news. The Red River expedition was still labouring hundreds of miles to the east. He spent several days gathering intelligence and then made ready to travel on by canoe to meet the expedition. Unexpectedly, he received a message from Riel inviting him to come up to Fort Garry for a meeting. The emissary stressed that the Métis were a peaceful people, loyal to Canada and concerned only to secure their rights in the Dominion. Butler made the most of his position, seeing Riel as the supplicant and himself as the representative of Her Majesty. He asked for three assurances before he would visit Riel: his baggage, impounded with the steamer, should be returned to him; Dreever, still in custody, should be released; and the Union Jack alone should fly over Fort Garry. His first two conditions were met and, with an escort provided by Riel, he travelled to Fort Garry.

In daylight the surroundings of Fort Garry were unimpressive. The fort itself was ramshackle, 'the whole aspect of the place desolate and ruinous'. It had two flagstaffs. From one hung a tattered Union Jack, from the other the new Métis flag. It was white and had two emblems, a fleur-de-lis representing the French ancestry of the Métis, and a shamrock, representing the Fenian aspiration of republican separatism. The secretary to the Métis government was one of Riel's former teachers, an Irish mathematician called William O'Donoghue.

Butler had a private meeting with Riel. He took an aversion to this 'short stout man with a large head, a sallow puffy face, a sharp restless, intelligent eye'. And he noted sardonically that Riel's gentleman's attire, black frock coat and trousers, was 'not a little marred' by his moccasins.

The potency of that composite dress image for the modern reader – the cultural inclusivity which it represented – was lost on Butler.[16] Riel stressed that he wished to retain power only until he could hand it over to a proper government: the recently arrived English-speaking settlers were not going to trample on the historic rights of the Métis. As he spoke, Riel grew declamatory, something which 'only made him appear ridiculous'. Yet Butler's disdain for Riel did not blind him to the fact that the Métis leader appeared devoid of self-interest:

> ... the question uppermost in his mind was one of which he did not speak, and he deserves the credit of his silence. Amnesty or no amnesty was at that moment a matter of very grave import to the French half-breeds, and to none so much as their leader. Yet he never asked if that pardon was an event on which he could calculate. He did not allude to it at all.[17]

Butler took his leave of Riel well satisfied with his mission to date. His intelligence gathering over the previous days had been thorough and he had had the bonus of meeting the Métis leader face to face. Furthermore, over the previous few days he had been making his first tangible contacts with Indians, for below Stone Fort there was an Ojibwa settlement. He had addressed, through an interpreter, an assembly of two hundred Ojibwa, exhorting them to take no part in the disturbances, telling them that the soldiers of the 'Great Mother' were on their way to establish peace. Butler's relish for this meeting is strikingly clear from his account of it. This was the stuff of boyhood fantasy made real. He lists the names of the elders: Kechwis, The Big Apron; Sou Souse, Little Long Ears; We-we-tak-gum Na-gash, The Man who flies round the Feathers. And he noted humorously that there was no Pahaouza-tau-ka, Great Scalp-taker.

The settlement was at the limits of constrained living. From here the Red River wound into the lonely expanses of Lake Winnipeg. The evening after his meeting with Riel, Butler pushed off from Stone Fort in a birch-bark canoe with a four-man crew. He carried basic supplies for his journey: tea, biscuit, flour, and the staple diet for wilderness travel – pemmican, a compound of dried meat, berries, sugar and fat. His paddlers drove their fragile craft with speed and dexterity down the marshy estuary towards Lake Winnipeg. The following day:

> Emerging from the sedges of the Red River we shot out into the waters of an immense lake... Not a wave, not a ripple on its surface; not a breath of

breeze to aid the untiring paddles. The little canoe, weighed down by men and provisions, had scarcely three inches of its gunwale over the water, and yet the steersman held his course far out into the glassy waste, leaving behind the marshy headlands which marked the river's mouth.

... The sun began to sink towards the west; but still not a breath rippled the surface of the lake, not a sail moved over the wide expanse, all was as lonely as though our tiny craft had been the sole speck of life on the waters of the world. The red sun sank into the lake, warning us that it was time to seek the shore and make our beds for the night ... As the night shades deepened around us and the red glare of our drift-wood fire cast its light upon the woods and rocks, the scene became one of rare beauty. As I sat watching ... there suddenly emerged from the forest two dusky forms. They were Ojibbeways, who came to share our fire and our evening meal. The land was still their own.[18]

Crossing to the south-east corner of Lake Winnipeg, Butler asked at a trading post if there was any news of the expedition. Nothing. By now it was late July. He decided to go up the 160 miles of the Winnipeg River to its source in the Lake of the Woods. The next five days were to be a revelation, 'filled from dawn to dark with moments of keenest enjoyment, everything was new and strange and each hour brought with it some fresh surprise of Indian skill or Indian scenery'.

The Winnipeg River drops steeply through heavily wooded country in its violent journey from source to mouth. Increasing his crew to five, Butler set off upriver. His canoe was a light frame of cedar covered with birchbark whose overlapping strips were gummed with pine resin. Paddlers and craft blended in the water, working up rapids and navigating turbulent currents. After any particularly arduous and adroit paddling session, 'the Indians rest on their paddles and laugh'. On the frequent portages the canoe was handled with extraordinary gentleness. At night, Butler's crew would rig a simple shelter for him from branches and a piece of sailcloth. Each morning the embers of the previous night's fire would be fanned to flame and the day would start with the smell of woodsmoke and the sound of birdsong. The immensity of the woods, the might of the river, the abundance of nature – all these provided a reserve of emotional sustenance for Butler that was to prove inexhaustible.

Reaching the Lake of the Woods, Butler found no trace of Wolseley. He made a sixty-mile crossing of the lake to the estuary of the Rainy River and here, at last, there was definite news. To the east a young Indian had seen a great army of white braves ... like locusts'. Butler pressed on. At Fort Frances, near the source of the Rainy, he learnt that Wolseley was 'expected for breakfast'. Ascending the last two miles of the river, he intercepted him.

It was 4 August 1870, eight weeks since Butler had had his assignment confirmed in Montreal. During that time the Red River expedition had been inching its way through the woods and waters of northern Ontario. Some two hundred boats carrying troops and supplies were crewed by civilian voyageurs. The rallying cry of the troops was 'On to Fort Garry', while the motto of the classically schooled officers was the first line of the *Aeneid*, 'Armaque, virumque cano' (I sing of arms and the man), punningly translated as 'Arms, men and canoes'.

Butler's reports were invaluable to Wolseley: strong support in the Red River Valley for the expedition, the Métis confused, their leader vacillating. His account of his meeting with Riel added a touch of glitter to an assignment very competently executed. By 23 August he was back at Stone Fort with fifty boats carrying Wolseley and the advance of the expedition. Six miles short of Fort Garry, the force spent a very wet night, and the next morning, with rain still falling, the sodden expedition reached its climax:

> ... the troops began to disembark from the boats for the final advance upon Fort Garry. The preliminary arrangements were soon completed, and the little army with its two brass guns trundling along behind Red River carts commenced its march across the mud-soaked prairie. How unspeakably dreary it all looked! The bridge, the wretched village, the crumbling fort, the vast level prairie, watersoaked, draped in mist, and pressed down by low-lying clouds.[19]

The Métis offered no resistence. That morning Riel and his officials had fled across the Assiniboine from where they listened to the cannonade that announced that the Red River, since 15 July the province of Manitoba, was secured for the Dominion of Canada. For the expedition, it was a damp and disappointing finish to months of toil. Militiamen, troops and voyageurs went on an orgy of drinking and 'men became perfectly helpless, lying stretched upon the prairie for hours as though they were bereft of life itself'.

By the first week in September, when Adam Archibald, the first Lieutenant Governor of Manitoba, arrived at Fort Garry to take up his responsibilities for the province and the Northwest Territories, the expedition had already begun to return east. Wolseley returned to a hero's welcome in

Montreal and Ottawa. Back in London the prospect of dizzying career heights began to open up for him, and he would be knighted for his leadership of the bloodless expedition.

And what of Butler in 1870? There is a line-drawing from *The Great Lone Land* which shows him at the source of the Rainy River on 4 August. He stands alone on a large rock outcrop, caught by the morning sun. Tall, full bearded, he waves his hat towards the large Iroquois canoe that is carrying Wolseley towards him. From the canoe a figure waves back. Behind Wolseley, strung out across the lake, is the advance of the expedition's flotilla. Butler belongs in that world of order and regulation, yet he is apart from it. Beneath him, by the side of the outcrop, out of sight of the approaching flotilla, kneel three Ojibwa in a small canoe. They are a symbol of the life beyond order and regulation which Progress, that most confidently held nineteenth-century belief, cannot see.

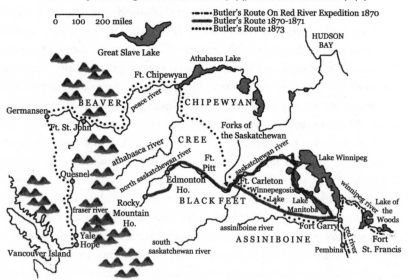

BUTLER'S CANADIAN TRAVELS 1870 - 1873
From the maps illustrating 'The Wild North Land' (1874) & 'The Great Lone Land' (1872)

Chapter Four

SEARCHING FOR A ROAD

Butler did not accompany Wolseley's expedition on its homeward journey from Fort Garry. Instead, he decided to return to Montreal as he had travelled out, via the United States, because it would allow him some extra time for wildfowl shooting in the marshes of the Red River. Towards the end of September 1870 he finally, as he thought, left Fort Garry, crossing into the United States on the *International*. During a chance conversation with a member of the Canadian bench, who was on his way downriver, the jurist asked Butler to return to Fort Garry with him to take delivery of several despatches for Ottawa. A routine request, it would add ten days to Butler's schedule, and he was happy to accede to it. It was, however, to have momentous repercussions, for back at Fort Garry he was presented with a dazzling opportunity by Governor Adam Archibald:

> 'I am so glad you have returned,' said the governor, Mr. Archibald, when I met him on the evening of my arrival, 'because I want to ask you if you will undertake a much longer journey than anything you have yet done. I am going to ask you if you will accept a mission to the Saskatchewan Valley and through the Indian countries of the West. Take a couple of days to think over it, and let me know your decision.' 'There is no necessity, sir,' I replied, ' to consider the matter, I have already made up my mind, and, if necessary, will start in half an hour.' On the 24th of October I quitted Fort Garry, at ten o'clock at night, and turning out into the level prairie, commenced a long journey towards the west.'

Butler's commission from Archibald involved an assessment of the state of law and order in the region, the effect of a recent smallpox epidemic on the Indians, and the state of the fur trade. Having been sworn in as a Justice of the Peace, Butler left Fort Garry in October 1870 with five horses, and a cart whose contents included two large crates of medical supplies and a stack of printed directions for the treatment of smallpox. These supplies were for distribution to the isolated forts on his itinerary, and to any small settlements he might come across. He was accompanied by the first of a succession of Métis guides, and by an official of the Hudson's Bay Company who happened to be travelling the early stages of his route. This was the journey out of which came *The Great Lone Land*, the book that would bring Butler emphatically to the attention of the reading public in the United Kingdom and in North America when it was published in 1872.

The great lone land of the title referred to the new Canadian territories of Alberta, Assiniboia, Athabasca, and Saskatchewan. Here were the prairies, extending westwards to the Rocky Mountains, and bounded to the north by the mixed woodlands below the evergreen forests of the sub-Arctic. The heart of the prairies was the interior plains. This was the ancestral home of the Plains Indians – Assiniboine, Blackfeet, Cree, Crow, Salteaux and Snake; the land of the bison and the mounted chase, the eagle-feathered war bonnet, the teepee and travois. Butler travelled this country by wagon, on horseback and by dog sled. It was a journey that took him over 1200 miles westwards into the foothills of the Rockies before circling back, via the valley of the Saskatchewan River and across frozen Lakes Manitoba and Winnipeg, to Fort Garry. His total trek covered over 2700 miles through an area with a population of a mere thirty thousand.

Readers of *The Great Lone Land* met an author with strong sympathies for victims of nineteenth-century Progress, a writer of considerable power, with forthright views and the ability to express himself trenchantly. *The Great Lone Land* vividly presents the nomadic world of the First Nations as being on the edge of near-extinction. Butler observed what he believed was the terminal decline of the traditional peoples of the Great Plains. He did not temper his words in apportioning culpability:

> The whole white world is leagued in bitter strife against the Indian ... The
> most curious anomaly among the race of man, the red man of America, is

passing away beneath our eyes into the infinite solitude. The possession of the same noble qualities which we affect to reverence among our nations makes us kill him. If he would be as the African or the Asiatic, it would be all right for him; if he would be our slave he might live, but as he won't be that, won't toil and delve and hew for us, and will persist in hunting, fishing and roaming over the beautiful prairie land which the Great Spirit gave him; in a word, since he will be free – we kill him ... I know that it is the fashion to hold in derision and mockery the idea that nobility, poetry, or eloquence exist in the wild Indian. I know that with that low brutality which has ever made the Anglo-Saxon race deny its enemy the possession of one atom of generous sensibility, that dull enmity which prompted us to paint the Maid of Orleans a harlot, and to call Napoleon the Corsican robber – I know that that same instinct glories in degrading the savage, whose chief crime is that he prefers death to slavery.[2]

This passage is interesting for more than what it says about the fate of the First Nations of Canada. When it is considered that Butler was as yet merely a lieutenant in the army with his career still before him, the references to Joan of Arc and Napoleon above are indicative of his strong independence of mind. Separately, there is his unambiguous reference to himself as Anglo-Saxon, 'that dull enmity which prompted *us*'. This self-labelling could merely be an *ad hoc* reference for the purpose of his argument. However, it is more likely to be an exercise by Butler in self-definition: he was an active participant, as a British officer, in the expansion of imperial rule across vast new territories of which Saskatchewan alone covered 250,000 square miles.

The Great Lone Land was published in London in 1872 to great acclaim. It was the scale of Butler's journey and the natural constraints of winter prairie travel that caught the attention of the reading public. The book was hailed in the *Annual Register* as 'a fascinating volume ... a thrilling narrative ... of dangers manfully faced and hardships cheerfully endured', and it was to remain a strong seller over the following decade, running into eleven impressions.

While the trials of trail life are well rendered in *The Great Lone Land*, Butler is also good on the routine aspects of his itinerant existence. With the full onset of winter he fought the cold by discarding his hat and boots for a parka and moccasins. He wore moose-skin mittens, and covered his stirrup irons with strips of buffalo skin. In temperatures as low as minus twenty degrees Celsius he would often sleep in the open on a buffalo robe, wrapped in a seven-foot deerskin sleeping-bag whose outer layer was of canvas.

Readers of *The Great Lone Land* were impressed with Butler's energy and resourcefulness. He came across as physically robust and as a man of considerable courage and assertiveness, willing to give most things a try. What *The Great Lone Land* did not do was give much sense of the impact he made on those who met him. There is, however, an account of Butler from that time. One of his longest days on horseback was the fifteen hours he spent in the saddle on the last stretch to Fort Pitt on the North Saskatchewan River. The final weary wintry miles were at night, and when he and his companions eventually found the hospitality of the fort, they were treated to a hot meal of buffalo steaks and potatoes before an open hearth crackling with an aromatic pinewood fire. They were served at table by an attractive young woman called Mary Sinclair, of mixed Scots and Cree parentage. A lifetime afterwards Mary Sinclair reminisced among friends about the might-have-been:

> ... once long ago, when I was a young girl, there was an officer who came to Fort Pitt. He was tall and very goodlooking, and he could talk so well. I thought I could have loved him. He came out of the snow and storm one night like someone from a different world. He went on to Fort Edmonton and when he was away I thought of him often. Afterwards he came back and I was glad. He spoke to me about his home in Ireland and asked me to marry him and go with him to the Old Country. I did like him very much but I was a child of the North-West and what would I do in other lands? Perhaps I cried a little, but I sent him away without me.[3]

It is not credible that Butler, enthusiastically engaged on a special commission which focused his restless energy and stretched his methodical intelligence, could have been serious about returning with a backwoods bride of mixed racial parentage to 'the Old Country'. He was probably interested in no more than a dalliance. Yet Mary Sinclair's words still radiate something of his irrepressible vitality.

The foothills of the Rockies were the westernmost limit of Butler's journey. When he turned his back on the 'mighty barrier' it was with a determination to return. His commission allowed him to chose his own route back to Fort Garry. He backtracked to Fort Edmonton (modern Edmonton, the capital of Alberta), where, instead of simply retracing his steps farther, he followed the north branch of the Saskatchewan River down towards Lake Winnipeg. At first he stayed close to his outward route, revisiting several of the forts, but his new course soon brought him towards the northern limits of the prairies. He did this sub-zero winter journey with dogs, often 'toiling from dawn to dark through blinding drift and intense cold'. Butler was initially appalled at the beatings his drivers administered to their animals but soon came to the conclusion that this brutality was a result of the combination of poor drivers and poor dogs. The best drivers relied on tongue lashings. Dogs and dog driving were the staples of campfire conversation. A man able to drive huskies for up to fifty miles a day without injury to them was highly respected. Butler himself learnt to drive dogs until, for the last six weeks of his journey, he had his own dog team, a quartet of pure-bred huskies whose leader was Cerf Volant. Cerf was untiring and intelligent, and Butler developed a special bond with him.

Over everything in *The Great Lone Land*, stark and unmitigated, hangs what Butler saw as the hopelessness of the condition of the Indian. Towards the book's close Butler presents his short and controlled narrative of the old Cree. He relates how one day he came across a solitary birch lodge in the snows. Inside a Cree is keening. The old man has lost his son-in-law to over-exertion in hunting. The dead man's widow and child silently watch the flames that flicker towards the conical roof from a small fire. 'He hunted for us; he fed us,' the old man said. 'I am too old to hunt; I can scarce see the light; I would like to die too.'[4]

Unlike the Indians, the Métis of the Northwest Territories did not engage Butler's sympathies. His disdainful attitude to Riel has already been noted. In general, he was dismissive of the Métis:

> The half breeds are a race easily offended, prone to sulk if reproved ... I had never been a believer in the pluck and courage of the men who are descendants of mixed European and Indian parents. Admirable as guides, unequalled as *voyageurs*, trappers and hunters, they nevertheless are wanting in those qualities which give courage or true manhood.[5]

Butler's assessment of the Métis points up his own mid-Victorian ideals of masculinity; 'true manhood', an obsolescent phrase today, conjures up a range of attributes that includes chivalry, personal honour and valour, attributes exemplified in robust action and straight-dealing. Against these standards, Butler found the Métis wanting. Their ambivalence and emollience appeared to him as negatives in the catalogue of virtues. He viewed them with some distaste, neither victims nor victors in the march of progress. His description of them as 'prone to sulk' captures that condescension found among men of empire towards peoples who were not urbane.

The 13,000-word official report[6] of his journey which Butler wrote for Governor Archibald underscores this condescending attitude and exposes the certainties that drove European expansion into what Butler described as 'an abundance of fertile regions admirably suited to colonialism'. How were these regions to prosper? asked Butler. Not through the Métis who, when not employees of the Hudson's Bay Company, are 'removed from the means of acquiring knowledge and civilization [which] has tended in no small degree to throw them back in the social scale and to make the establishment of a prosperous colony almost an impossibility'. The Northwest Territories – ordered and regulated – would develop through 'the immense wave of human life which rolls unceasingly from Europe to America ... destined to reach those beautiful solitudes, and to convert the wild luxuriance of their now useless vegetation into all the required elements of civilized existence'.

Butler's commission from Archibald included ascertaining the effects of a recent smallpox epidemic which had ravaged the area; assessing the state of the fur trade; and taking a crude census of Indian populations between the Red River and the Rockies. In reporting the scourge of smallpox, Butler's compassion breaks strongly through the constraints of official prose. The appalling sufferings of Cree and Blackfoot, and their stoicism in the grip of pestilence, are strikingly portrayed. There had been previous epidemics of smallpox in these areas. This one, in combination with the slaughter of the buffalo, heralded the end of the nomadic culture of the plains. Butler calculated that the total Indian population on the Canadian plains was only 26,800.

Butler's commission also involved an examination of the situation along the Saskatchewan with regard to troops being sent there to maintain order. He made three recommendations: the appointment of a peripatetic civil magistrate or commissioner; the establishment of two government stations; and 'the organization of a well-equipped force of from 100 to 150 men, one-third to be mounted, specially recruited and engaged for service in the Saskatchewan, enlisting for two or three years' service, and at expiration of that period to become military settlers, receiving grants of land, but still remaining as a reserve force should their services be required'.

It was that last recommendation – for a well-equipped force, mobile and one third *mounted* – that gave Butler his niche in Canadian history. His proposal was endorsed in a further report in the following year, presented by Colonel Robertson-Ross of the Canadian Militia to the federal government in Ottawa (Federal Prime Minister, Sir John A. Macdonald, had himself examined the feasibility of such an idea late in 1869[7]). In May 1873 the new force was established as the North-West Mounted Police, under Lieutenant-Colonel George Arthur French from Co Roscommon; it was armed and fully mounted, not as a military force but as a civil one. The initial intake was 150 men, the upper limit of the strength suggested by Butler. The first red-coated Mounties, as they became known, were deployed from Fort Garry in November 1873 and became an indispensable part of the new Canada.

On 20 February 1871 Butler, having mushed across the white wastes of lakes Winnipegosis and Manitoba, arrived back at Fort Garry. As one of his priorities, he found a good home for Cerf, his lead husky. He completed his report in less than three weeks and presented it to Archibald, who was highly appreciative and wrote to Ottawa recommending Butler's assignment in some capacity to the Northwest Teritories.

When Butler got to Ottawa, he met Sir John A. Macdonald, and other influential figures:

> They were highly complimentary, said nice things about the three thousand miles travel in the wilderness ... hemmed and hawed when it came to Governor Archibald's recommendation ... these excellent colonial ministers had wives, sons, and daughters. An army officer who married a minister's daughter might perchance have been a fit and proper person to introduce the benefits of civilization to the Blackfeet Indians on the western prairies, but if he elected to remain in single cussedness in Canada he was pretty certain to find himself a black sheep among the ministerial flock of aspirants for place, no matter what might have been the value of his individual services.[8]

Butler's speculative venture with Horatio Case was yielding nothing. The 69th had been posted to Bermuda and Butler thought it would be a retrograde step to rejoin them. He had outgrown regimental routine as a lieutenant, and he believed that his services to Canada must be worth a captaincy without Purchase. He decided to put his case in London, and crossed the Atlantic forearmed with the knowledge that both the Colonial Office and the War Office had been formally advised by Ottawa of his meritorious service.

In London in May he was accepted as a Fellow of the Royal Geographical Society on the strength of his Canadian travels. He did not fare as well in terms of his career development. Ostensibly his chances of promotion were good, not least because he was prepared to take an unattached captaincy on half-pay. The Purchase system was also about to be abolished as part of the reform of the army being carried out by Edward Cardwell, the Secretary of State for War in the first government of William Gladstone. However, Butler found himself ensnared in the coils of bureaucracy. It was explained to him that he could not be promoted on merit to captain before Purchase was abolished; if he were, he would be unable to sell his commission, and he would have the right to be compensated for this. Further, following the abolition of Purchase, scheduled for the autumn of 1871, there would be a moratorium on promotions until 1872. Butler would have to wait. Garnet Wolseley, now Sir Garnet, recently appointed by Cardwell as an assistant adjutant general at the War Office with responsibility for modernizing disciplinary practice in the army, was unable to help his talented protégé.

Suddenly, in late May, London was agog with the news that Paris was burning. Civil war had broken out between the bourgeois republican government based at Versailles and the radical workers' commune of Paris. Butler crossed over to France to see for himself what was happening. It was to be a traumatic experience. In the period since his first visit at the end of 1869, France had been repeatedly convulsed as the new Germany, the Prussia of Bismarck, struggled for mastery in Europe with the France of Napoleon III. Butler's sympathies were anti-Prussian; he saw Germany as the bully-boy of Europe. In September 1870 Napoleon and 100,000 French troops had surrendered at Sedan, the Second Empire had fallen, and a demoralized France had proclaimed a republic. Germany had then overrun France and laid siege to Paris. Following the capitulation of Paris, German forces stayed on and watched while the communards took over the city in defiance of the National Assembly at Versailles. In April 1871 violence erupted when the National Assembly determined to regain Paris. The five-week siege which followed exceeded in viciousness anything that had occurred during the German siege of the city, and it culminated at the end of May in *La Semaine Sanglete*, the Week of Blood. It was this final phase of the conflict that brought Butler to France.

What he found shocked him. This was the week in which 17,000 people died in Paris. In 1871 technology was beginning to radically alter warfare: breech-loading rifles were already leading to the emergence of the sniper; rifled cannon were trebling the range and accuracy of artillery fire. France gave Butler a glimpse of what would routinely become the future of warfare: large-scale and prolonged disruption of civilian life, massive destruction of civic and commercial buildings, indiscriminate injury and death.

He secured lodgings at Versailles where the French goverment was directing operations against the city. Towards the close of his second day, he witnessed a remarkable procession coming out of Paris:

> ... a great straggling band of Communist prisoners, men, women, and children, ragged, fierce, powder-marked, streaming with perspiration; such people as I had never seen before; and have never seen since; faces at the last gasp of exhaustion; faces that looked scornfully at the howling mob of bourgeois, that shouting, racing crowd which ran under the elms on either side and ran out of the cafés, throwing vile epithets over the heads of the soldiers. At the end of this dismal column came the carts with the wounded. In one of these there sat, bolt upright, a woman in the prime of life; her black hair hung loose upon her shoulders, her olive face had a gash across one cheek from which the blood was still flowing, her hands were tied behind her back; two or three wounded men lay at her feet helplesssly stricken, but had there been a thousand dead or dying around her it would not have mattered. It was her face that held the eye. I have never forgotten the face and figure of that proud, defiant, handsome woman.[9]

The following day he managed to get into the city. The destruction appalled him. In the Place de la Concorde, where he had stood and marvelled in the brilliance of gaslight only seventeen months before, the buildings were roofless and charred. The Tuileries was nothing but bare gaunt walls behind which floors and rafters still burnt. The effect of the glare was 'like that of lighted candles set within a colossal skull'. The listless French troops occupying the city were demoralized former captives of the Germans. 'The moral rivets of their individual bodies and souls seemed to be as loose as were the social and political screws in the collective fabric of the state.' In the warm summer air, the city reeked with the smell of decomposing corpses. The government summarily executed prisoners. At La Rocquette Prison, Butler, sickened by 'a horrible smell as of a shambles' which filled the execution yard, had the process of trial coolly outlined for him by a young lieutenant:

'We strip their right shoulders,' he said. 'If the skin of the neck and shoulder shows the dark mark produced by the kick of the chasepot rifle the court pronounces the single word "classe"; if there is no mark or discoloration on the shoulder the president says "passe", and the man is released. Those to whom "classe" is said are shot. One hundred and fifty men were shot at daybreak this morning in this courtyard."[10]

Butler left France gripped with melancholy and doubt. Was this the soldier's life he actually wanted? More than that:

> The thought that had been growing in mind above every other thought in those days and amid those scenes was the hopelessness of all this social world of our so-called civilization. Was this all we had been able to do for the people, for the men who had nothing, for those poor whom we were always to have with us? Nations fought themselves into victory on one side and the other, dynasties rose and disappeared, religions ebbed and flowed; but in this war there was no cessation, no equilibrium, no end. The have's and the have not's were always face to face, ready to shoot down or to rush in."[11]

Butler badly needed an antidote to the sordidness of Paris. He still had some leave left, so he came back to Ireland where he began to write *The Great Lone Land*. At the expiry of his leave, he was ordered to report to the 69th's home base in London. The regiment was still in Bermuda and there was little for Butler to do. He continued writing and in a 'little dingy red-brick subaltern's quarter ... at Chatham I lived again in the wilds'. Early in 1872 he unsuccessfully put his name forward to the Royal Geographical Society to join a small expedition preparing to go to east Africa in search of David Livingstone, who had disappeared some years previously while seeking the source of the Nile. However there now came a unexpected turn-of-events: a letter from Horatio Case in Canada to the effect that it was time for the three partners, Butler, Case and Wodehouse, to sell their plot of land near Petrolia to a commercial syndicate. The deal netted Butler $1000. Meantime in April the finished manuscript of *The Great Lone Land* was accepted for publication by Sampson Low, and his promotion to captain finally came through. Promotion was on half-pay to an unattached company, which meant he would have to wait for a vacancy to arise. Butler did not sit still. After repaying his debts in Tipperary, he still had a substantial amount of disposable income; 'I was free to go where I chose and I chose to go to the wilds again.'

Butler decided to go back to America. Still unsettled by his experience of the destruction and butchery of Paris, he was unsure about wanting to stay a soldier. Around this time his old friend Mansfield resigned from the army, adding to Butler's uncertainty about the course his life should take. America alone had given him the purpose and excitement that he was seeking. Perhaps his future lay there.

He crossed the Atlantic to New York in early May, visited Boston, and travelled on into Canada. Over the summer in Ottawa he made several un-successful representations for some kind of civil post. In the early fall he retraced his old route down the Red River to Fort Garry which, in the short time since he had first visited it, had been swallowed by Winnipeg, grown from small town to capital city. There he was reunited with Cerf. Buying two more dogs, and a cart and horses, he set out once again across the prairies. The weather was at its autumnal best. The dogs ran free; they would come into their own for winter travel. Butler was headed for the Forks of the Saskatchewan River to meet Mansfield and another old col-league of the 69th. The three men proposed to winter in a log cabin in the heavily wooded country of the Forks, and with Butler's arrival at the end of October, they set out on a month-long hunting expedition to the plains of the South Saskatchewan River to provision themselves with meat 'be-fore the fierceness and desolation of the prairie winter set in'. It was early December before they returned to their cabin in the woods.

The three were not totally isolated. Two Cree families built a lodge across the river from them and frequently crossed the ice for handouts. Trappers occasionally passed by, and within a day's hard travel either up or downriver there was a small trading post. The posts did not impress Butler. Between the old life of the Indian and the ordered life of European settle-ment was the world of 'the brutish pioneers of Anglo-American freedom':

> Civilization, or what we term such, rolls with queer strides across the American continent ... To civilize a new land is the easiest of tasks if we but set about it after the American model. Here is the recipe. Given a realm from which the red man has been banished, tricked, shot, or hunted out; from which the bison or the elk have been chased; a lonely tenantless land with some great river flowing in long winding reaches silently through its vast plains and mountain gorges: here then is what you have to do:
>
> Place on the river a steamboat of the rudest construction. Wherever

the banks are easy of ascent, or where a smaller stream seeks the main river, build a drinking house of rough hewn logs; let the name of God be used only in blasphemy, and language be a medium for the conveyance of curses. Let every man chew when he isn't smoking and spit when he isn't asleep; and then when half a dozen persons have come to violent ends – when killing has literally become 'no murder' – your new land will be thoroughly civilized.[12]

The 'brutish pioneers' were not the only harbingers of 'civilization' on whom Butler focused a critical eye. Christian proselytizers had a fundamental shortcoming:

I believe, gentlemen missionaries, you mean well by this Indian. I will go further; you form, I think, almost the only class who would deal fairly by him, but you go to work in a wrong direction; your mode of proceeding is a mistake. If you would only be a little more human and a little less divine – if you would study the necessities of the savage races amidst whom you have cast your lot – what good might ye not effect? ... Make him a good man before you attempt to make him an indifferent Christian. In a word, do more for his body.[13]

Those two quotations are from *The Wild North Land*. While wintering at the Forks, Butler spent some of his time writing up notes towards a second travel book. He needed something distinctive if he was not literally to retrace the ground covered by *The Great Lone Land*. He decided on a journey into the north-west across the ancestral lands of the Chipewyan, Cree and Beaver Indians. Using dog sleds, he would travel to the foothills of the Rockies, cross those great mountains on foot and come down to the Pacific coast of British Columbia. He calculated that the journey could take four months. His two companions were not interested in this scheme; they wanted to return to the Red River. Butler was not deterred, and at the start of February

all my preparations were completed, dogs fat strong and hearty, copper kettles, a buffalo robe, thermometer, 3 to 4 rounds of ammunition, a little tobacco and painkiller, a dial compasss, a pedometer, snow shoes, about 15 pounds of baggage, tea, sugar, a little flour and lastly the inevitable pemmican.[14]

He headed northwards into 'the vast stillness'. His nine-foot sled was of oak and birchwood, the frame held together with thongs. His dog team was led by Cerf. On a good day the dogs would cover thirty-five miles without hardship.

Travelling towards Lake Athabasca, Butler entered heavily wooded country. Fort Chipewyan at the western end of the lake was the northernmost limit of his journey. There he replenished his stores before turning westwards along the frozen Peace River accompanied by three unprepossessing sled drivers who 'met on a common basis of rascality'. They continually pilfered from him and incessantly complained. Matters were not helped when he succumbed to *mal de racquette*: he overdid his use of snowshoes and by the latter part of March his feet were very swollen. Nightly massage had little effect and soon he was hobbling. Stopping on the trail to recuperate was out of the question for time was against him: he had to take full advantage of the still-frozen river system which provided a level surface for dogs and sleds. Already the increased daylight hours were turning the snow to slush for longer each day. For an entire week Butler was reduced to huddling on his own sled as he was hauled slowly westwards. By the beginning of April he had reached British Columbia, which had joined the Dominion of Canada in 1871, and shortly after he arrived at the settlement of Fort St John on the Peace River in the foothills of the Rockies. He paid off his surly drivers and spent a restful week getting fully back on his feet.

By this time the spring thaw was well advanced. At Fort St John Butler sold off all his dogs except Cerf. He had grown even fonder of the dog during the past months and did not want to part with him. 'A man', he wrote, 'can seldom feel alone if he has a dog to share his supper, to stretch near him under the starlight, to answer him with tail wag, or glance of eye, or prick of ear.' His affection for his husky prompted two separate sets of sentimental verses in *The Wild North Land*. He pre-empted criticism of these by entitling them *Doggerel* and *More Doggerel*.

Butler's route from Fort St John was directly west into the mountains. With a guide and two local men as hauliers he left the station on 22 April 1873 for what turned out to be the toughest four weeks of his entire journey, pushing him to mental and physical extremes. He dislocated a thumb leading horses across ice. Then, while crossing the semi-frozen Peace River in a small canoe he overturned, and found himself trapped beneath his craft. Terrified of being dragged below the four-feet of solid ice which bordered the rushing midstream section of the river, Butler managed to kick himself free of the canoe, injuring his leg in the process. Two weeks later the party lost their heavy canoe in a fruitless attempt to navigate a canyon against the turbulent Ominica River which was swollen with icy meltwater from the mountains.

Once away from the Ominica River, the worst was over. Butler was now high in the Rockies, in the goldmining country of the Columbian plateau. Germansen, where he spent some days, was a typical mining town: less than twenty sturdy wooden houses with ditches and drains crisscrossing the hillsides. The miners endured 'almost incredible hardships' hunting for gold. Butler's reaction was typically practical-minded:

> When one sees this wonderful labour, this delving into the bowels of rock and shingle, this turning and twisting of river channel, and sluicing and dredging and blasting, going on in these strange out-of-the-way places, the thought occurs; if but the tenth part of this toil were expended by these men in the ordinary avocations of life, they would all be rich and comfortable.[15]

From Germansen, Butler travelled on foot and horseback 330 miles south to Quesnal on the Fraser River. He had crossed the continental watershed by now and was descending towards the lowlands of the Pacific coast. His trek had taken four months. It had been travel of a most arduous kind and he was exhilarated by his achievement. He crossed into the United States and indulged in the luxury of being a tourist: he visited Yosemite, went down to San Francisco and crossed the continent to the east by the recently completed transcontinental railroad. Cerf stayed with him, alert and lively, a continual source of attention in hotels and city streets. Man and dog were finally to part only when Butler left America for Europe in the early Fall. Meantime he worked steadily on the manuscript of his travels.

He also wrote an appendix[16] for the book, in which he argued that Canada's proposed transcontinental railway should run through the Rockies north of the 55th parallel, foreseeing that to the north of the Saskatchewan lay some of Canada's richest agricultural land (political and short-term commercial interests were to ensure that the transcontinental line would run much closer to the border with the United States). Butler also stated that time constraints did not allow him to more than mention that there were 'many subjects connected with the settlement of Indian tribes of the West and their protection against the inevitable injustices of the incoming settler'.

The Wild North Land was published at the start of 1874, prefaced with a quotation from Tennyson's *Ulysses*:

> *I cannot rest from travel. I will drink life to the lees.*
> *I am become a name for always roaming with a hungry heart.*

It was a success, but it suffered in comparison with its predecessor. It lacked both the novelty of the earlier book, and the topical interest which the Métis resistance at Red River had lent it. More importantly, *The Great Lone Land* was written out of a yearning for the wild which suffuses its pages while *The Wild North Land*, written while Butler was still in America, lacked that emotional sweep. There is a tedium in some of the ornate passages describing the immensity of the Canadian landscape and a noticeable development of a tendency, evident in *The Great Lone Land*, to pile on stock adjectives to achieve an effect.

Prominent in both books is the portrayal of Indians and of Indian life. A passage from the final chapter of *The Wild North Land* ends with this sombre image:

> One evening I stood in a muddy street of New York city. A crowd had gathered before the door of one of those immense buildings which our cousins rear along their thoroughfares and call hotels. The door opened and half a dozen dusky men came forth. 'Who are they?' I asked. 'They are the Sioux chiefs from the Yellowstone,' answered a bystander; 'they're a taking them to the the-a-ter, to see Lester Wallick.' Out on the great prairie I had often seen the Red man in his boundless home. Savage if you will but still a power in the land, and fitting in every way the wilds in which he dwells. The names of Red Cloud and his brother chiefs from the Yellowstone were household words to me. It was this same Red Cloud who led his five hundred whooping warriors on Fetterman's troops, when not one soldier escaped to tell the story of the fight in the foothills of the Wyoming Mountains; and here was Red Cloud now in semi-civilized dress, but still a giant 'midst the puny rabble that thronged to see him come forth; with the gaslight falling on his dusky features and his eyes staring in bewildered vacancy at the crowd around him.'[7]

Red Cloud or Mahpiua Luta, the Oglala Sioux, was one of the foremost of nineteenth-century First Nations leaders. Nine years after that sad spectacle, Butler gave the name Red Cloud to the eponymous hero of his one work of fiction, the classic boys' adventure story of life on the prairies.

Chapter Five

THE WHITE MAN'S GRAVE

Towards the end of his life, in the rural tranquillity of Bansha across the river Suir from Ballyslatteen, Lieutenant-General Sir William F. Butler, working on his autobiography, reminisced on his introduction to Africa and Africans thirty-five years before. His mood was reflective. 'Looking back now' he wrote, 'I can perceive things that I did not discern then ... We were looking for more than we had a right to expect.'

Butler's army career from late 1873 is a vivid illustration on an individual level of the unprecedented growth of the British empire during the last quarter of the nineteenth century. At that time a European expansionist movement, unparalleled for speed, size and thoroughness, swept across Africa. In 1872 Africa, almost entirely under African rule, was for Europe the Dark Continent. European settlements tended to be coastal enclaves, with the exception of southern Africa where Dutch-descended Boers had trekked away from British control in Cape Colony to set up the Orange Free State and the Transvaal. Over a period of less than twenty years, this situation was radically transformed as the great powers of Europe carved the continent into its modern political shape. Between 1873 and 1900 the British empire increased in size to embrace one-fifth of the land area of the globe, becoming the largest empire the world had known. Butler's eight African assignments during this period illustrate Britain's increasing involvement with the continent, while his own writings give a personal picture of what it meant to be a part of this extraordinary movement.

Butler's first experience of Africa was on the Gold Coast, part of modern Ghana. The Gold Coast was a British Protectorate and was under threat from the forest-dwelling Asante. The Asante empire was one of the most cohesive in Africa, claiming suzerainty over 95,000 square miles of land. Its capital, Kumasi, was 145 miles from the coast. Here the Asante ruler, the Asantehene, lived in a palace whose main function room could hold a thousand people. The empire was administered with a high degree of bureaucratic skill, and in the court at Kumasi were speakers of Arabic, Dutch and English.

In January 1873 the young Asantehene, Kofi KarKari, sent an invasion force of 12,000 soldiers across the Prah River under his foremost general, Amanqua Tia, to gain control of the coastal strip. In London there was widespread debate as to the best response to make to the crisis. It was accepted that the coastal strip itself should remain under tight British control. However, the Liberal government of Gladstone was opposed to getting involved in the hinterland of the Gold Coast: it would suffice to teach the Asante a lesson by driving them back across the Prah. The government was strongly opposed to using British troops for this purpose. The foetid coastal swamps and the dark, impenetrable forests had a fearsome reputation for fever and malignancy.

West Africa was known as the white man's grave. If the Asante were to be repulsed, it would have to be by the tribes of the protectorate. It was a matter of choosing the right man to lead them. In August 1873 the task was given to Garnet Wolseley. Wolseley was limited to taking thirty-six officers with him: these men became known as the Asante or Wolseley Ring, a sparkling band of talent whose exploits captured the imagination of the Victorian public. Among them was Butler.

Butler had come up from New York to Ottawa by late August 1873. There, while sitting in a hotel reading an evening paper, his eye was caught by a brief report from England: an expedition under Wolseley was about to leave for the Gold Coast. As he had done once before, Butler telegraphed Wolseley and crossed the Atlantic without waiting for a reply. In London he found instructions to follow Wolseley, who had already left for Africa. In the short time intervening before the next available sailing, Butler placed *The Wild North Land* with Sampson Low. It was accepted on the strength of *The Great Lone Land* which was already into its fourth impression. He dashed off a preface which concluded with a reference to his new venture that is a good example of the sometimes fatuous self-assurance of the mid-Victorians:

Long ere this story finds a reader I hope to be on my way through the man-grove swamps which lie between the Gold Coast and Coomassie [Kumasi]. To others must fall the task of correcting proofs, while I assume my part in the correction and revision of King Koffi Kancali and the administration to his subjects of that proof of British prowess which it has been desirable to give them.'

With this neat conceit Butler was tempting fate. He reached Cape Coast Castle, capital of the Gold Coast Protectorate, after a three-week voyage on a commercial steamer which joined the line of ships anchored in the roadstead outside the reef. Access to the shore was impossible for large craft. It was night, and Butler caught the sickly-sweet smells of equa-torial vegetation that wafted across the lagoons. With daybreak he took his place in a rowboat and was propelled through the thunderous waves of the reef to reach land in a surge of surf.

Wolseley had arrived three weeks earlier and was setting a frenetic pace. For the duration of the expedition, he had been made commander of British forces in all the West African settlements, and with this appoint-ment went the temporary rank of major-general. The timing of the expe-dition had been Wolseley's decision. October to January was the dry sea-son and, once the heavy rains came, campaigning would be impossible. Wolseley had also been convinced from the first that a substantial body of British troops was essential to success: native levies alone would not drive the Asante back from the coastal strip nor force the Asantehene to come to terms. Before leaving England Wolseley had got from the Secretary of State for War, Edward Cardwell, a statement that 'nothing but a convic-tion of necessity' would induce Her Majesty's Government to commit British troops to the Gold Coast. Wolseley was satisfied with this appar-ently unhelpful directive for he was confident that, once on the Gold Coast, he could contrive such a necessity.

His staff included several veterans of the Red River, among whom was Redvers Buller as Director of Intelligence, as well as a number of men ex-perienced in battle, including Brevet-Major Baker Russell and Colonel Evelyn Wood. Wood had been in the Crimea and had gone on to win the Victoria Cross in India during the Mutiny. The son of a clergyman, he was the elder brother of Katharine Wood, better known as Katharine O'Shea, the future wife of Charles Stewart Parnell. In addition, Wolseley chose a number of officers known for their writings on various aspects of army re-form: Captain Henry Brackenbury from the staff of Woolwich Military

College was appointed as military secretary, while Brevet-Colonel George Pomeroy Colley, a junior colleague of Wolseley's at the War Office, would join the expedition in mid-December. From Rathangan in County Kildare, Colley was the only officer of the expedition with previous African experience, having spent some time in the healthy uplands of southern Africa. All these men were under forty years old. Their selection had caused some resentment within the military establishment, much of which viewed Wolseley as an opinionated upstart.

As he steamed southward towards Africa, Wolseley had one major irritant: Captain John Glover of the Royal Navy. Glover was the administrator of the Lagos Protectorate on the Bight of Benin, and the most experienced British official in West Africa. He understood local politics and was an unofficial policeman along the area of the Volta River east of Asante. When Wolseley had been given command of the Asante expedition, Glover had been authorized by the Colonial Office to raise native levies along the Volta and proceed towards Asante in support of Wolseley. Glover was nominally under Wolseley's orders for the duration of the Asante campaign, but Wolseley was concerned that Glover would eclipse him. There was to be a consistently cool tone to all Wolseley's official references to Glover, and this was reflected in the general attitude of the Ring, Butler included.

Once arrived at Cape Coast Castle, Wolseley contrived a short engagement with an Asante force which exposed weaknesses in the native troops under his command. He was then able to send a despatch back to London claiming that, if the Asante were to be defeated, two or three battalions must be sent from England as the core of a 10,000 strong army that would be raised from the local tribes, a proposal to which the government agreed. The decision was popular in England: the lead up to the Asante campaign had been reported by the press in strongly partisan terms, with prominence given to the repugnant aspects of the Asante empire: despotism, human sacrifice, and the blood rituals of public executions.

An impressive cohort of British war correspondents had accompanied Wolseley to the Gold Coast. They included the independent-minded and temperate Winwood Reade of *The Times*. Wolseley had a low opinion of journalists. His *Soldier's Pocket Book* described them as a nuisance and bluntly advocated deceiving them with regard to military intentions but, aware of the value of good publicity to his own career, he tolerated their presence.

There was, however, one correspondent with no establishment ties, who had not travelled to Africa with the Ring and whose arrival Wolseley awaited with some concern. This was the correspondent of the *New York Herald*, a man with an unrivalled reputation for scoops. One year previously, the same year as the publication of Butler's *The Great Lone Land*, his *How I Found Livingstone* had caused a sensation in Britain. The very title of this book had infuriated sections of the establishment, that 'I' summed up everything that was wrong about Henry Morton Stanley. He was meddlesome, brash, pugnacious and pushy, the epitome of the New American – except that Stanley was not American at all but British.[2]

At the time of the Asante campaign, Stanley, only thirty-two years old, already had an extraordinary career behind him. He had fought – on both sides – in the American Civil War, before becoming an outstanding newspaper reporter. In 1867, the year Butler had first visited the American West, Stanley had reported on the First Nations of the Great Plains, describing them in a memorable phrase as 'wronged children of the soil'. He had found David Livingstone in November 1871 on the eastern shore of Lake Tanganyika, and furnished the English language with a new catch-cry, *Dr Livingstone I presume?*

Stepping ashore from a surf boat at Cape Coast Castle, Stanley was approached by an English-speaking Fante who introduced himself as the servant of Captain Butler. A room had been made available at Butler's quarters in the Colonial Surveyor's residence and dinner would be sent across there to Stanley from Government House. Butler and Stanley took to each other when they met and, instead of having his first meal on the Gold Coast alone, Stanley was escorted by Butler to Government House. Of Butler, Stanley told his readers in one of his earliest reports that 'the author of *The Great Lone Land* needs no introduction from me. He is a favourite of Sir Garnet ... he is one of those energetic men who by their example infuse vital force in others.'[3]

It was this energy of Butler's that Wolseley proposed to tap by giving him a special assignment in the forthcoming campaign. Wolseley's objective was to push the Asante back across the Prah River, cross the river at Prahsu, invade the Asante heartland and capture Kumasi seventy-four miles beyond the Prah, and force the Asante to acknowledge British supremacy over the coastal strip. It would be December before British troops would arrive. The interim would be used to clear a crude roadway to the Prah with local labour, and to build depots along it so that troops could be moved quickly inland.

The drive into Asante would be on four fronts. There would be a direct thrust by Wolseley and the main column along the new road. On the left flank Wolseley proposed a levy of local tribesmen to be raised and led by one of his own staff, a Captain Dalrymple. The extreme right flank, moving well to the east along the line of the Volta, would be Glover's responsibility. Between Glover and the main column, Wolseley decided on a second right flank formed from the Akim tribes of the forest. It is not difficult to see this decision of Wolseley's as being prompted by his wariness of Glover. Instead of pulling Glover's route closer to the main column, Wolseley wanted his own man on his immediate right flank. That man would be Butler, the only officer of the expedition to 'dwell wholly and entirely among the natives'. On 2 November, eleven days after his arrival in the Gold Coast, Butler was given his formal instructions:

> You will proceed on the 3rd instant, in one of her Majesty's men-of-war, to Accra, *en route* for western Akim ... and you will use your best endeavours to raise the whole of the fighting men in western Akim for the purpose of closing in upon Amonquatier's [sic] army, as it is endeavouring to recross the River Prah into Ashanti [sic]... The major general relies upon your zeal and discretion, and on your knowledge of barbarous peoples to carry out quickly the objects of this most important mission which has been confided to you.[4]

The eighty-mile passage to Accra was a rough one and Butler was wretchedly seasick, an apt prelude to his mission.

To read Butler's account of the following three months in *Akim Foo*, his book on the expedition, is to enter the mind of someone suffering from severe culture shock. Written shortly after the expedition, when he was despondent and in poor health, *Akim Foo* shows Butler's revulsion against almost everything he experienced, particularly during his first weeks as a lone whiteman in the forest. There was the claustrophobia, the enervating damp and humidity, the weird insect life. That 'knowledge of barbarous peoples' referred to in his commission did nothing to soften his reaction to his new environment. The people repelled him. Again and again he refers to their 'jabber', their 'jabbering noises', and their 'ceaseless gabble'. The African is 'stupid', his features 'repulsive'. In a crude and vivid racist setpiece, Butler presented a stock caricature of the African:

> ... the law of earning one's bread by the sweat of one's brow. Of all the earth's inhabitants this negro is the only man who denies this ordinance.

He makes his woman work, and he earns his bread by sitting on his heels and hams staring vacantly at space. He is as strong as a hippopotamus, and quite as ugly; but despite his strength, the summit of his labour is to grease himself until his black hide glistens like coal tar, and his immense mouth grins from ear to ear with the huge animalism of his delight.[5]

The portrait of the African as drawn in *Akim Foo* is found nowhere else in Butler's writings.

At Accra, 'white and foul under a blazing sun', Butler hired twenty-seven porters for his extensive baggage, and quit the town with little delay. The two main kingdoms in west Akim were those ruled by Kofi Ahenco-ra and Kwabina Fuah. Butler's priority was to go to the courts of these men and persuade them to join him in a march to the Prah. To his dismay he heard that both kings were on their way to Accra to meet with Glover. By coming to Accra, they were turning their backs on the Asante. Unless But-ler could prevail on them to turn back, his chances of raising a substantial Akim force would disappear. He pressed forward to intercept them. His meeting with the first of the kings, Kwabina Fuah, on 7 November 1873, was an encounter between white and black that would be replayed with variations across Africa in the next quarter century. First Butler encoun-tered the king's advance guard coming towards him on the trail. It was a small procession of soldiers, ceremonial bearers, drummers and musicians playing strident horns. Butler refused all salutation with this company and told them bluntly through his interpreter, 'your faces should be turned to Asante', before striding on, a sweating, irascible whiteman in heavy tweed clothes and a pith helmet. Up ahead, sustained drumming signalled the ap-proach of Kwabina Fuah himself.

Butler halted under a palm tree in a small clearing. He had one of his two Union Jacks unfolded and erected as an awning, beneath which he seated himself on a draped box-seat. Kwabina arrived, 'a sober looking sav-age fat and well greased ... with a slow and not unmusical voice'. Kwabina was wearing a silk cloth around his lower body, with one end draped over a shoulder. During the lengthy palaver that followed, Kwabina kept point-ing out that he was on his way to Accra because of an invitation from Glover. Butler's attempts to explain that he himself was the emissary of Wolseley, the big chief at Cape Coast Castle, did not impress Kwabina, who knew of Glover's reputation. He put to Butler the obvious question: why were there two white chiefs with different views on what the Akim should do? In desperation, Butler was reduced to a bag-of-tricks approach to get Kwabina to follow him. He produced one of the three bottles of champagne he was carrying, opened a crate of rifles, fired off a full fourteen shots to demonstrate the superiority of the weapon over the standard muzzle-loaders available to the Akim, and offered six of the rifles and ten gold pieces as a pledge of how well Kwabina would be recompensed if he turned back to the Prah. The king, within two days travel of his destination, declined, and Butler lost patience. He had his flag folded and marched on into the forest 'plodding the dreary pathway in the enervating heat of afternoon'. The enormity of the task he had been given by Wolseley was beginning to hit him. Towards nightfall he crossed the Ayhnsu River on the shoulders of his porters. He had left all trace of the coastal strip behind and was starting a three-month sojourn in the equatorial forest:

> ... an eternity of sombre gloom ... The day and the night are the same to it; noiseless rivers steal along under dense layers of tangled foliage; huge poisonous fruits fall down from lofty close set trees, and lie beneath the undergrowth, emitting noisome odours; great orchids hang over the pathway, spiral creepers, hundreds of feet in length, twisted like huge serpents, cling from tree to tree; and far down below the mass of foliage, amidst these tangled and twisted evergreens, beneath the shadow of the great grey tree-trunks, man moves as though he slowly picks his way at the bottom of some mighty ocean.[6]

Two further days of travel brought Butler face to face with King Kofi Ahencora. He too was en route to Accra, though he was more amenable to Butler's persuasion than Kwabina had been. For one thing he was closer to home. For another, Butler offered him £18 a month for every soldier he supplied. This sum would be for his sole use, separate to the sixpence a day each of his soldiers would be paid. Kofi was interested. He asked for time to consider and, over the next two days, Butler experienced to the full his alienation from all those around him. In the village where he was waiting he was an object of unceasing curiosity for his skin colour, his height, his beard, his attire. He could not escape, even when he retreated into the hut provided for his use: 'all day long crowds came to stare at me; through windows, round corners, by the edges of doors, black eyes and woolly heads popped and peered ... reading, writing or eating, the black eyes looked on'.[7]

After two days Butler extracted a promise from Kofi that he would raise a force against the Asante. With this secured, he set out westwards once more only to be prostrated by bush fever. For days he lay 'in a hot and filthy hut' overdosing himself on quinine. When his fever began to abate he had his bearers carry him onward in a hammock. He calculated that he was within three days of the road of Wolseley's main column to Prahsu on the Prah. If he could get to the depot of Mansu, almost midway between the coast and Prahsu, he could secure sufficient arms and money for the Akim chiefs and headmen whom he hoped would join him. Forcing himself to his feet for the last part of his journey, he reached Mansu on 23 November 1873. He found it to be little more than a collection of rough huts and was startled by the appearance of the first British officer he met, 'with hollow cheeks and long drawn chin, and with eyes that looked so widely and wildly at one'. It was a description that applied to himself.

The news at Mansu was mixed. None of the British troop transports had yet arrived at the coast. The Asante army under Amanqua Tia had moved back to the Prah river. This had not been a retreat but a tactical withdrawal in keeping with Asante policy of avoiding heavy engagements in areas not fully secured. Wolseley's advance force, coastal troops led by British officers, had been continually harassed as they pushed into the forest whose cover the Asante used to scarifying effect with a succession of random attacks. Wolseley himself had been down with fever and had recovered only by spending almost a fortnight aboard the hospital ship, anchored offshore from the pestilential mainland. It was also proving impossible to recruit enough porters and labourers to open up the road to the Prah quickly.

Butler collected his supplies and marched back to Akim. He was too late to attack the Asante as they recrossed the Prah. He suffered another bout of fever, this time accompanied by delirium. Staggering on, he inspected the Prah before returning to the line of march of the main column at Yankumasi. The first transports had by now arrived at the coast but the eight depots which Wolseley had planned to open between the coast and the river were nowhere near completion. Unseasonal rain was turning much of the route into quagmire. Wolseley was increasingly conscious of the time factor, the bulk of the Asante army was already back in its heartland, and there was no enthusiasm among the coastal tribes for active pursuit of an invasion force that had withdrawn from disputed territory. However, by 31 December 1873 the British troops, numbering over 2000, had all been landed, and Wolseley was on his way to the front. In a decision that provides an emphatic measure of his worries, Wolseley had, in mid-December, sent a despatch to Glover on the Volta ordering him to alter course and march directly towards Asante to provide support for the main column's push to Kumasi.

Meanwhile Butler had gone into Akim for the third time. Wolseley was still holding to his plan for a four-pronged thrust and now Butler was assisted by four white officers, one of them a banjo-playing surgeon with a limited musical repertoire. All these newcomers were hit by fever and had at various stages to be carried on the march to the Prah. Butler's new instructions were to cross the river with as many Akim as possible. He reached the Prah by 15 January 1874 and, watched by about sixty Akim, crossed the river at Antea, twenty-five miles upriver from Prahsu. Technically he had invaded Asante.

Over the next few days more and more Akim arrived at the south bank and they eventually decided to cross after him. Immediately north of the river was country from which the Asante had driven them a generation previously: this might be an opportunity to reclaim it. Keeping their options open, the Akim allowed Butler to lead a force of over 1500 men into Asante. Progress towards Kumasi was slow and unnerving. The forest tracks were spotted with fetishes to deter strangers. Skulls, bones and the occasional grotesquely placed full skeleton unnerved the Akim as they moved farther into the dense bush.

Despite his frustration with his allies, Butler seldom resorted to physical rebuke, having 'learnt the utter uselessness of coercion' in his early days in the forest. Once, during the final days of the march towards Kumasi, he caught up with his vanguard led by the surgeon and Kofi Ahencora, to find the king, who had decided to pitch camp for the night, being threatened at gunpoint by the surgeon: 'The moment was critical. I stopped the tumult, ordered that on no account should a weapon ever be drawn upon king, chief or soldier and quieted the outraged honour of Ahencora'.[8]

The last days of January saw Butler's efforts moving towards a grim climax. The forest was filled with menace. The long equatorial nights throbbed with the sound of Asante drums and with strange cries and screams. Butler pushed his Akim force within a day's march of Wolseley and the main column whence, muffled and distorted by the forest, the occasional sound of cannon and gunfire could be heard as the Asante finally began to come to grips with the British expedition. Butler's Akim had their own intelligence network, and analysis of its information showed them that their long-term interests would be best served by not engaging with the Asante. They decided secretly on withdrawal.

The blow fell on Butler on 30 January in his well-secured hill camp of Akina when 'these reluctant and cowardly savages' simply vanished into the forest. Sick at heart, he began to sink into a morass of despondency. He had been singled out for this Akim commission and he had failed – not once but twice. For his first commission, when he went to Accra, had been to close in on the Asante army as it was recrossing the Prah. His second commission, when he had returned to Akim in December, was to raise and conduct a force to Kumasi. As if to push him beyond the limit of emotional endurance, the one redeeming possibility left – action with the main column – was now to be denied him. One day's direct march westward was the main force of the expedition. However, to take this route without his Akim allies would be suicidal. He had no choice except to work back in a semicircle and recross the Prah. This cost him five days, during which Wolseley's campaign came to a bloody close.

Wolseley himself had invaded Asante on 15 January, and over the following week 1500 British troops and 1000 native levies had crossed the Prah. The Asante resistance now became total. Their methods of warfare took full advantage of their environment. Advance guards would attack, retreat, feint, attack, in a pattern whose purpose was to draw the enemy on and elongate its ranks. Meanwhile strong flanking forces would converge through the screen of forest foliage and, at the optimum time, fall on the enemy from two sides with devastating effect. The main Asante weapon was the muzzle-loading flintlock musket; in the confines of the forest where close fighting was the norm, this weapon was not as ineffective against breech-loading rifles as it would have been in open country.

Through incessant skirmishing and ambush, Wolseley kept relentlessly on, calculating that, if he persisted, the Asante eventually would be forced to confront him in a pitched battle to stop his progress to Kofi KariKari's royal city. This would give his troops the chance to fight in traditional formation. His prognosis proved correct when on 31 January, while Butler was stumbling southwards from Akina, the Asante war reached its climax at the battle of Amoaful. Both sides fought with tenacity, and it was superior firepower that finally gave victory to the British whose casualties were four dead and almost 200 wounded. As a proportion of the expedition, this was high. Asante losses were estimated at about 1000, a small proportion of the forces available to them, but their commander, Amanqua Tia, had been killed at the close of the battle.

Wolseley spent that night discussing with his staff officers what he should do. Outside his headquarters, in crude operating theatres, a small team of army surgeons sawed and stitched the limbs of the maimed. Kumasi lay just over twenty miles in front. Behind lay a tenuous supply line which might be cut at any time. Wolseley decided to risk going on. His gamble paid off. On the afternoon of 4 February 1874 the Union Jack flew, briefly, over Kumasi. It was a ghost city. Kofi KariKari and his court had abandoned it, stripping it of most of its valuables before leaving. A thorough search for booty yielded only £11,000 of golden ornaments, a pittance contrasted with the fantasies about Kumasi as a city of gold. The expedition itself had cost London ten times that amount. Wolseley appointed two of his staff as prize agents to transport booty back to the coast. By custom, the booty would be auctioned, and profits divided among the expedition members according to rank.

To bring the campaign to a formal conclusion Wolseley needed Kofi's acceptance of treaty terms. He sent messengers after Kofi, but to no avail. The Asantehene simply procrastinated, knowing that Wolseley's position would grow precarious if he delayed in Kumasi with insufficient supplies and with the rains washing his road away. Thwarted, Wolseley destroyed the palace and burnt the city before beginning his return to the coast.

Four days after the start of his retreat from Kumasi, while camped at the village of Fommanah, Wolseley had welcome news. Emissaries arrived from Kofi to say that the Asantehene would accept terms if Wolseley called off his right flanking force. Ironically, this was a reference to Glover and his 750 troops from the Lagos hinterland. Glover was within a few miles of Kumasi, and Kofi, having lost his leading commander, was reluctant to engage him. Wolseley sent a draft treaty back to Kofi, proposing 'perpetual peace' between the Queen of England and her coastal allies on the one side, and the King of Asante and his people on the other. The treaty was returned to Wolseley duly 'x'd. The fact that Kofi had not appeared before any authorized British officer was a triviality for Wolseley, whose aim now was to get away from the Gold Coast with all speed.

Meanwhile Butler and his fevered companions had retraced their steps to Prahsu where they heard the news of Amoaful. Butler himself refused to rest and, 'hoping that I might reach the front before Kumasi was taken', he pressed on. His wretched emotional state was matched by his physical condition and skeletal appearance. He could join the thumb and forefinger of one hand and run the circle thus made the length of his arm from wrist to shoulder. As night fell on 7 February, he reached Wolseley's camp at Agemmaum. Wolseley's next despatch to the War Office had much of its content devoted to Butler:

To Secretary of State for War from Camp Amoaful. Sir. I had scarcely sent off my despatches yesterday when Captain Butler, half pay 69th Regiment arrived at my camp, and as his mission to the Western Akim is now completely closed, I feel it my duty to bring at once to your notice the admirable manner in which he conducted a most trying and difficult task. That Captain Butler failed in his effort to lead a force of Akims to Comaasie is not his fault, but is solely due to the ineradicable cowardice and sloth of the people with whom he had to deal ... The high opinion of Captain Butler which caused me to give him an independent command is strengthened by his conduct in this war; and I beg to recommend him especially to your notice as an officer of great ability, of remarkably ready resources and of untiring powers of action.[9]

Stanley, the outsider from the *New York Herald*, added his own gloss to this despatch when it was published:

Sir Garnet very frankly declares the cause of Butler's failure. Captain Butler is a gallant gentleman of such large nobility of heart, that he believes that kindness will enable a man to mould as he pleases an African savage. Over-leniency is as bad as harshness, indiscriminate kindness is fatal to discipline. If Captain Butler, with whom all sympathised in his misfortune, had been stern but just, he would have succeeded. – Always spare the whip. But firmly grasp the reins.[10]

Any fair assessment of the outcome of Butler's commission to Akim must be placed in the context of what was achieved by the other two flanking columns, Dalrymple's on the left and Glover's on the extreme right. Dalrymple raised 200 men and, in Wolseley's words 'utterly failed to induce any man to cross the Asante frontier'. Glover did take a force of 750 to the environs of Kumasi, but all these were trained mercenaries from the hinterland of Lagos far to the east. It was Winwood Reade who described Butler's commission best: 'it was a failure of which any man might be proud. The wonder is that he did so much.'[11]

Butler collapsed at Agemmaum and had to be carried out to the coast. He left West Africa on 27 February 1874, a week after Wolseley who had rushed ahead to beat the correspondents back to England. Once at sea Butler's condition rapidly deteriorated. It was as if what had sustained him was an overwhelming will not to die on the Gold Coast. Having achieved that, he sank into prolonged semi-consciousness with fever and dysentry.

Winwood Reade, travelling on the same vessel, described him 'as being in a most precarious condition'. Day followed day with no abatement of his acute illness until he appeared to capitulate totally to fever, and he underwent the phenomenon of an out-of-body experience:

> I dimly remember people gathered about the cot, and one good comrade asking in my ear for my last wishes. I remember, too, suddenly declaring that I died a Catholic. Then there is a blank, but not altogether, for I can recollect that after the usual final settlings of face and limbs had been made – the eyes closed, and the sheet drawn over the laid-out figure – there was a curious indistinct idea in my brain that it was not as people supposed; that I was still conscious, and even that I was being carried by invisible hands, or being floated on towards a great cloud veil, the passing through which it seemed was to be the final passage out of life. There was no sensation of bodily pain. How long I lay in this condition I don't know, but I remember men coming about the cot, lifting the sheet, and touching me and talking to each other. Then I thought, – these men are about to prepare my body for the sea – ; and as in these hot latitudes the time between death and burial in the ocean was a very short one, I felt the extreme horror of the situation and longed to be able to make some sign or movement by which they might know that I was not really dead. Next I heard one of the men who was moving my limbs say to his comrade, I don't think he is dead.[12]

At Madeira a priest came came on board to give Butler the last rites. When the ship reached Portsmouth on 28 March his condition had improved only slightly and he joined the sick and wounded in the Royal Victoria Hospital at Netley by Southampton Water. It would be two months before he was strong enough to be discharged and his youngest sister, Frances, came over from Tipperary to help nurse him.

During his first weeks at Netley, he was largely oblivious to the acclamation that was greeting the return of the Asante expedition which was hailed as a triumph for civilization. There was a review at Windsor Castle, after which decorations and promotions were lavishly distributed. Wolseley was invested as a Knight Commander of the Bath and had his rank of major-general made permanent. All the key oficers of the Ring were decorated and promoted. Butler became a Companion of the Bath and was promoted to major. In the House of Lords the Duke of Cambridge, Commander-in-Chief of the Armed Forces, specifically named him as 'one of those gallant officers who acquitted themselves well of the task assigned to them'.

On 16 April Queen Victoria herself came to Netley to visit the hospitalized veterans, and she spoke with Butler. The expedition officers received invitations to the social event of the year, a May Ball at Buckingham Palace to celebrate the visit to London of the Emperor and Empress of Russia. Butler was too weak to attend and shortly afterwards he was invalided back to Ireland to recuperate. He was placed on half-pay, nine shillings and sixpence a day.

The ball at Buckingham Palace was not the only excitement of the London social season that Butler had to forego because of his illness. In May 1874 the discovery of a formidable new painting talent was drawing unprecedented crowds to the Royal Academy's annual exhibition. Item 142, *Calling the roll after an engagement, Crimea*, depicted a war scene. There were no jingoistic heroics in the composition. The haggard faces of the soldiers were a strong testimony to the suffering and endurance of the rank and file; the pain as well as the valour of soldiering was captured. Praised by the Prince of Wales, the painting received a private viewing in Buckingham Palace by the queen, who subsequently bought it. That the painter of *The Roll Call*, as it became known, was one Elizabeth Thompson – a shy, twenty-seven-year-old spinster living quietly in London – captivated its viewers; she had, to brilliant effect and without any direct experience of army life, entered an artistic sphere that had been the preserve of men.

Butler's return to health was slow and painful. For over a month he could walk only a few tottering yards before collapsing. He convalesced in the west and south-west of Ireland where he was overcome, perhaps for the first time in his life, by the wild natural beauty of his native land. His wrote that his doctors were 'the outside car, the great cliffs of Moher and the heathery glens of Kerry'.

With his strength gradually increasing, he began to come to terms with the biggest personal crisis of his life. Africa had taught him a hard lesson. He had gone there in a mindframe common among young men of sound health and good expectations – an unthinking certainty of his own indestructibility – but the reality of his own mortality had been agonizingly brought home to him. More than that, Africa had forced him to see that his utmost was not necessarily enough. And, crushingly, it had humiliated him at a deep private level. No amount of sympathy from colleagues, no amount of public recognition for his efforts, could compensate for the frustration of not carrying out his commission and the bitterness of losing his first opportunity to lead men into batttle – the highest ambition and ultimate test for every young officer.

It was no surprise that the book he began to write in Kerry of his West African experiences should have been subtitled *The History of a Failure*. Published in 1875, *Akim Foo* has a sustained emotional intensity which is not found in any other of Butler's biographical writings. It is as if writing the book was a catharsis, releasing a flood of revulsion for almost everything about West Africa, its peoples, climate and topography. In the book's opening pages, he pithily summed up his feelings by stating that 'the best thing I ever saw on the coast of Africa was the line of steamers waiting to take you away from it'.

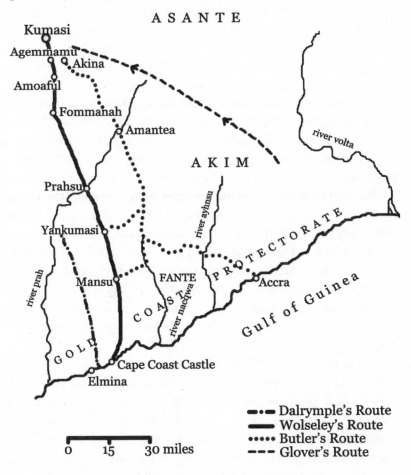

Dalrymple's Route
Wolseley's Route
Butler's Route
Glover's Route

THE ASANTE CAMPAIGN 1873-74
From the map illustrating 'Akimfoo' (1876)

Chapter Six

SOUTHERN AFRICA

'The poison of the Gold Coast', wrote Butler, 'was not yet out of my veins' when, in February 1875, he was again on his way to Africa. This was another mission led by Wolseley. As on the two previous occasions, the Red River and Asante, it was the despatch of a cable that signalled the start of Butler's involvement. Only this time there was a difference which marked a significant change in his status, for now it was Wolseley who cabled Butler. At thirty-six, Butler was at last firmly on the military career ladder, and as a protégé of one of the leading reformers at the War Office. As a Wolseleyite, Butler's fortunes would, to a great extent, ebb and flow with those of his leader, whom he had publicly acclaimed in *Akim Foo* as another Wellington. But Butler's outspokenness and independence of mind would prevent his ever becoming a close confidant of Wolseley, for whom the highest loyalty encompassed obsequiousness – a quality foreign to Butler's nature.

At the start of 1875 Wolseley was preparing to go out to Natal Colony in southern Africa as governor. Natal was the antithesis of the Gold Coast. It had a healthy climate, spectacular open country and a thriving population of 18,000 whites, most of them English, with their own legislature. However, the black population outnumbered the whites by fourteen to one and the legislature had been failing to preserve the rights of the black majority. In 1874 the Colonial Office decided to recall the governor and replace him with a short-term appointee whose function would be to get the Natal legislature to agree to a lessening of its powers. Such a policy, besides redressing black grievances, could ease the road to federation of the three colonies and two Boer states of the region. Federation had worked for Canada. It was thought it could work for southern Africa.

To minimize the disaffection this proposed change would cause in Natal, it was essential that the colonists be confronted with a high-status figure in their new governor. Early in 1875 Wolseley accepted the post. He did so reluctantly and only for a period of six months. Although he was an intriguer, diplomacy was not his forte. He was allowed a staff of five. He had one civilian imposed on him, but apart from this he was free to choose his own team. He needed intelligent, articulate persuaders. He turned to the Ring and chose four veterans of the Asante expedition: Major Henry Brackenbury, Colonel George Pomeroy Colley, Captain Lord Edric Frederick Gifford and Major William Butler. Brackenbury had been military secretary to the Asante campaign, on which he had already written a two-volume history. Colley's proven zeal and efficiency were complemented by his previous experience of southern Africa. Gifford had received one of the two Victoria Crosses awarded for the campaign.

Wolseley and his entourage reached the port of Durban on 1 April 1875. The excitement of the colony at the arrival of the new governor and his party was intense. John Robinson, a member of the Legislative Council, later to become Natal's first premier, wrote that 'never before had a representative of the Crown come to South Africa attended by such a galaxy of able and famous men. Arms, diplomacy, administration, literature and pluck were all notably represented.'[1]

In the capital Pietermaritzburg, Wolseley engaged in a softening up of the white colonists and 'drowned the independence of the colony in sherry and champagne'.[2] There was no lack of female attention for Wolseley's retinue. The cachet of a flirtation with one or more of these metropolitan gods, who played the recently invented game of lawn tennis, and danced the polka and the waltz, meant that there was no shortage of women keen to move beyond the formalities of etiquette to less constrained relationships. Colley held aloof from these opportunities; he had a strong attachment to an Edith Hamilton from Queen's County (modern County Laois) in Ireland, whom he would eventually marry. Brackenbury, Butler and Gifford made the most of their happy situation. A passing reference by Wolseley in one of his letters to his wife Louisa mentions Butler as 'having another affair on his hands'.

Wolseley's preparations for legislative change were not entirely confined to social functions. He had to get the Legislative Council to vote for

a curtailment of its own power, and he made use of every device at his disposal to achieve his aim. By the expedient of giving two of the nominated
members paid leave of absence, he brought Butler and Colley on to the executive, with Colley as Treasurer and Butler as Protector of Immigrants. In
the short time available to Wolseley, neither of his appointees had time for
their nominal portfolios; their job in and out of the chamber was to argue
the case for a weakened council. Wolseley himself showed marked defects
as a diplomatist as he variously blustered, cajoled and threatened. By contrast Butler, although not temperamentally a negotiator, was consistently
forceful and courteous.

The bill to enlarge the Legislative Council by ten nominated members
had a dramatic second reading. Colley, was unable to deliver his carefully
honed final speech because of his sympathy for the colonists' position.
Butler had no difficulty in delivering his contribution and he represented
'of course, the imperial point of view'.[3] This point of view reminded the
colonists of their duties as British subjects. It stressed that the black in-
habitants of Natal were entitled to the protection of British justice, and it
argued that it was in Natal's long-term interest to surrender some of its independence now, in order to have the benefits of federation later. The
colonists were averse to any weakening of their power, but they were sen-
sitive to their situation. Natal had been established scarcely a generation
earlier at the expense of the two land-locked Boer republics, the Transvaal
and the Orange Free State. Again, much as the colonists might have
wished to, they could not deal with the issue of black settlement from
their own resources. They needed London. Wolseley got his bill passed.

While the immediate spur to the changes in the Legislative Council
had been the colonists' disregard of native rights, Wolseley and his team
had little concern with racial issues in the abstract. Wolseley held strongly that imperial policy towards southern African blacks was too much influenced by idealistic pressure groups in Britain – imperial policy on native
issues was so benign that it encouraged blacks to migrate to the colony
where they were swamping the whites. Butler's view was different:

> The equality of all men in the eyes of the law finds poor favour in the sight
> of an English colonist in countries where black and white men are thrown
> together. To too many of our race the sentiment of equality has reference
> only to a set of beings above them in the social scale: apply it equally to all,
> let it affect a dark race or another people and the sentiment instantly
> changes to one of repressive superiority.[4]

There was also a change in Butler's views, as he had crudely expressed them in *Akim Foo*, on the African aversion to work. Now he pointed up the contradiction to be met with everywhere in the views of whites on black labour. For every white who believed that the African was 'the laziest brute on earth', there was another who could get as much good black labour as he needed. Butler was not optimistic about the long-term future for south Africa: white expansion, driven by greed and the gun, was unstoppable.

With the enlarged Council secured, Wolseley's party visited western Natal. At the frontier, Butler and Colley left the main party, separately but with similar commissions. While Colley headed for the Transvaal, Butler set out by waggon for the Orange Free State with letters of introduction to President Brand. His commission was to survey life and political attitudes in the country. He journeyed for five days, up through the passes of the Drakensberg Mountains and across the high veldt, to meet Brand in Bloomfontein. From there he travelled to Griqualand West to visit the diamond mines of Kimberley. The mining area was on a scale vaster than anything he had seen in Canada. Over a thousand claim-holders, mainly whites, swarmed about four gigantic open pits directing the operations of thousands of black diggers who, for £4 a month, dug and shovelled and carted. From the rims of the pits a myriad of light steel ropes criss-crossed down as much as two hundred feet to the workings on the mine floors.

Butler was ambivalent towards the Boers. He found they had some admirable qualities – simplicity, homeliness, strong family attachments and 'certain characteristics of solid determination and love of independence', but these 'modern Israelites' were uncouth, and their misuse of the land was a disgrace; 'to make the earth a waste and call it a farm is the first rule of Dutch agricultural policy'.

On the Boers as fighters, Butler expressed the conventional view about a people who for more than a generation had continually moved on rather than confront Britain. The Boer would fight Africans where 'he will have the Wesley-Richards breech-loading rifle against a rusty musket when fighting Zulu or Bechuana or Basuto'. However, he would not take on Empire forces. 'He is not a soldier and he never will be,' wrote Butler, adding with unconscious irony, 'though he is a fearless and practised rider and an unerring shot.'" Butler was also dismissive of an Afrikaans word which had entered military parlance. This was *commando*, which he described as 'merely a new name for an old thing. It was war without any of the usages or restraints which civilisation has imposed on war.'

Butler ended his solo mission to the Orange Free State by returning to Natal on horseback through the hazardous mountain passes of Basutoland. When he got back to Pietermaritzburg in mid-August, it was to find all his colleagues busy writing up their final reports.

During those last weeks in Natal, Wolseley and his party were joined by the English historian James Anthony Froude. Froude, a convinced federalist, was the most influential unofficial adviser to the Colonial Office on southern Africa. It was not for his views on Natal that he engaged Butler's attention during those weeks in Pietermaritzburg, but because of his views on Ireland. It is paradoxical that it was while he was in Natal on an imperial mission that Butler should have first been singled out as being somehow different to the rest of his colleagues because of his Catholic Irish background. Froude had recently completed a history, *The English in Ireland*. He held that the Act of Union of 1801, which had abolished the Irish parliament and established the United Kingdom of Great Britain and Ireland, had saved Ireland for the Empire. The thrust of his views was that British laws and institutions would be safe in Ireland only in the hands of a Protestant ascendancy. Since this would be impossible in the late nineteenth century because of the widening of the franchise, it followed that the security of the United Kingdom would be maintained only if a local parliament were never restored to Ireland. Froude's view of Ireland was the conventional one in Britain – Wolseley shared it – though there were dissenting voices.

During his final weeks at Government House in Pietermaritzburg, Butler found himself the focus of some sharp-edged bantering by Froude, twenty-two years his senior. Butler was well able to deal with this, and on one occasion stopped Froude with a devastating riposte. Froude 'liked to try little bits of religious or political badinage upon me. I remember his asking me in a large company if I had gone when at Madeira to see the Portuguese statue of the 'Winking Virgin' which was said to be there. I said that I had not and gave as my reason that I had seen so many winking ladies in England that the sight had ceased to have any novelty for me.'[6]

There is a contemporary account of Butler just before he left Natal: when Sir Henry Bulwer, the new governor, arrived to take over from Wolseley, he had a gangly, uprepossessing youth in train as his secretary. This was H. Rider Haggard, who was later to turn his African experience to good account in the adventure novels *King Solomon's Mines* and *She*. Haggard found Butler to be 'a most agreeable and sympathetic man, who took the trouble to talk a good deal to me although I was but a lad. I recall that with much graphic detail he told me the story of how, when he was suffering from fever, he was nearly thrown overboard off the west coast of Africa.[7]

Shortly after Butler's return to England in the autumn of 1875 the Duke of Cambridge approved his assignment to the War Office on Wolseley's recommendation. It is significant that Butler was not assigned to quasi-diplomatic work after Natal. His strengths were not those of a negotiator, and he was not suited to the amoral shadings of political compromise and the ambiguities of diplomatic manoeuvre. At a time when the Colonial Office and the War Office were collaborating heavily, he was not asked to become involved in discussions on possible federation for southern African.

At the War Office, Butler was appointed as a deputy assistant quartermaster general and was initiated into army supply systems and procedures. He found himself in 'a great congeries of confusion'. Edward Cardwell, the Secretary of State for War between 1868 and 1874, had introduced major reforms. Purchase, as mentioned, had been abolished. Recruitment policy for the rank and file was being changed, causing a downgrading of the old regimental system. The Commander-in-Chief had been made subordinate to the Secretary of State for War and this was symbolized by the relocation of military headquarters from the Horse Guards in Whitehall to the civilian War Office in Pall Mall. Butler found the civilian and military bureaucrats co-existing in mutual mistrust in a warren of offices 'a mass of old and confused buildings ... typical of the confused work itself'. Half-a-dozen or so houses had been

> ... thrown into intercommunication by means of three-step doorways and devious stairways ... Men spent the greater part of their time in official hours in writing minutes from one dingy room to another across these dusty passages and dark corridors. The clerk who could write the sharpest minute in the most illegible handwriting was a valuable reinforcement to his particular side, and he had never to be at a loss in finding opportunity to discharge his minute guns into the ranks of some opponent. Plenty of fighting could be had all round.[8]

This grossly inefficient bureaucracy irritated Butler, but his reaction to the 'evils of the contract system' was anger. The contract system was a venal, often blatantly corrupt supply procedure, run mainly for the benefit of civilian contractors, and for which the army rank and file ultimately paid with their health, if not with their lives. Butler's exposure to the process, by which over-priced, shoddy materials and unsuitable equipment were foisted on army regulars, would put him in implacable opposition to army contractors for the rest of his life.

Though Butler found the War Office frustrating in many ways ('a vast wheel was going round, and all men, big and little, were pinned upon it'), he was among old comrades. Wolseley was there with responsibility for streamlining the auxiliary forces. Buller, Brackenbury and Gifford were also in London, and Butler was firmly part of a cadre zealous for modernization. Butler's concerns were wider than army reform. He took a strong and active interest in contemporary international politics. Two regions of the world, Afghanistan and the Balkans, dominated strategic military and diplomatic thinking in the United Kingdom in the late 1870s.

Afghanistan was an independent kingdom on the north-west frontier of British India, a vital buffer between India and the expanding Russian empire to the north. In 1878 Britain, under the Conservative government of Disraeli, invaded Afghanistan to protect its Indian interests. The invasion was preceded by intense public debate, to which Butler contributed with a magazine article arguing against an invasion.[9] He stated baldly that an earlier British occupation of the country had been a calamity. It had led in 1842 to one of the most disastrous retreats in European history when 5500 troops and 15,000 civilians perished on the march from Kabul back to India. From this disaster, mainly caused by 'the indecision of character and faltering purpose of the British leaders,' there was, Butler told his readers, only one survivor – a Dr William Brydon.

In the Balkans, nationalism was creating huge fractures in the declining Ottoman empire. This instability drew in the Great Powers of Europe, and in 1877–8 the Russians were at war against the Turks, reaching the outskirts of Constantinople before being stopped by the sight of a British fleet in the Sea of Marmora. It was this occasion which introduced, in Butler's phrase, 'the music hall god Jingo' as an object of worship in England. The most popular political refrain of the time was

> *We don't want to fight but by Jingo if we do,*
> *We've got the men, we've got the ships, we've got the money too.*

From the Congress of Berlin of June–July 1878, Disraeli returned to London, claiming to have brought back 'peace with honour'. He also brought back the right for Britain to occupy Cyprus and, within weeks,

the island had Garnet Wolseley as its first High Commissioner and Commander-in-Chief, accompanied by Brackenbury and Gifford. It was a
wretchedly uncomfortable posting. Butler came out at the year's end on a
visit, enduring three days of seasickness *en route*. He found his old comrades bored and frustrated. If he had entertained thoughts of getting an assignment to Wolseley's staff, he did not pursue them.

Something altogether different was about to open up for him. As he
passed through Trieste on his way back to England, there was unbelievable
news from Africa. At Isandhlwana, north of Natal, 1300 empire soldiers,
800 of them British, had fallen under the assegais of the army of the Zulu
king, Ceteswayo. The immediate cause of this disaster was the reckless
over-confidence of a British invasion force of 17,000 men which in January 1879 crossed into Zululand from Natal. Isandhlwana was, in the words
of the *Annual Register*,

> A shock for which the nation was totally unprepared. It was as complete
> and almost as horrifying a surprise as the Indian Mutiny, and nothing had
> occurred since then to stir public feeling about imperial affairs so pro-
> foundly.[10]

The Zulus were the foremost black power in southern Africa. Their king,
Ceteswayo, was concerned to have friendly relations with Natal on his
southern border as an insurance against the threat of Transvaal expansion
on his western border. The Natal colonists themselves were apprehensive
about this powerful black kingdom to the north. However, Zululand was
underpopulated; if subdued, the surplus black population of Natal could
be resettled there. Meantime, diamond mining was changing southern Africa. Mining meant money and money meant guns for blacks and whites.

In December 1876 Sir Bartle Frere was appointed British High Commissioner for southern Africa. Frere, a federationist, came to Africa with
two objectives: to annex the Transvaal – a policy sanctioned by London –
and to break the Zulus by military means, a policy not sanctioned by London. In April 1877 the Transvaal, to the anger of the Boers, was proclaimed
a British colony. This transformed the relationship between the British
and the Zulus. Overnight, by annexing the Transvaal, Britain had taken on
responsibility for Boer encroachments along the western frontier of Zululand. The Boers were continuing to settle on disputed lands and Ceteswayo was growing increasingly concerned. Early in 1878 he succeeded in

getting Frere to set up an independent boundary commission. The commission vindicated all Zulu claims. Its findings were kept secret for five months before being disclosed to a Zulu delegation at the Natal border on 11 December. The findings were well received but their disclosure was accompanied by a set of impossible demands from Frere; the most swingeing were that the Zulu army, estimated at 50,000 strong, was to disband, and that the defence of Zululand was to be the joint concern of a Zulu Council of State *and* imposed British advisers. Ceteswayo was given thirty days to comply, something which Frere knew he could not do.

On 11 January 1879 an imperial army of 17,000 troops under Major-General Lord Chelmsford, Commander in Chief of the South African Armed Forces, invaded Zululand, only to suffer disaster at Isandhlwana when a Zulu impi of 20,000 smashed down on its main column in an unparalleled four-hour attack – 'the Washing of the Spears'. Chelmsford retreated in disarray to Natal, leaving his two flanking columns exposed in Zululand. The westernmost of these was led by Evelyn Wood, and in it was Redvers Buller in command of a 200-strong troop of colonial cavalry.

In the immediate aftermath of Isandhlwana occurred one of the most extraordinary defensive actions of British imperial history, when on 22 January 139 soldiers (25 of them Irish), members of the 24th Battalion of the 2nd Regiment of Foot, held off a 4000-strong impi through twelve hours of attack on their crudely fortified mission station on the Buffalo River at Rorke's Drift (later commmemorated by Elizabeth Butler in her painting of the name). Eleven of the defenders won Victoria Crosses.

Disraeli's government reacted quickly to the news of Isandhlwana. Natal itself appeared to be under threat from the Zulus. Heavy reinforcements of imperial troops would have to be got out to South Africa without delay. Butler had cabled the War Office from Trieste, volunteering for service, and on 28 February he sailed from Southampton on the S.S. *Egypt*, posted to the port of Durban in Natal as assistant adjutant general with responsibility for supplies. Returning to Natal after almost four years, Butler found the colony in a near frenzy:

> The state of confusion existing within Natal could scarcely be exaggerated. To the extreme of over-confidence which had, indeed, been the primary factor in the disaster of Isandula [Isandhlwana], had succeeded the dread of a Zulu invasion. You will usually find that the term 'picnic' at the rising of the curtain upon one of these little wars is readily changed to 'panic' before the completion of the first act."

Butler was hugely disappointed at not being at the front. He was hungry for action. His role in the Asante War had not involved actual combat. To be stuck in a stifling office in Durban was doubly disappointing when colleagues from the Asante War were getting more than their fair share of chances. Both Wood and Buller had played key roles in Chelmsford's left-flanking column during the January invasion of Zululand. At the end of March they had distinguished themselves in a bloody engagement, for which Buller would receive the Victoria Cross.

However, Butler threw himself with typical energy into his job at Durban, where his work exposed him to the full venality of the contract system of supply. The army was being 'robbed right and left'. He instanced, as one typical minor example of the corruption practised, the purchase of a water-can, cost 5/= , which was invoiced as a water *cart*, cost £25.

Meanwhile, Disraeli's government had found a scapegoat for the Zulu crisis in Bartle Frere. Frere's public rebuke signified the abandonment of federation policy. Official thinking was that the security of Natal and the Transvaal could be guaranteed only by the smashing of Zulu power. Southern Africa was a mess of problems in need of firm leadership from one who would be above local politics and untainted by policy misjudgments. Wolseley, who had been lobbying for months to escape from Cyprus, was called on. In late May he was appointed as Governor of Natal for the second time. He was also given the local rank of full general so that he would outrank Chelmsford.

Wolseley's appointment was hugely popular in Britain. He had come to be known as 'our only general' and was about to be written into *The Pirates of Penzance* as Major-General Stanley, 'the very model of a modern major-general'. Paddington Station was thronged on 29 May 1879 when he left to thrash the Zulus. He took with him Brackenbury as his military secretary and secured Colley as his chief-of-staff.

During Wolseley's last week in England, Chelmsford was putting the final touches to the plans for a second invasion of Zululand. This time there would be no unnecessary risks taken. The invasion force would move carefully. It would have a twelve-cannon artillery battery, rockets, and Gatling guns. Wood was once again given command of the left flank, assisted by Buller who would lead the mounted volunteers. On 1 June 1879 the second British invasion of Zululand got underway.

The Zulu power was severely weakened. Losses at Isandhlwana had been more than 2000 elite warriors, and Ceteswayo, in a despairing utterance, had described his pyrrhic victory as 'a spear through the belly of the nation'. However, the invasion got off to an ominous start, sending shock-waves through Britain. Eugene Louis Napoleon, the Prince Imperial and the main hope for opponents of the Third French Republic, died in a skirmish with a small party of Zulus just across the border from Natal. The prince was the son of the deposed Napoleon III, who had died in exile in England. His widow, the Empress Eugenie, had become warmly accepted by British society, and her young son, while waiting for the call of destiny from France, had attended the military college at Woolwich where he distinguished himself as a horseman and won the affection of his fellow cadets. In 1878 he was commissioned as a lieutenant in the Royal Artillery. When the prince volunteered for service in Natal there was much discussion at the highest levels before his request was granted on the explicit understanding that he would not be exposed to situations of risk. He had reached Durban shortly after Butler arrived there and Butler was briefly responsible for him before he travelled up-country to join Chelmsford's staff. Butler found him 'a splendid young soldier, handsome, active, brave to a fault'.

The prince's death was a freak occurrence. He had ridden out with a small escort to an area supposedly free of Zulus. In the heat of mid-afternoon, his party had dismounted when they were suddenly fired on at close range from the veldt. Safety lay in flight, but in the panic the prince's horse bolted, leaving him to face his pursuers alone. His body was recovered lacerated with assegai wounds, all borne on the front, and was returned by ceremonial stages to Durban where Butler was charged with the obsequies. The special order he issued to the troops illustrates the unconventionality of his thinking and his independence of mind: few, if any, British army officers would have referred so publicly to the 'mighty name' and 'great military renown' of Napoleon Bonaparte.

10th June 1879

The mortal remains of Prince Louis Napoleon will be carried, tomorrow, at half-past 9.a.m., from the Roman Catholic Church, in Durban, to the Wharf, at Port Natal, for embarkation in H.M.S. *Boadicea* to England.

In following the coffin, which holds the body of the late PRINCE IMPERIAL OF FRANCE, and paying to his ashes the final tribute of sorrow, and of honour, the Troops in garrison will remember:

First: That he was the last inheritor of a mighty name, and of a great military renown.

Second: That he was the son of England's firm ally in dangerous days.

Third: That he was the sole child of a widowed Empress, who is now left throneless and childless, in exile, on English shores.

Deepening the profound sorrow, and the solemn reverence that attaches to these memories, the Troops will also remember that the PRINCE IMPER-IAL OF FRANCE fell fighting as a British soldier.

W.F. BUTLER
A.A. General
Base of Operations
DURBAN, NATAL,
South Africa.[12]

Butler was openly critical of the manner of the death. He was scathing of the prince's escort and their abandonment of him, but he reserved most of his anger for those in higher authority:

It was afterwards said by way of excuse that the prince was brave to rashness, and that it was his reckless daring which led to his death. What an excuse! Making the fault of those who were responsible for the escort and its leadership only more glaringly apparent.[13]

Wolseley arrived in Durban on 28 June. He was hungry to get to the front, but Chelmsford was determined to take the Zulu capital, Ulundi, himself before Wolesley could reap the glory of certain victory. On 4 July 1879, 5000 British soldiers marched ponderously on Ulundi in classic hollow-square formation with mounted cannon at its corners and rockets and Gatlings at its front. Twenty thousand Zulus hurled themselves at the square in a final futile attempt to preserve the independence of their state against the might of modern armaments. Ten British soldiers died at Ulundi. Zulu losses ran into an estimated 2000. Chelmsford's victory was only slightly marred by his failure to capture Ceteswayo. For Wolseley, making his way up from the coast, this was something to be made the most of. He announced that the king was deposed and sent messengers into Zululand to demand his unconditional surrender. Ceteswayo refused to accept this humiliation and went on the run.

Chelmsford formally handed over command to Wolseley and left for England. With Chelmsford gone, Wolseley concentrated all his efforts on capturing Ceteswayo. Privately, he would have preferred a simpler option to that of capture. Writing to his wife in mid-August, he said: 'I shall get him. If he would only resist and be killed, the result would be still more satisfactory."[4] Ceteswayo was captured on 28 August. Some fifty years of age, of striking presence, barefoot and dressed in a rough robe, he made a dignified appearance before Wolseley and was rushed to the coast and captivity in Capetown Castle.

Wolseley then turned his attention to the truculent Transvaal. He was determined to quieten that country by a display of military might. The troublesome Pedi tribe, on the northern border of the Transvaal, gave him his opportunity. Wolseley calculated that a campaign against them would both make the Boers grateful and show them that Britain was not to be trifled with. He struck successfully against the Pedi, but his victory had the opposite effect on the Transvaal to that intended. With the Zulus and the Pedi no longer a threat, the Boers were free to devote their energies to obstructing British control of their country. Wolseley's strengths as a military man were in no way matched by his strengths as an administrator and the following months were not easy ones. When he finally left Natal, he came home to the disappointment of not getting a hoped-for peerage.

In Durban, Butler, who had some respite when troops were upcountry, found himself in the latter part of 1879 extremely busy organizing the billeting and embarkation of the troops returning to England, and the payment and discharge of the irregular forces. It was not until January 1880 that he left Durban. His last mission in South Africa was one that showed the breadth of his sympathies. His ship was due to call at Cape Town and he received a request from the officer responsible for Ceteswayo, to bring a supply of rushes from Zululand so that the king, 'unable to sleep in an English bed', could have mats woven for him. When his ship docked at Capetown, Butler personally brought the rushes on the roof of a cab to Cape Town Castle where Ceteswayo was confined:

> I was soon in the room where the unfortunate Ceteswayo was kept. He was delighted to get this little bit of his beloved Zululand in his dreary four-walled prison. It was the same as putting a little bit of green sod into the cage of a lark; only the unfortunate king wept when he saw these reminders of his old home, and he said to the interpreter as he shook my hand 'Say to him that he has brought sleep to me: now I can rest at night.'[5]

In an article that he wrote on his return from Natal in 1880, Butler expressed his views on Zululand with customary clarity and emphasis. Britain had ignored the fact that the Zulus had not been a serious threat to the stability of either Natal or the Transvaal. Further, Britain had actively supported Ceteswayo's claim to the Zulu throne in 1872, at the expense of the development of a communal government system. Butler now went further than before in publicly recognizing the common humanity of black and white:

> Not withstanding the wide gulf which we fancy lies between us and this blackman, he is singularly like us. He will cry if you stick a pin into him, he will be thankful for a gift, he will resent an injury, he will weep for the loss of a wife or child, he will fight for his homeland – and he can even die for what he believes to be the right. And mark you this vast difference between him and the other aboriginal races with whom your spirited colonisation has brought you into contact: he does not die out before us.[16]

By this time the Wolseley Ring was causing strong resentment among those outside of it. Wolseley was accused of gross favouritism in selecting the same officers again and again for service. He responded to these criticisms by saying that, to ensure lasting army reform, a ring of officers such as he had developed was an essential leaven. The army possesed no General Staff Unit and this allowed cliques to thrive. (Wolseley's main rival clique was headed by his contemporary Frederick Sleigh Roberts, 'Bobs'.) By the close of 1879 the individual officers in the Ring were becoming differentiated, not so much by their closeness to Wolseley as by their relative distance from him. Colley was nearest. Brackenbury, Buller, Wood and Frederick Maurice, who had been Wolseley's private secretary on the Asante campaign, formed a lower tier. Butler, Gifford and Hugh 'Baby' Mac-Calmont, another veteran of the Red River, made a third tier. In keeping with his policy of watching for new talent, Wolseley had become mentor to Captain Herbert Stewart, a cavalry officer who had served under Chelmsford in Natal.

Butler's position in the Ring at this time was largely due to his posting at Natal four months before Wolseley left Cyprus. However, the differing views of the two men on the responsibilities of Imperial Britain towards subject peoples ensured that, had Wolseley taken Butler on to his own staff for the duration of his South African assignment, Butler would probably have moved no closer to him. This difference of opinion manifested itself with startling clarity in the aftermath of the Egyptian revolt of 1882.

Chapter Seven

'YOUR LIFE IS STILL BEFORE YOU'

On his return to England from Natal in February 1880, Butler was invited to meet the Empress Eugenie Napoleon to give her the details of her son's obsequies in Durban. This meeting had an extra melancholy frisson since Butler, on his voyage home, had again visited St Helena. Eugenia was deeply touched by Butler's warmth and sympathy, and their meeting marked the beginning of a long friendship.

In April he was promoted to lieutenant-colonel for services in Natal. That month, following a general election, the Liberals swept back to power under Gladstone. One result of this was the appointment of a new viceroy, the Marquess of Ripon, to India. Butler, publicly identified as non-interventionist with regard to the recent Afghanistan invasion, was proposed as his private secretary. However, Ripon was a recent convert to Roman Catholicism and Gladstone vetoed Butler's appointment: in Butler's words 'he considered that a Catholic viceroy in India was sufficiently experimental without further endangering the position by the appointment of another of the same creed to a subordinate but still influential post'.[1] The secretaryship to the viceroy went to Colonel Charles Gordon. Butler, instead, became Assistant Adjutant General, Western District, on an annual salary of £600. His position was third in the regional military hierarchy at Devonport, Plymouth.

In tandem with his career over the preceding few years, his personal life had undergone significant change, for he was now a married man and a father. On 22 April 1876, while mired in the routine of War Office bureaucracy, he had gone to a lunch party with the purpose of being introduced to the battle artist Elizabeth Thompson. He later told Elizabeth that it had been while hospitalized at Netley in 1874 that he had heard about *The Roll Call* and its remarkable creator, and how 'he said one day in utter fun under his reviving spirits to his sister, "I wonder if Miss Thompson would marry me?" '[2]

Elizabeth Southerden Thompson was born on 3 November 1846 in Lausanne, Switzerland. She was the elder of two children, both girls, born to Thomas and Christiana Thompson. Elizabeth and her sister Alice were to achieve artistic fame in their twenties, one as a painter, the other as a poet. They were the offspring of unconventional parents. Thomas Thompson was a thirty-two-year-old widower of independent means when, early in 1844, he attended a concert in Liverpool with his friend, the novelist Charles Dickens. One of the musicians was the nineteen-year-old Christiana Weller, an accomplished concert pianist. Both men were smitten by her vivacity and charm. Dickens wrote Christiana some verses in mock apology for having bestowed the name Weller on his splendid comic creation in *The Pickwick Papers*:

> *Lines for Miss C. Weller's Album.*
> *I put in a book once by hook and by crook*
> *The whole race (as I thought) of a 'feller'*
> *Who happily pleased the town's taste much diseas'd,*
> *And the name of this person was Weller.*
> *I found to my cost that* one *Weller I lost,*
> *Cruel destiny so to arrange it !*
> *I love her dear name which has won me some fame,*
> *But great Heaven how gladly I'd change it.*[3]

Thomas Thompson and Christiana Weller were married in 1845. During the 1850s the family lived for long periods in Italy. Elizabeth and Alice's parents lavished affection on them. They were known by their pet names, Mimi and Babe; Elizabeth retained hers all her life and used it in all her intimate correspondence. Christiana kept a gushing and erratic diary during those years in which the children are depicted as 'little angels', 'sweet babes', and 'as gay as larks'. Thomas Thompson was of a more reflective nature than his wife. Both parents had an unusual degree of involvement in the education of their daughters. Christiana taught them how to sketch and play the piano, while the more routine aspects of their education were the responsibility of their father.

In 1853 Dickens, on a tour of Italy, called unannounced on the family at Nervi outside Genoa. He reported to his wife:

> I found them living in a beautiful situation in a ruinous Albaro-like palace. Coming upon them unawares I found T[homas] with a pointed beard, smoking a great German pipe, in a pair of slippers; the two little girls very pale and faint from the climate, in a singularly untidy state – one (heaven knows why!) without stockings, and both with their little short hair cropped in a manner never before beheld, and a little bright bow stuck on the top of it. ... We had disturbed her [Christiana] at her painting in oils, and I have rather received an impression that, what with that, and what with music, the household affairs went a little to the wall. T was teaching the two little girls the multiplication table in a disorderly old billiard room, with all manner of maps in it.[4]

Elizabeth was robustly independent and self-confident. She inherited her mother's gaiety, tempered with her father's desire for private space. As she grew to maturity, her strength of character was belied by her appearance. Slightly built and just five feet in height, she suffered from a minor hearing defect which made her self-conscious with strangers. At the age of nineteen she began an intensive three-year-course at the Kensington Female School of Art, where she outshone most of her co-students. By the time she graduated in 1869 Elizabeth was devoting much of her time to military subjects. This was a genre largely ignored by other British painters and was an unusual one for a woman artist. Her choice of subject matter was both shrewd and courageous, and she brought intuition and sensitivity to her paintings. 'My own reading of war', she wrote, ' – that mysteriously inevitable recurrence throughout the sorrowful history of the world – is that it calls forth the noblest and the basest impulses of human nature.'[5] She pursued her chosen *metier* methodically, using the contacts of her father to observe army life. In 1873 she had her first oil painting accepted by the Royal Academy. Entitled *Missing*, it portrayed an imaginary scene from the Franco-Prussian War of 1870. *Missing* was a modest success. It allowed Elizabeth the freedom to rent her own studio in Kensington and here in December 1873, while Butler was staggering through the forests of Akim, she began *The Roll Call*.

Elizabeth remained closely attached to her family and moved in social circles that embraced the resurgent world of English Roman Catholicism. Her parents were from an evangelical Protestant tradition, but long sojourns in Italy had drawn the entire family towards Catholicism. They had gone to Rome for the opening of the First Vatican Council in 1869, and Christiana converted to Rome around this time. She was followed by Alice in 1872, and by Elizabeth in 1873. The Thompsons now became part of the London circle of the Archbishop of Westminster, Henry Manning, yet another convert. In September 1873 Elizabeth and Alice were part of the first pilgrimage since the Reformation to leave the shores of England. The chartered cross-channel steamer on which the pilgrims travelled from Newhaven to France flew three flags, the Union Jack, the pontifical flag and a banner of the Sacred Heart of Jesus. The pilgrims were waved off from the quay by a small good-natured crowd and a single protestor, '... brandishing a bludgeon and shrieking at us, "You're a disgrace! You're a disgrace to your country!"'[6]

In 1874 *The Roll Call* brought Elizabeth Thompson overwhelming public acclaim, and when Alice published her first volume of verse, *Preludes*, the following year, the sisters became something of a celebrity duo. John Ruskin, Slade Professor of Fine Art at Oxford, and an influential writer and critic, praised them generously. Tennyson, the Poet Laureate, invited them to afternoon tea. He did not impress Elizabeth; she found him patronizing.

Among Tennyson's most popular narrative poems was 'The Charge of the Light Brigade'. At the time she met Tennyson, Elizabeth was working on her painting of Balaclava. *Balaclava* was not a recreation of the charge but of its dreadful aftermath. The painting was exhibited in a commercial gallery, the Fine Arts Society in Bond Street. During the private viewing in April 1876 she was invited to lunch by a Mrs Mitchell, 'next door to Lady Raglan, her great friend. Two distinguished officers were there to meet me and we had a pleasant chat.' Looking over that faded diary entry in old age she commented, 'And that is all I say!'[7] One of those officers was Butler.

The couple met frequently over the following months and Butler attended several of the musical afternoons held in the Thompson family home in Kensington. The attraction between them was immediate and strong, and they soon became Mimi and Will to one another. Elizabeth found in the articulate Butler an attractive social confidence, while he found in her a quiet warmth and lack of pretension, unusual on the London social round. They laughed easily together. Their shared intellectual interests included military history, a rare joint pursuit for a Victorian courting couple. They each had an awareness of the cost of British pre-eminence in world affairs, as that cost was paid by the lesser servants of empire or its subject peoples. For both, religion was a binding force. Elizabeth was zealous for her new faith, and she drew Butler into the cerebral world of lay Roman Catholicism that flourished in the London of the 1870s. Through Alice Thompson, Butler became friendly with the journalist Wilfrid Meynell, another convert, shortly to become secretary to Archbishop Manning. For Butler the Catholic revival had an added attraction: its minority status made it, *ipso facto*, a worthwhile cause.

By autumn, five months after they had first met, the couple had made their courtship public. They announced their engagement on 3 March 1877, and decided on a June wedding. The preparations for it did not interrupt Elizabeth's painting; through the winter she had been working on her third Crimean subject, *Return from Inkerman*. It was nowhere near as powerful as her earlier Crimean paintings and was her last on the subject.[8]

Monday 11 June 1877 was a superb summer day. The wedding of Major William Butler and Miss Elizabeth Thompson took place in the Servite church on the Fulham Road. Manning, now a cardinal, officiated, while Alice and a Protestant friend of the Thompsons, a Dr Pollard, were the witnesses. Guests included Wolseley and several officers of the Ring. A group of Elizabeth's student friends scattered flowers in the aisle as the couple came down from the altar.

Although launched with the customary religious and social trappings, Butler's marriage was not a conventional one. Commissioned officers of Her Majesty's Forces tended to marry in their mid- to late-thirties, and in this Butler conformed to type, but his choice of partner was unusual for an army man. His wife had a highly successful and very public career of her own. She had little interest in the tight social round of the typical officer's wife, with its rivalries and petty snobberies, and she could never play more than a peripheral part in her husband's advancement, for she had no military connections. One other aspect of Butler's step into matrimony is worth comment. He was thirty-eight years old, and his mother had died when he was nine. From his early teens, with a few brief exceptions, his world had been a male one. The transition to being a husband and father would not be without its share of strains.

The Butlers spent their honeymoon in Ireland. From London the couple made a leisurely and broken journey to Hollyhead to catch the steam packet to Kingstown. Elizabeth, as was customary for travelling ladies, was accompanied by a personal maid. From Warwick in the English midlands she found time to dash off a short letter to her mother. Something of the depth of her emotions is caught by it. It is the only extant letter of Elizabeth's which opens without the formality of addressing its recipient. Instead, in an overspill of feeling, it begins:

> Oh! 500000 exclamations won't express the state of things. A greater darling never was than this Will of mine and I know that everyday he will develop some new excellence. I am very well, though sleep and appetite are at a discount at present. Will looks magnificent and is so engaging. Anne [the maid] is the greatest comfort to me. When we are in Kerry though she will not be wanted so much. She is to go to see friends at Clonmel during our rustic sojourn in the hills of Glencar ... Please send my bathing dress and chemisettes.[9]

The couple spent a month in Ireland. They visited the Suir Valley and Butler's old home at Ballyslatteen, but it was in Kerry, where Butler had regained his health after the Gold Coast, that Elizabeth found 'the land that held a magnet for us'. They stayed at Glencar at the foot of the Macgillicuddy Reeks, in a converted shooting lodge, the Glencar House Hotel. It was in the glen that Elizabeth sketched two local men who would become the centrepiece of her first painting with an Irish theme, '*Listed for the Connaught Rangers*'. The honeymooners returned to London for the autumn wedding of Alice Thompson to Wilfrid Meynell.

Early in 1878 the Butlers' first child, Mary Patricia, was born, only to die within months. They went to Europe that summer, visiting Lourdes and Lausanne – Elizabeth's birthplace. Then it was on to Germany and a steam trip down the Rhine to Rotterdam. *En route* there were opportunities to observe the new militarism, which they found both comical and menacing. In a Dusseldorf café they watched officers at a nearby table saluting and counter-saluting with stiff and ostentatious discipline. On the steamer there was an row one evening in the dining salon over seating arrangements.

> 'Will found an epauletted disciple of Bismarck in my place at supper. He told the epauletted one of his mistake, much to the latter's manifest astonishment, who didn't move. I suppose there came something into the British soldier's eye, but anyway the sabre rattler eventually got up and went elsewhere: things felt electric.'[10]

When Butler sailed for Natal in February 1879, Elizabeth, pregnant again, stayed behind in London with her parents. She made a triumphant return to the Royal Academy in May of that year when she had two paintings exhibited. The first was *'Listed for the Connaught Rangers'*, the second the stunning *Remnants of an Army*, depicting the arrival at the haven of Jalalabad Fort in 1842 of Dr William Brydon, an exhausted horseman on a mount near collapse. (Brydon, it will be recalled, had been referred to by Butler in his 1878 essay against British military involvement in Afghanistan. Husband and wife were at one in their thinking on this matter.) Elizabeth gave birth to her second child, christened Elizabeth, in September, while Butler was still in Natal.

With Butler's return to England in 1880, his promotion to lieutenant-colonel and his appointment as Assistant Adjutant General, Western District, he and Elizabeth moved with their baby daughter to Plymouth, to a fashionable house on the historic Hoe overlooking Plymouth Sound. In Plymouth, on 7 November 1880, their son Patrick was born.

Devonport was a leisured existence which Elizabeth found 'conducive to lotus eating'. Such life was insufficiently challenging for both husband and wife. Elizabeth was never far from her easel. She had been asked by the queen to paint a subject from a contemporary war. She had always avoided the depiction of actual violence 'because it was against my principles to paint a conflict'. She proposed the scene at the finding of the body of the Prince Imperial in Zululand. Victoria's advisers pointed out that it would not be appropriate to have the queen commission a portrait that symbolized the end of French monarchist hopes. Elizabeth was pressed for another subject from the Zulu War. She chose the defence of Rorke's Drift, depicting mainly the defenders, and representing the attackers off-centre as an indistinct surge with only one Zulu warrior fully delineated.

Butler himself was flattered to be included in the fourth volume of *The Cabinet of Irish Literature*, published in 1880. The volume carried five excerpts from his writings. He also expended some of his energies on the publication in 1880 of *Far Out: Rovings Retold*, his first book since *Akim Foo* in 1875. This collection of essays, which was praised by Ruskin, included impressions of Cyprus and the United States, a lighthearted account of travels with Cerf Volant, and several essays on aspects of southern Africa. It also carried the stirring 'A Plea for the Peasant', showing Butler's thinking on conscription, a heavily debated aspect of army reform. 'A Plea' argued for short-service conscription – something that would not come about until the First World War – and for the preservation of a propertied peasantry as the backbone of the army: there was a world of difference between 'the coster and the cottier'.

Butler also found time to contribute to a popular sub-genre of apocalyptic writing on the weakness of Britain after the Franco-Prussian War of 1870. His short *The Invasion of England*, published anonymously, described an England of the 1890s taken over by Germany, a situation brought about not from a lack of courage on the part of British troops but from insufficient contingency planning and training, outdated equipment, lack of supplies and hopelessly inadequate transport systems. Butler's views on the state of Britain's defences were shared by most of his colleagues.

Wolseley was still to the fore in effecting change. He had returned from Natal in 1880 to the post of Quartermaster General, the third most influential post in the army. He clashed continually with the Commander-in-Chief, the Duke of Cambridge, 'Old Bumble Bee'. Cambridge believed that Wolseley and his kind were ruining the army. Several of the recent reforms were contentious. For example, the abolition of Purchase in 1871 had led to the practice of promotion by seniority. Wolseley disagreed with this, arguing for promotion by merit. He was vehement in the expression of his opinions, belittling his opponents at every public opportunity. At the end of 1881 he was appointed Adjutant General, second only to Cambridge, by a government eager to keep up the momentum of reform.

Gladstone had fought the 1880 election on a policy of imperial retrench-ment and his attacks on the Conservatives included a scathing indictment of the annexation of the Transvaal as 'insane and immoral'. Once in power however, Gladstone did nothing to rescind the annexation, arguing that matters would only be worsened by such a move. Wolseley, on his return from Natal, had lobbied successfully for his protégé Colley to succeed him in Africa. Colley was offered the joint post of Governor of Natal and High Commissioner to the Transvaal. In the summer of 1880 he and his wife of two years sailed as Sir George and Lady Colley for their new life. It was to prove brutally short.

The Transvaal was seething. The Boers had placed much of their hopes in a return to power of Gladstone. But Gladstone had failed them. In December 1880 the Transvaal proclaimed its independence, and the first Anglo-Boer War began. In the new year Colley took personal command of the British troops that marched into the Transvaal to quell the rebellion. Back in England, Butler followed events in South Africa closely and in February 1881 *The Contemporary Review* carried a 5000-word article by him entitled 'The Boers and the Transvaal'. Most of the article was given over to tracing Boer history since the days of the Great Trek. Butler was sympathetic to the Boers: current British policy was wrong. The annexation of the Transvaal in 1877 had made a mockery of the Sand River Convention of 1852, by which Britain had agreed to the establishment of the Transvaal as an independent state. Further, it was not only the Boers of the Transvaal who had been disaffected:

> ... there had been created in the mind of the Dutch community inhabiting South Africa a spirit of deep and angry hostility towards our rule. The old animosities which had fallen asleep during the quarter century of quiet, have been aroused to bitter wakefulness and a blow has been struck against the possibility of fusion between English and Dutch or even of friendship and political confederation, which will take more time to efface than the present generation has before it."

The Boer War came to an abrupt and bloody conclusion at Majuba Hill in the Drakensberg Mountains on 27 February 1881 when Colley was killed and his small force routed, from a site of his own choice and in a fight of his own timing. It was a Sunday, a fact not lost on the Boers: Colley had profaned the Lord's Day.

In London, the government decided against continuing to use force. The Transvaal quickly agreed to an armistice whose terms were negotiated by Evelyn Wood, Colley's chief-of-staff. By July, independence was restored to the Transvaal, Britain reserving to itself the right to control foreign relations. Wood's conduct of the negotiations had been astute but there were many in the army, Wolseley included, who saw the armistice as a betrayal of imperial interests, and who looked forward to a time when the humiliation of Majuba might be avenged. As for Colley himself, the cause of his death was analysed for years. Butler dealt charitably with Colley's memory in his 1899 biography of his fellow Irishman, but H. Rider Haggard would be less sympathetic to Colley:

> One of Wolseley's darlings, every advancement, every honour, was heaped upon him. At last fortune offered him a soldier's supreme opportunity and he used it thus! Had he been content to wait, it was said at the time – and I for one believe – that the Boers would have melted away. Or if they did not he would soon have found himself at the head of a force that might have commanded victory ... But he had theories and he lacked patience."

With southern Africa quiet, the second great issue of public import which had been prominent in the general election of 1880 came centre stage. This was the condition of Ireland. In the opening sentences of his 1881 article on the Transvaal, Butler had linked these two parts of the world, some 6000 miles apart, saying of the Transvaal that it was 'another and a larger Ireland; a region in which conflict had become chronic, opposition a habit, friction a necessity'.[13]

The general election of 1880 had been fought in Ireland on the land question. A series of poor harvests in the preceding years had culminated in a wretched harvest in 1879. This in turn led to a steep increase in the eviction rate of small tenant farmers. However, a generation on from the Great Famine, this class was less fearful of the power of the landlord and eligible to vote in elections by secret ballot. In 1879 the Land League was founded. It threw its weight behind the Nationalist or Home Rule Party, which was already benefitting from the tacit support of many of the old Fenians, who were prepared to try constitutional methods to advance republican ideals. Ireland had 100 seats in the imperial parliament and in the 1880 election it returned 61 Home Rulers, one of whom was the obstructionist MP Charles Stewart Parnell, who was soon voted chairman of the party. What became known as the Land War gripped Ireland; the withholding of rents, evictions, agitation, coercion, outrage, reprisal. Evictions ran into thousands each year through the early 1880s. Tipperary, Butler's home county, had a high level of outrages.

Butler followed the Irish situation with informed interest. In July 1881 *The Contemporary Review* carrried a second article by him. Entitled 'They Were a Great People, Sir', it did not propose solutions to the problem of Ireland. As yet, Butler, like so many others sympathetic to Ireland's plight, was suspicious of Parnell's credentials and apprehensive of the whiff of physical force from many of the newly elected nationalist MPs. His article was largely an historical overview to explain the current situation. The plantations of the seventeenth century had altered a workable system by bringing 'a new breed of proprietors' into Ireland, the 'rough troopers' of Cromwell:

> ... men who stood almost completely isolated from their fellow beings beneath them as though they had been the white garrison of a western prairie fort amid a wilderness of Red Indians ... of the kinship that comes of common race, the bond of a faith held together, the union that holds hopes, fears, and dangers past and to come, linked in an undivided destiny, there

was not to be one chord of sympathy vibrating through the social structure of Ireland. On the one side, the 'new interest' would find itself year by year forced into more exclusive isolation, but growing weaker through absenteeism, the spirit of modern opinion, and the influence of modern ideas. On the other, the people, ever drifting further away from the memory of obedience and regard for their old masters, would become more hopelessly estranged from the classes above them, more prone to wander after wild experiments, to listen to the teaching of dangerous doctrines, to catch the echo of distant democracies, remaining deaf to the solid sound of sense that also comes from them.[14]

The reference to 'a western prairie fort amid a wilderness of Red Indians' is interesting: Ireland may have engaged Butler's attention but in 1881 the strongest emotional pull on him was still from Canada. In the autumn of that year he was actively pursuing the possibility of joining an expedition to the Mackenzie River in the Canadian Arctic. In November 1881, with Elizabeth halfway through another pregnancy, he wrote to Wolseley:

> I thank you most sincerely for putting forward a memo on the subject of the Mackenzie River expedition. I grudged asking you to help me in the matter at a time when I know you must have had on your hands plenty of far more important work public and personal. If the expedition comes off I should be willing to give up my staff pay for the period of absence and they can scarcely refuse to give me 6 or 8 month's leave for such a purpose.[15]

Nothing came of these hopes and Butler was in Plymouth for the birth of his second son, Richard, on 15 March 1882. During this time he was completing his only novel, *Red Cloud*, an adventure story for boys. Published in 1882, when Butler was forty three, *Red Cloud* was a salute to the departing nomadic world of the North American Plains Indians. It was also Butler's personal retrospective on the passing of the years of his early maturity, a time when for long stretches he lived life close to nature with an intensity never to be recaptured. In writing *Red Cloud*, Butler was doing more than providing an adventure story for his own and other children: he was bidding farewell to his youth. For the book's eponymous title he went back to that scene from years before in the gaslight of a New York street. He took the name, but none of the pathos or humiliation, of that bewildered figure in 'semi-civilized dress'.

The novel springs not from Butler's head, but from his heart. Both *The*

Great Lone Land and *The Wild North Land* belong to the canon of nineteenth-century British imperial literature. It has already been seen from his 1871 report to Governor Archibald in Fort Garry how firmly Butler believed in ordered colonial expansion into the fertile Canadian plains 'admirably suited for cultivation'. His appendix to *The Wild North Land* had argued for the construction of the Canadian transcontinental railway across the Saskatchewan prairies to open them up for cultivation. Tellingly, in his autobiography he would describe the valley of the river Platte, where in 1867 he had first encountered the prairie and the bison as having been transformed within seven years into 'a smiling plain of farms, waving crops and neat homesteads'. (It will also be recalled that Butler's strongest criticism of the Boers was that they did not cultivate their lands.)

Yet Butler, unlike most of his peers and colleagues, recognized and acknowledged the high costs of Progress. He valued much of what was being lost. The riches of the traditional life of the Plains Indians, particularly their relationship with nature, impressed him deeply. If in *The Great Lone Land* and *The Wild North Land* this sounds out as a constant motif, it becomes the dominant key in *Red Cloud*.

The story is told in the first person by an unnamed young Irishman who leaves his cottage home in Kerry to wander the American prairies. There he mets with a lone Sioux, Red Cloud. The Sioux is searching; for nine years he has been trying to confront a villainous white trader called McDermott, a man who, under the guise of friendship, had sold Red Cloud's father to his death. The Irishman is drawn into the search and a close friendship grows between himself and the Sioux.

Butler runs the story through the seasons of a full year, and underscoring the storyline are graphic descriptions of Indian craft. This makes for something much more substantial than a *Boy's Own* adventure. The reader is drawn into a celebration of a natural world of great richness and diversity. Into the novel, Butler distilled everything that had attracted him to the North American west: its vastness, its variety, its freedom, and its aboriginal peoples who lived as part of nature.

At the end of *Red Cloud* McDermott is dead. The Indian and the narrator prepare to part, but the Irishman cannot will himself to cleave this friendship and to leave the life he has come to love.

The novel's final lines build towards a poignant climax as Red Cloud speaks. And it requires no great leap of imagination to hear in the words which Butler gives the Sioux – *We cannot change our colours* – an ambivalence in Butler himself about the life path he is now firmly embarked on:

'You look upon your life as closed. My friend you are wrong. Your life is still all before you. You are only setting out upon its prairies. Many long years from now when you are in sight of the Mountains of the Setting Sun you will know that I, Red Cloud the Sioux, showed you the right trail, though he could not follow it himself. We cannot change our colours. The Redman cannot give up the wilderness; he dies amid the city and the fenced field. You cannot make this wildlife your own, even though you may wish to do so. You have other work to do; you must go back and do it.'

... Far down in the plain a light haze of smoke hung above the treetops. We shook hands in silence.

'See,' he said, 'the smoke of your people's fires far below; there is your road and here is mine ...'

'And is there nothing then that I can do for you?' I said. 'You have done everything for me: let me do something in return.'

'Well, my friend,' he replied, 'sometimes think of me. When I am camped at night far out on the great prairie I would like to say to myself, my white brother remembers me. That is all.'

Then he turned off to the North leading his horse by the bridle up the mountain path. I stood watching him as step by step the void of space grew between us. Think of you!, I said, speaking half aloud. Yes, that I will. Whenever the wind stirs the tree branch or rustles the reeds and meadows, whenever the sun goes down over a distant land or sea, in the moonlight of nights; in the snow of long winters you will be near me still.

At a bend in the trail he turned to look back. It was but a moment, and then the mountain path was vacant and I saw him no more.[16]

Chapter Eight

THE EGYPTIAN CAMPAIGN
AND ITS AFTERMATH

It was not Canada but Egypt which next freed Butler from the boredom
of garrison life at Devonport. Egypt was a province of the Ottoman empire and in 1882 it was in crisis. During the 1860s and 1870s its ruler, Khedive Ismael, had plunged his country into enormous debt through elaborate modernization schemes, the most expensive of which was the hun-
dred-mile canal cut through the Isthmus of Suez. By 1875 Egypt owed
£70,000,000 to European creditors and, to alleviate the situation, Ismael
sold his canal shares. They were bought for Britain by Disraeli, who told
the Commons: 'We are obtaining a great hold and interest in this important part of Africa because it secures to us a highway to our Indian empire
and other dependencies." The shares cost Britain £4,000,000 and this
money was borowed from Rothschild, the international financiers. Earlier
in his life Disraeli had half-joked that Europe was run by seven Great Powers: Austria, Britain, France, Prussia, Russia, Baring, and Rothschild.

Britain became the largest single shareholder in the Canal and within a
year Ismael was forced to accept an arrangement known as the Dual Control, whereby Britain and France together tried to regulate Egyptian finances. The debt continued to soar and in 1879 the Sultan in Constantinople deposed Ismael and replaced him with his son, Tawfiq. The rural
masses groaned under excessive taxes. In the cities, small-scale money
lenders and property-owners, most of them foreign – in Butler's words

'Jews and Gentiles, Turks, Arabs, Greeks, and Syrians; all of those extra-ordinary, astute human units grouped under the name of Levantines' – charged exorbitant rates for loans and tenancies. Within the national assembly opposition to Khedive Tawfiq was led by a Colonel Ahmad Urabi, a man of peasant origins. By January 1882 Urabi was the most popular man in Egypt and in that month he became Under-Secretary of State for War. He attracted some public attention in Britain, most of it critical. To many he was a destructive demagogue, though there were others, most notably Wilfrid Scawen Blunt,[2] who saw him as an Egyptian nationalist. Egypt seemed to be teetering on the brink of a descent into turmoil.

There were 90,000 Europeans living in Egypt, and their alarm at the deteriorating situation caused London and Paris to send an unsolicited joint memorandum to the khedive assuring him of their support and encouraging him to deal firmly with dissent. The effect of this note was the opposite of what was intended: it proved that Tawfiq was nothing more than a puppet controlled by Europe. Urabi wrested control of the national assembly from him. For Butler, the development of the crisis and the manner in which it was resolved showed beyond doubt that the prime movers were international financiers 'letting loose the dogs of war'.

By mid-May 1882 an Anglo-French fleet of four warships was anchored in the outer harbour of Alexandria. To the mass of Egyptians this was a menacing insult and on 11 June serious rioting broke out in Alexandria. Urabi demanded an end to European interference in Egypt and began to strengthen coastal fortifications. Gladstone's government split over what response it should make. Compelling factors for intervention included the threat to the Suez Canal – through which four-fifths of the traffic was British – and pressure from Rothschild.

London tried without success to get the Ottoman Sultan involved. France had been satisfied to be part of a small intimidatory fleet but would not go further. Britain decided to act alone. On the morning of 11 July, twenty-eight ships of the line began a bombardment of the ancient city of Alexandria. By night fall, the city was a flaming ruin. British marines came ashore the following day to scenes of appalling destruction. Urabi's forces fell back inland. In Butler's view, the bombardment was 'a strategic and tactical error of the first magnitude'. It failed to break the revolt, allowing Urabi to concentrate his army away from the coast in a position of his choice, and it left exposed the long line of the Suez Canal to the east. Urabi rallied the provincial governors in Egypt and conscripted thousands of fellahin. Britain had no alternative but to invade to overthrow him.

The command of the invasion force was given to Wolseley. His Chief-of-Staff, General Sir John Adye, was imposed on him, but he was able to chose the remainder of his personal staff. Butler, on the strength of his work in Durban, was appointed Assistant Adjutant and Quartermaster to the expedition. Buller was made responsible for Intelligence. Brackenbury was not available, though he would join the expedition later. Field commands were given to Evelyn Wood and Herbert Stewart, among others. Queen Victoria's son Arthur, Duke of Connaught, was assigned to the headquarters staff. Wolseley, commanding a force of 40,000 men, came to Egypt with two priorities: to secure the Suez Canal, and to destroy Urabi's army. From Alexandria he moved a decoy force under Wood towards Cairo, masking the movement of the troop transports to the canal with a diversionary night bombardment. On 19 August the canal was seized, and within two days Wolseley and his personal staff, with 10,000 men at their back, were at the port of Ismailia at the southern end of the canal, which was linked by rail to Cairo seventy-five miles to the west.

With the canal secured, Wolseley prepared to tackle the Egyptian army. He was determined on a major engagement that would bring the revolt to a decisive finish. He would advance steadily through the desert along the line of the railway, pushing against all resistance until he reached Urabi's heavily fortified position of Tel-el-Kebir, 'The Great Hill'. There he proposed to crush the enemy. On his first reconnaissance from Ismailia, Butler accompanied him into the desert:

> I have never forgotten that first morning out from Ismailia. Here, as day broke, was the desert at last, the first sight I had ever had of it. There is nothing like it in all the world – only sand, the sand of the hour glass, but made infinite by space, just as a tumbler of sea water becomes infinite in the ocean. Sand, drifted into motionless waves, heaped in ridges, scooped into valleys, flattened, blown up into curious cones and long yellow banks, the tops of which the winds have cut into fretted patterns as it blew over them. And all so silent, so withered, and yet so fresh; so soft, so beautiful and yet so terrible.[3]

Wolseley inspected the line of the railway. Parallel to it ran a narrow sweet-water canal supplying fresh Nile water along the route between Cairo and Ismailia. Every few miles, the Egyptians had artillery posts; one by one these capitulated over succeeding days, as the British cavalry under General Drury Lowe pressed relentlessly forward with artillery support.

The heat in the delta was intense, the sun scorching, and officers and men sweated in their serge tunics. Supplies were plentiful, however – no small tribute to Butler's organizational ability – and the men were well equipped, with adequate cover and messing arangements. There was sufficient water from the canal, and communication lines back to Ismailia were kept open at all times. Four days after Wolseley's first reconnaissance from Ismailia, the advance of the British force was entrenching at Kassassin, only six miles from Tel-el-Kebir, and over the next week the mass of Wolseley's disciplined force streamed up from Ismailia. Throughout Butler's account of those days and nights are references that underscore how much the contemporary industrialized world impinged on the campaign: steam trains plying the permanent way, the laying of a tramline at Ismailia, ships at the entrance to the Suez Canal 'packed like herrings in a barrel' and their lights at night visible from the desert.

On the morning of 9 September Wolseley moved his headquarters to Kassassin and over the next few days prepared for an attack on Tel-el-Kebir. Tel-el-Kebir was heavily defended. Its fortifications stretched some 6000 yards across the length of a low ridge. To the south of the ridge and at a right angle to it ran the railway and the canal. Tel-el-Kebir was held by 20,000 men with 75 heavy guns. Wolseley had 11,000 infantry, 2000 cavalry and 61 guns, but his troops were better equipped than the Egyptians and they were more experienced. He examined his options for an attack on Tel-el-Kebir. An artillery bombardment would have to be carried out from an exposed plain, open to the entrenched Egyptian guns. To attack in a flanking movement around the ridge would be heavily contested, and would also allow a tactical retreat by the Egyptians if it succeeded. The only decisive action would be a frontal assault on the fortified ridge which would invite severe casualties from Egyptian artillery as the British crossed the open plain; unless, of course, the plain was crossed at night preparatory to a dawn attack.

Wolseley ascertained that the Egyptians did not mount pickets below the fortifications during the hours of darkness and, in what became a classic military action, determined on a night advance. Surprise was critical. Discussion of the plan was confined to his personal staff at first, and explained to the field commanders on a need-to-know basis. Only on the last day, 12 September, did the troops become aware that that something was about to happen. That afternoon the British encampment at Kass-assin looked much as it had done over the previous few days. Egyptians scouts saw no evidence of preparations for action on the part of the enemy. As darkness fell the campfires of the British flamed into the moonless sky as if the troops were settling down for the night, but the camp was in a fever of quiet activity as the huge force prepared to move into the desert in attack formation, a formation that would have to be held for up to eight hours since it would be impossible to manoeuvre at Tel-el-Kebir without alerting the Egyptians. The early part of the march took the army to within three and a half miles of their objective. Here, an hour before midnight, Wolseley personally checked that the lines had held, before advancing again in total silence. Harnesses were muffled, all lose metal secured. The desert absorbed the sound of horses' hooves and carriage wheels.

By half past two on the morning of 13 September, 13,000 massed infantry and cavalry made a final halt. Timing was critical: too far from the entrenchments just before dawn would leave them exposed to Egyptian artillery; too close and it would be too dark to attack and they would be discovered while they waited.

The final advance, described by Butler as 'a gigantic bolt of flesh, steel and iron shot westward into the darkness', began shortly after 3 a.m. It was Butler who navigated by the stars for the staff group around Wolseley. Two incidents from that fraught final march caused near panic. The first was 'a peal of wild and hilarious laughter' which was abruptly terminated. It came from a Scots infantryman who had filled his canteen with rum instead of water and had imbibed liberally throughout the night. His comrades quickly overpowered him and he was chloroformed by a medical orderly. The second incident threw Wolseley and his staff into momentary panic. During the last hour of the advance Wolseley had meticulously observed the time ticking away. The attack was timed for just a few minutes before dawn. With some ten minutes to go and everyone in a heightened state of tension the eastern sky was shafted with a golden glow of light. Thought was frozen, there was a sickening feeling of miscalculation, but then the glow dissipated. The luminous eastern sky was not the dawn but the great Crul's Comet of 1882. Minutes later the battle of Tel-el-Kebir began.

The British forces were so close to the entrenchments that the Egyptian artillery barrage which opened up fell way behind them. They swept inexorably over the fortifications. The main assault was by Highland infantry led into close combat by sword-bearing officers. They had the sun behind them. The Egyptians, an inexperienced conscript army, caught off guard, defended the ridge but were hopelessly ill-prepared for the British onslaught. Butler later told his wife that the taking of the fortifications was like 'going through brown paper'.

Within half an hour it was clear that the British would have total victory. Urabi himself had been in bed when the battle started. He later remarked that the English had not given him time to put his boots on. The hopelessness of his situation was quickly apparent and he fled towards Cairo. When Wolseley and his staff rode up through the captured fortifications into the Egyptian camp, the extent of their conquest was plain. Two thousand men had died, the wounded were never tallied; there were 480 British casualties. Wolseley's victory marked the apogee of his career. The inevitable victory painting was called for and Elizabeth Butler executed it. It was entitled *After the Battle*. Against the background of the long ridge over which the British have poured, two groups of infantry line the approach to the canal bridge at Tel-el-Kebir. The focus of the painting is Wolseley and his entourage in their red tunics. A piper plays and helmets are raised in salute to Wolseley, a straight-backed, stern figure on horseback dominating the foreground. Slightly behind him are his staff officers: Adye; Buller, his horse shying; Butler, leaning from the saddle to exchange words with a soldier. Small touches dampen the triumphalist impact of the painting. Outside the left parapet, two soldiers have their backs to Wolseley. A horse and rider lie dead in the foreground. Wolseley is aloof, quizzical. At his side, Adye seems to be urging him forward, but to what?

Butler himself never liked the painting. He thought that it was jingoistic, that it glorified what had been in the end a rout. His own account of Tel-el-Kebir ended with a eulogy of the Egyptians:

> There is one thing I should like to put on record regarding this battle of Tel-el-Kebir. Complete surprise though it was to the Egyptian soldiers behind their entrenchments, they nevertheless fought with the greatest determination against overwhelming odds. Not a moment was given to them to awake, form up, prepare, or move into position. The assault fell upon them as a thunderbolt might fall upon a man asleep. The leaders in whom they could trust, were, like themselves, fellaheen; few among them knew anything of war, its arts, manoeuvres, or necessities; they were betrayed on every side, yet they fought stoutly whenever ten or twenty or fifty of them could get together in the works, in the angles of the lines, and in the open desert between the lines. The heaps of dead lying with and across their rifles facing the upcoming sun bore eloquent testimony to that final resolve of these poor fellows. Peace be to them, lying under these big mounds on the lone desert ... They died the good death. Dust to dust. They did not desert the desert, and Egypt will not forget them.[4]

Tel-el-Kebir marked the end of the Egyptian revolt. Urabi was hotly pursued by British cavalry units. The collapse of the Egyptian army had been so complete that Cairo surrendered the following day. Urabi surrendered on 15 September. A few days later, he was moved for his own safety into one of the khedival palaces, the Abdin, where there was a heavy concentration of British troops. His arrival was watched by a throng of curious officers among whom was Butler. Urabi alighted from the carriage which had brought him to the palace and, before he was ushered away, he observed protocol by saluting the onlookers. He received only two salutes in response, one from Drury Lowe, the other from William Butler.

Butler's responsibilities included securing tents for the 10,000 troops pouring into the city: 'the filth and vermin in the permanent barracks made it perfectly impossible to put European troops into them'. To the normal bustle of Cairo was added the tension induced by foreign occupation. Two ammunition trains exploded in the central station, killing thirty people, and for a time officers and men moved warily about the narrow streets. Nevertheless, life had its lighter side. Wolseley threw an extravagant picnic at Memphis, which included an over-long guided tour of the pyramids. The party travelled up the Nile to Memphis and rode donkeys to the picnic site. Butler described the company, under the heat of the sun, as being 'satiated with sarcophagi and with a thirst for tea such as only six thousand years of mummy powder could give us'.

As September drew to a close, the fate of Urabi dominated discussion. Khedive Tawfiq and his court, reinstated in Cairo, spoke openly of the need to execute him and his co-conspirators as traitors. Of course there would be a trial, but it would be held *in camera* as soon as Urabi was handed over by the British. Among officers of the occupation force there was much heated talk, most of it anti-Urabi. Wolseley thought Urabi should be hanged. Butler, one of the strongest dissenting voices, urged clemency and used every device open to him as Urabi's death appeared more certain.

As mess talk became more vehement, Butler proved himself a man for whom protocol was insufficient restraint for impulses born of strong convictions. On 4 October General Adye was due to leave Cairo for England. A man of balanced views, he was expected to counsel moderation towards the rebels when he met Gladstone, with whom he was personally friendly. But he might be too late. Urabi was to be handed into Egyptian custody on 5 October. On the night before Adye's departure Butler sat up composing a letter which he pressed on him during the formal farewell on the platform at Cairo Railway Station:

Nothing but a very strong belief in the necessity of doing what I can to avert what I believe would be a national crime makes me now write to you upon a subject far removed from the sphere of military duty which has hitherto given me a claim as an officer of your staff to communicate with you. I write to urge you to telegraph from Alexandria to England to stop the execution of Arabi [*sic*] Pasha (should the court which is sitting or about to sit, condemn him to death) until you have arrived in England and are in a position to place before the Government a full view of the Egyptian question as it will by then have taken place in your mind, in just and true proportion.[5]

Butler went on to make four pragmatic arguments for sparing Urabi's life: execution would keep Egypt festering, bring the judgment of history against Britain, lower Britain's military prestige in the world, and hurt Gladstone's reputation. Butler's intervention with Adye angered Wolseley, and when news of it reached the War Office, it was viewed as presumptuous. Butler's own view of his action would have been that it was no time for niceties; besides, he had gone through his chief-of-staff on this extreme matter.

The Urabi incident is an example of that combination of outspoken concern and impetuosity which helped make Butler's reputation as an officer who was not quite pukka. He was clearly not a lone voice among the military in Cairo: Adye himself was sympathetic to Urabi's position and could be relied upon, as Butler acknowledged, to do everything possible in London to mitigate his fate. A more cautious man would have held back, satisfied that the time between Adye's departure from Cairo and a government decision being telegraphed from London to Egypt was enough to resolve a situation which, though serious, was not yet critical.

Butler's intervention was unnecessary. Urabi's plight had already raised concern in Europe; in France public opinion ran in his favour, while in England an Egyptian Prisoners' Fund received contributions from people as varied as Charles Gordon, and Lady Augusta Gregory who had spent the winter of 1881–2 in Egypt. Gladstone was resolutely against Urabi's death. The khedive was pressured into convening an open court martial, and Urabi and his fellow officers were given the services of two experienced British counsel. Urabi had in his possession papers highly embarrassing to the khedive, as well as papers implicating Constantinople in his actions. These were skilfully used behind the scenes. A range of accusations against Urabi, including the charge that he was responsible for the

Alexandria riots, was dropped. He finally faced one charge, that of armed rebellion, and on this he was found guilty on 3 December 1882. Sentence of death was pronounced but was immediately commuted to perpetual exile. Urabi was deported to Ceylon.

By the time Urabi's trial had concluded in Cairo, most of the British expeditionary force had returned home. Butler had liked Egypt and he left it 'with feelings of keen regret'. On 18 November 1882 there was a royal review in Whitehall, during which thousands of onlookers jammed the streets. Three days later, Wolseley, newly ennobled as Lord Wolseley of Cairo and Wolseley, presented his staff at Windsor. Several of them, including Butler, were made aides-de-camp to Queen Victoria. The aides were an honorary corps of some forty army officers who were called on for a range of ceremonial occasions.

The next few months were a heady social whirl which brought the Butlers close to the centre of high society. Victoria's youngest son, Arthur, Duke of Connaught, had been on the Egyptian campaign. Now the Butlers made the acquaintance of her eldest son, Albert Edward, 'Bertie', Prince of Wales, a man with a reputation for fast living whom Wolseley was to label 'Edward the Caresser'.

Butler retained his post at Devonport and his home on Plymouth Hoe. He came frequently to London by train. In the spring of 1883 Elizabeth was again pregnant and much of Butler's socializing was done unaccompanied. In April he attended a public function in honour of Wolseley and there he met Lord and Lady Colin Campbell. He had known Lady Campbell when she was Gertrude Blood – her father's family came from County Clare. Twenty-six years old, tall, elegant and unhappily married, Lady Campbell invited Butler to call on her some afternoon. He took up her invitation with consequences that were to return to haunt him.

Meantime there was an unexpected coda to Butler's Canadian experiences. In late summer he was approached by a British commercial syndicate to go out to the Saskatchewan Valley and report on the 'agricultural capabilities' of a million-acre block of land lying immediately north of the North Saskatchewan River. He jumped at the chance. His companion was Thomas Wyndham Quinn, fourth Earl of Dunraven[6], who was personally interested in the venture. The two men were friendly through their shared love of Canada, and Dunraven had suggested Butler's name to the syndicate. By the early autumn of 1883 the trip was finalized. It was necessary to undertake it before winter descended on the North Saskatchewan.

Butler curbed his impatience to get away to Canada while Elizabeth's pregnancy progressed. Their daughter Eileen was born on 3 October 1883, and three days later Butler left Liverpool for New York. From there he travelled by train to the rail town of Troy, three hundred miles west of Winnipeg. At Troy something of the feel of the old days returned when he transferred to a stagecoach for a five day journey to the North Saskatchewan River. It was not a journey of unalloyed pleasure. His several coach companions were 'apostles' of the new civilization, exemplars of 'a dull, heavy, cursing, spitting, eructating and smoking kind of savagery'. However, old memories were revived for him as they rattled towards the wilderness.

In North Saskatchewan Butler met Dunraven and inspected the territory in which the syndicate was interested. It was good land, but its remoteness was too big a drawback for Butler to be able to recommend the investment. The inspection took less than a week and when it was completed the old Butler, slipped from the harness of domesticity and routine, reasserted himself briefly. Instead of returning by stage to Troy, he decided to head west towards Edmonton, from where, by turning due south, he could reach the transcontinental railway at Calgary and come back east. With a buckboard and three horses, he and two companions set off north of the Saskatchewan, on the first leg of a 600-mile journey.

> We camped that night by some large willows between two frozen ponds. When twilight came and the wind blew in gusts through the willows from far off, and I saw the horses feeding on the ridge against the afterglow, I felt a silent joy such as I had not known this time in its fullness. Here at last was the lonely land still untouched."

That night he wrote in his diary that 'savagery lies south of the river'. The journey, retracing his 1870-trek to Edmonton, was something of a pilgrimage. He spent a night at Fort Pitt, where he had twice captivated Mary Sinclair. It now had a North-West Mounted Police post whose senior officer was none other than Frank Dickens, the third son of Charles. Butler found that 'he bore a striking resemblence to his illustrious father'. Fort Pitt also had an Indian reservation, a last refuge for destitute and despairing Crees. Everywhere on his journey along the Saskatchewan Butler saw and heard the same evidence: the old nomadic life was over.

Butler's party went south to Calgary by snow sled. Then it was east to Winnipeg and on to New York. By mid-December he was back in England where once more Egypt was the main topic of international news. The British invasion of 1882 had brought unforeseen developments in its wake. When the revolt was crushed, it had proved impossible to make an immediate withdrawal. The authority of the khedive had been greatly weakened and the Egyptian army could not be allowed to resume its former strength. The civil administration was in a shambles and, to overhaul it, Evelyn Baring was appointed Consul General to Egypt in September 1883. Baring was an autocrat, known to his own subordinates as 'Over-Baring'. He brought with him to Egypt a host of ex-India officials to work as advisers in the various ministries. Their task was expected to be short-term.

What changed matters were events in the Sudan, the vast desert country south of Egypt, turning this short-term British occupation of Egypt into what became, in all but name, a seventy-four year colonization. Since the early part of the nineteenth century the Sudan had been ruled by Egypt. Its capital Khartoum, 1650 miles up the Nile from Cairo, was the headquarters of the Governor General of the Sudan. As Egypt moved towards crisis in the 1870s, the Sudanese began to assert themselves and by early 1882 a messianic movement was sweeping the Sudan. It was led by Muhammad Ahmad of Dongola, who proclaimed himself to be the Mahdi, with a divine mission to drive out all foreign influences. In January 1883 the Mahdi's dervishes captured El Obeid, the capital of the prosperous province of Kordofan. Khedive Tawfiq sent a large force of Egyptian troops up the Nile under a retired British officer, Colonel William Hicks. Hicks and his 10,000 men headed into the deserts of Kordofan only to be annihilated by the Mahdi. This disaster led Britain to the realization that the occupation of Egypt would not be short-lived.

When Butler arrived back in England from Canada in December 1883, the main topic of public interest was the Mahdi, who was reported to be marching towards the Arab city of Omdurman, across the river Nile from Khartoum, from where he would begin a siege of the capital. England endured a frenzy of debate. It was argued that if the Mahdi was not stopped immediately he would eventually invade Egypt, utilizing the discontent which had been so much a feature of Urabi's revolt. The possibility of another North African Campaign raised speculation to the highest pitch in the War Office. From Devonport, after his lengthy leave of absence, Butler let Wolseley know that he was keen to return to Africa. Gladstone's Cabinet was, as usual, divided over the issue of intervention. Gladstone himself held that the invasion of 1882, reluctantly sanctioned, was sucking Britain into a continent where it had little business to be.

By mid-January a solution of sorts was reached. There would be no British force sent to the Sudan, but the Egyptian administration in the country would not be abandoned. It would be evacuated from Khartoum and the small provincial towns, and brought safely down the Nile to Egypt. General Charles Gordon was the man chosen for the task.

Seven years earlier, in January 1887, while 'pinned' to the 'vast wheel' of the War Office, Butler had met Charles 'Chinese' Gordon. One night he and a fellow officer, Major Robert Owen Jones, had had an intimate club dinner with Gordon, who was temporarily back in London after three years working as governor of Equatoria, Egypt's remotest province. Gordon was forty-three years of age, but looked older. He had quit Equatoria disillusioned by his inability to stop the trans-Saharan slave trade. Uncharacteristically, Butler found himself largely silent as this extraordinary man, a combination of mystic and pragmatic soldier, talked of God, the Sudan, the lake regions of East Africa, and the volatile politics of the Balkans. Gordon

> ... spoke in low but very distinct tones, and his voice, varying with its subject, carried to the ear a sense of pleasure in the sound similar to that which the sight of his features, lit with the light of a very ardent soul, gave to the listener's eye. I never heard human voice nor looked into any man's eye and found similar tone and glance there, nor did I ever meet a man who had equal facility for putting into words the thoughts that were in his brain. You had never to ask an explanation; the thing, whatever it might be, was at once said and done. That night was the only one in my club life in which I saw the man with the bull's-eye lantern come to say the hour of closing had come and gone.[8]

Chapter Nine

THE GORDON RELIEF EXPEDITION

Gordon was a man viewed with some caution by his colleagues. He had great ability, courage, imagination, and a keen sense of justice, but he was also unpredictable and rashly single-minded. For his Sudanese venture, he was assigned as his assistant a Colonel J.D. Stewart, a level-headed veteran who had been about to leave England for Canada. Some days later in Devonport, Butler received a cable to attend the War Office. Coming up to London, he was certain that it would be something to do with the Sudan. Instead, to his great disappointment, he was asked to go to Ottawa in Stewart's place on 'a confidential civil mission'. Butler's transatlantic journeys were by now something of a joke among his colleagues: Wolseley, when he occasionally mentions Butler in his extensive private correspondence with his wife, refers to him as 'Acrass the Atlantic', an impish take-off of Butler's pronounced Irish accent. Cork-born Louisa Wolseley's private view of Butler was that he was 'an im-perfect gentleman – if you can call him one at all'.

Butler's short visit to the War Office convinced him that something other than an evacuation of the Sudanese garrisons by Gordon might be in the offing. From Queenstown, where his ship stopped briefly before the Atlantic voyage, he wrote to Wolseley on 8 February 1884: 'I leave in a couple of hours for New York. The last phase of the Egyptian game of pull-Baker pull-Mahdi is not one such as one cares to be away from on the Western Continent. I hope that if anything should arise you will not forget that the cable can find me at Ottawa in a couple of hours."

Gordon reached Khartoum on 18 February 1884 and shortly afterwards cabled that he was not going to evacuate the city but hold it. 'Mahdi must be smashed' was one of the typical phrases he kept telegraphing to Cairo before the copper wire was cut just below the city on 12 March.

In London, Queen Victoria intervened with Gladstone's government on Gordon's behalf. He could not be abandoned. Britain's honour was at stake. Gladstone resisted: an expedition would be 'a war of conquest against a people struggling to be free'.² But the pressures against this stance began to mount. Contingency plans for a rescue expedition were discussed and Wolseley lobbied to lead it. Against the advice of Lieutenant-General Sir Frederick Stephenson, Commander-in-Chief of the Armed Forces in Egypt, who favoured a shorter overland route via the Suez Canal, Wolseley argued that an expedition to relieve Khartoum should follow the course of the Nile. The Nile was well-established as a route to Khartoum; for almost 1300 miles, as far as Dongola, it was defended by a string of small Egyptian military posts; masses of troops could be transported by water to Dongola, where a mere parade of strength would be enough to intimidate the Mahdi and allow the orderly evacuation of Khartoum 300 miles farther south.

In anticipation of approval for the expedition, Wolseley began his preparations. He would re-run his Red River campaign but on a much grander scale, with several thousand troops moving up the Nile in a great flotilla. The Nile had only a small number of paddle-steamers but hundreds of native boats or nuggas, each of which could carry forty men. However, the nugga's draught was deep; it was easily impeded by shallows and could navigate rapids only in high water. Wolseley turned to the Ring for recommendations. Butler, who had come back from Ottawa in April, was among those consulted. He had not gone beyond Memphis during the 1882 campaign, but his view was that 'water is water and rock is rock whether they be in America or Africa'.

Everything now hung on Gladstone's government which on 5 August 1884 cautiously voted £300,000 for the relief of Gordon. Wolseley summoned Butler from Devonport and gave him responsibility for securing sufficient boats in England to be shipped out to Alexandria. Four hundred were needed. On 7 August Butler and a Colonel Alleyn of the Royal Engineers were in Portsmouth inspecting standard ships' boats which they found unsuitable. Instead, the two men designed a thirty-foot 'Nile whaler', to be fitted with a lug sail and twelve oars, and which would carry ten soldiers and two crew, plus 1000 lbs of stores and ammunition. Butler then engaged forty-seven boatbuilding firms and in four weeks, a month earlier than official estimates had allowed, 400 boats, carried on eleven steamers, were on their way to Alexandria. The expeditionary force would comprise 7000 men. Public debate over the best route continued. There were peppery letters to the leading newspapers about the foolishness of trying to ascend the Nile at a time of year when the river level would be falling; June and July – not October – were the months of highest water level. It was pointed out that the expedition was six times as large as that on the Red River; and that logistical problems would be magnified accordingly.

The number of whalers ordered now doubled. Engrossed in preparations, Butler had his own views about the boats, endorsed from an unexpected quarter when he was visited by Henry Morton Stanley:

> One day I was at work as usual over the details of the expedition when there entered my room a man second to none in the roll of discoverers and explorers of this century. We had not met for years ... 'You are very busy I know and I won't stay long. I only looked in to shake hands and tell you I have seen all those letters against the boats you are building. I have also read a description of the boats themselves and in my opinion they are not only the right craft for the work you have to do but they are the only means by which you can do that work. I have tried boats like that on the Congo and found them all right.'

One aspect of the boats had originally presented Wolseley with an unexpected problem: the matter of crews. He pursued his parallel with the Red River to an extraordinary degree when he asked Ottawa to engage 400 voyageurs (at $40 per man per month). The men hurriedly recruited were a motley group which included Métis and Iroquios, as well as British immigrants who knew little about river navigation. They sailed from Quebec for Alexandria on 5 September to play their part in what some were now calling the Circus on the Nile. Butler arrived in Cairo on 25 September. Wolseley was already there. The Ring was back in Egypt. Buller was Chief of Staff, Brackenbury Deputy Adjutant and Quartermaster. Herbert Stewart was to command the land forces that would move to Dongola, while Evelyn Wood was charged with keeping communication lines open. Butler was assigned to the river column, the most physically arduous of the posts held by the old guard and the post that involved least contact with Wolseley.

Wolseley had already upset the regular occupyng forces in Egypt by being appointed, however temporarily, to the senior military post in the country. The Ring itself caused further anger among the lower-ranking officers on the expedition, who were conscious of being kept firmly outside it. The future General Sir Ian Hamilton, with experience in India, found that 'nothing could have been more inhospitable or forbidding than the response from the special preserve of the Wolseleyites ... any attempt to cut in from any benighted country like India would be summararily dealt with ... I was an intruder. I was alone in a hostile camp.'[4]

But if the Ring was closed to outsiders, it had its own dissensions. Its members were no longer young and eager solely for fame and glory, but were middle-aged men, conscious of status and career prospects, and watchful of each other's preferment. By this time Brackenbury, Buller, Stewart and Wood all had knighthoods. On the Gordon Relief expedition, Wolseley had the conferring of local rank within his gift. Butler had expectations that were not met. He was given the temporary rank of full colonel, while others received greater preferment. Buller, for example, was given the local rank of major-general and Brackenbury that of full general.

Wolseley's decision to move his forces to Dongola by two routes, river and land, was to further split the Ring. The land column, mounted infantry and cavalry – a 'camelry' in Wolseley's phrase – made a leisured and lighthearted progress up to the Sudan border. Its senior officers had personal baggage trains of up to forty camels. In contrast, the river column was to have little opportunity for leisure. As he left Cairo, Wolseley was still loudly confident that there was little need to rush. The expedition would proceed to Dongola where the situation would be reviewed.

For Butler and the river column, the itinerary was simple on paper. Whalers and troops would be towed by coalburning paddle-steamers up to Aswan, below the first of the Nile cataracts. Once through the first cataract, there were 200 miles of easily navigable waterway to Wadi Halfa, just below the second cataract. Wadi Halfa, which became known to the troops as Bloody Halfway, was at the Sudan frontier. There was a length of railway from Wadi Halfa around the obstacle of the second cataract, beyond which would be 270 unobstructed miles to the third cataract at Abu Fatmeh. Once through this, it would be plain sailing, or rowing, to Dongola, 300 miles from the besieged Gordon.

In theory the cataracts were navigable by light boats, but safe passage depended on the water level, which by late October would be sinking by six inches a day. On smooth stretches of the river, shoals and sandbanks would appear overnight, throwing navigation plans into complete disarray.

By 19 October Butler was at Wadi Halfa, where the immensity of his task became clear to him. The rapids of the second cataract, which extended for over twenty miles, held Bab-el-Kebir, the Belly of Stone, a ravine fifty yards long and some thirty feet wide, down which the Nile raged in a precipitous torrent. The thirty miles of railway which skirted the cataract had no rolling stock capable of transporting troops and whalers. The whalers either had to be hauled through the rapids or carried round them. In either case, it meant the removal and portage of each boat's supplies. Meantime a shortage of coal for the transport steamers was delaying troops and whalers downriver. The responsibility for this lay with Buller, of whom Butler was openly critical. By the time sufficient coal had been shipped to Egypt, several weeks had been lost.

Among those held up were the voyageurs. It was the end of October before they were deposited below the second cataract. At Gemai, above the worst reaches of the cataract, the river column had set up a supply base and its major boat repair yard. Here, on 4 November, Butler, busy in the dockyard, looked out to see something that added its own exotic quota to the Nile expedition:

> ... across the river a strange object caught my sight – strange only in this Nile land, for in other lands it had been a well known friend ... There hugging the back eddy of the muddy Nile a small American birchbark canoe, driven by those quick downstrokes that seem to be the birthright of the Indian voyageur alone, was moving up the further shore: when this strange craft had got well abreast of our dockyard it steered across the swift river and was soon underneath my tent. Out of the canoe with all the slow gravity of his race stepped a well remembered figure – William Prince Chief of Swampy Indians from Lake Winnipeg ... After him came seven other Indians and halfbreed voyageurs all from the same distant land.[5]

In 1870 Prince had been the best of Butler's crewmen as he ascended the Winnipeg River. The reunion between the two men was all the warmer for its unexpectedness. Prince became senior crewman on Butler's own whaler until sickness overtook him.

While Butler toiled at Gemai, Wolseley had gone up ahead of his main land force to Dongola where he established his headquarters. There, intelligence reports told him that Gordon's position was becoming perilous. The slow pace of the expedition's advance started to fret Wolseley. It was already mid November and his 'camelry' were now struggling to reach Dongola. Wilting under the desert sun, they made their increasingly painful way through the huge serrated rock platforms that flanked the Nile. Sickness was now beginning to take a toll of the expedition. Isolated cases of cholera, scurvy and typhoid had to be monitored as the numbers reaching Dongola increased.

Wolseley was under increasing strain and he had no confidants to ease it. Publicly he tried to sustain the pose of the assured commander, calm in the face of delay and uncertainty. In his private journal he fumed at the government in London, at the Cairo bureaucracy and most of all at Gladstone, the procrastinator. It needed only a spark for Wolseley to explode. The impetuous Butler was to provide it.

Butler had got the flotilla moving steadily. Almost half the boats, laden with men and supplies, were now progressing slowly upriver. On 16 November he pushed off from Gemai in number 387, his floating home. He reconnoitred the river as far as the third cataract, two hundred miles south, travelling through a landscape ever harsher and bleaker, under an increasingly powerful sun, the direct force of which was magnified by its reflected glare from the water. Butler and his crew wore goggles for much of the day. Number 387 used windpower when it could, and when the wind failed, the crew rowed. Towards dark they would come ashore, usually on an island, to throw up bivouacs and light a small fire from driftwood. Night was special; Butler immersed himself in the ambience of the cloudless skies, the brilliance of the stars, and the sweep of the great river from the continent's core.

Number 387 was the first whaler through the third cataract at Haffir. Above it, at Abu Fatmeh, Butler found orders to sit by the telegraph station and wait for a message from Wolseley. Butler telegraphed his arrival to Wolseley, waited overnight and, with no reply, decided to go upriver to headquarters at Dongola. He cabled ahead to announce what he was doing. His cable threw Wolseley into a fury. The delays, the enormity of the task he had brought on himself, the probable fall of Khartoum and the possible death of Gordon; all these were concentrated into a stinging written rebuke to Butler. Wolseley despatched a steam pinnace downstream to intercept him and tell him to get back to his post: his duty was the expeditious processing of the boats between the second and third cataracts.

Butler was stopped and turned back within sight of Dongola, 'the cruellest check of all my life'. He dashed off a short memo of remonstrance which the pinnace delivered to Wolseley, and later that evening wrote a lengthy letter to his chief in which he made specific suggestions for speeding up the progress of the boats. But he did not leave matters at that. He told Wosleley that by having been made turn back, he had been given 'a slap in the face'. And he continued:

> I freely admit that the orthodox English staff officer would have stopped at Haffir today, tomorrow and the day after, eyeglass in eye and cigarette in mouth; but on the other hand he would have taken sixteen to eighteen days to ascend the river from Sarras to Haffir, and when acting on your orders to have gone back on the seventeenth or nineteenth day to try and galvanise the slow moving mass of boats into quicker work, his words would have had about as much effect upon Tommy Atkins as his cigarette smoke would have had upon dulling the Egyptian sky. Unfortunately perhaps for me, these were not my methods of work; and I fear they never will be.[6]

He went on to complain that his mentor was treating him unfairly *vis-a-vis* other senior officers in the Ring, all of whom were with the land column. This missive did nothing to placate Wolseley, who recorded in his diary:

> I don't like its tone but it is quite Butlerian: he is in his own opinion the only wise man out there and anything that has gone wrong has been occasioned because I did not consult him more, take him more into my confidence and follow his advice ... The fact is Butler's talent is erratic it can neither work in any ordinary groove nor work in harmony, with the talents of other men in a team. This fact reduces his usefulness by one half. He is one of those men who imagine they have been and who are convinced that they are always in the right. He is an impulsive talented Irishman wanting in method and who will never rise to the position in the army he aspires to and which, if he had more ballast and more businesslike habits, might be within his reach. All my old companions, men whom I brought on, Wood, Redvers Buller, Butler etc. are now reaching that age and standing in the service when it is difficult to place them in a small army in the field, and when there, each and all are so jealous of the other that the team is a difficult one to drive. I have suspected a little captiousness more than once in my followers since I came to Egypt. Butler is the first upon whom my wrath has fallen and I hope he may be the last.[7]

It was sometime during these weeks that Butler was hit by a second blow that severely tested his resilience. The irregular mail delivery to

Gemai brought him a solicitor's letter from London. Lord Colin Campbell had just taken a civil action for divorce against his wife on the grounds of adultery. Three co-respondents were named: George Spencer Churchill, heir to the Duke of Marlborough; Captain Eyre Massey Shaw, Super-intendent of the London Metropolitan Fire Brigade; and Colonel William F. Butler, Assistant Adjutant Western Command. Butler reportedly reacted to this letter by flinging it into the Nile and emphatically saying he would have nothing to do with it.[8] The matter would tick away for two years as the law took its cumbersome course.

Butler spent an arduous month up and down the river, rankling at Wolseley's rebuff. 'I am to be the Moses of the expedition, not to enter the promised land', he noted in his diary. By now the whalers were a sizeable flotilla, 'pitched, patched and tin-plated', and the ferrying of troops and supplies upriver was steady. Butler and Alleyn, his colleague from the Royal Engineers, chivvied and cajoled, urging more speed and effort, something that did not impress the visiting *Daily Telegraph* correspondent, who sourly remarked of the two men that 'the celerity with which they are able to move about on the Nile has often been cited. It may be safely set down to two things. They travel with picked crews and in boats not loaded down with 100 days provisions.'[9]

Butler's disappointment at his exclusion from Wolseley's entourage became acute as Christmas approached and he was still confined to the river, while others went by land or water to headquarters, which had now been moved further south to Korti. He was particulary envious when he heard that Wolseley had given Herbert Stewart, his protégé from the Zulu War, the local rank of brigadier-general with responsibility for the advance guard of the expedition. 'I am out in the cold with a vengeance now', was one of his diary entries for Christmas Eve.

Most of the expedition had by now reached Korti, and for the new year Butler got the perfect present: a cable from Wolseley instructing him to come up to join him. As he wrote home to Elizabeth, 'I came like the wind'. He arrrived at Korti on 4 January 1885. There he found that everyone acknowledged the worth of the boats. Not only had they transported the men and stores of the river column, they had carried supplies for the camel corps for the push to Khartoum.

The expedition had already entered its final phase. Two advance columns, one on land and one on water, had gone forward towards Khartoum. Wolseley had no authority to proceed personally beyond Korti, but he had full discretion to deploy troops as he considered fit. It was the first occasion in his role as a commander-in-chief that he was not leading the field operation and this was exposing weaknesses in him. Intelligence from his spies had convinced him that Gordon's plight was indeed desperate, yet he was unsure what to do.

At Korti the expedition was 280 miles from Khartoum by the direct desert route. But at Korti the Nile bends, first to the north, then to the east before turning south again, describing a gigantic question-mark some 250 miles long. If the expediton continued to follow the river, it would be moving away from Khartoum for weeks before it again headed south. On the other hand, if the expedition struck directly across the desert to Khartoum, it would do so with huge shortages of baggage animals. It would also move into the type of terrain where the army of Hicks Pasha had been so recently destroyed.

Wolseley decided to send an advance column of the camel corps into the Bayuda desert on a trek of 180 miles to the Nile at Metemma. From there a dash could be made for Khartoum, only 100 miles upriver. Five days before Butler's arrival at Korti, Herbert Stewart had led the advance column out of the camp on what was to become known as the March of the Forlorn Hope. Two days earlier, on 28 December, Major General William Earle, one of the few senior officers imposed on Wolseley by London, had launched the river column from Korti: 2900 men with supplies for 100 days, transported in 217 whalers. Earle was accompanied on land by a force of hussars and Egyptian cavalry. Brackenbury had gone with Earle as his second in command.

Butler was at Korti for twelve days. He lost no opportunity to let Wolseley know how badly he felt he had been treated. A letter he wrote home to Elizabeth at this time shows something of his frustration:

> I sent you a few words of cheer at Christmas by wire, but my letters have been getting fewer. I really had not the heart to write bad news. I had suffered so much from what I must always regard as unjust treatment at the hands of my 'best friends' that I could only go on day after day working, and lying down each night with the hope, which work well done gives, that all would come right in the end ... I have indeed had ample recompense for the thought and labour given to these boats and to this expedition by the unspoken approval of the officers and men. The latter know well enough who works for them ... [My] pay and allowances for the last three months, only £160 or thereabouts. It is less pay all counted than I got at Devonport, and I have a lower position on the staff here than I had there. So much for what

you thought my 'sincere friends' would do for me by way of local rank. Still, I say to myself that it is 'all right'. War is the sum of all human wrongdoing and it also holds every possible injustice in it. Never mind, 'cheer up'.[10]

Wolseley could not deny that Butler had done a good job with the boats. That job was completed and Butler was near desperation for a chance at the front. Wolseley gave it to him. On 16 January 1885 Butler left Korti in number 387 to catch up with the river column. The expedition was entering its critical phase. Beyond Korti the power of the Mahdi was palpable.

As Butler and his crew raced to meet up with Earle, the 1500 men of the camel corps were facing 8000 Mahdists in the Bayuda at Abu Klea. There, on 17 January 1885, in what Winston Churchill was later to describe as 'the most savage and bloody action fought in the Sudan by British troops', the camel corps defeated the Mahdists, at a cost of 380 casualities. The Mahdists were armed mainly with swords or javelins, their fire-power was Remington rifles captured from Egyptian troops. In theory the camel corps should not have suffered the losses it did, but the Martini-Henry rifles with which it was armed jammed, while the bayonets, made of inferior metal, buckled on impact.

Two days after Abu Klea, as the advance column straggled on, Stewart was fatally wounded in the groin by a sniper's bullet. The column reached the Nile demoralized, exhausted and unsure how to proceed.

The news of Abu Klea eventually reached the river column, putting it into a state of constant alert. Butler was assigned 'to command the advance guard both by land and water'. He operated on the left bank of the river with forty British hussars mounted on Arab ponies, and a patrol of twenty Egyptians on camels. He inspected each day's section of river in advance, found suitable campsites for the boat-borne troops and oversaw the construction of simple fortifications. In tandem with this, he scouted the land ahead and to his flank. His nights were spent bivouacked several miles ahead of the main column. There was little sign of the enemy.

On 5 February he reached Kerbekan, a 400-foot ridge dominating a foaming stretch of rapids. From the top of the ridge, eating a lunch of mouldy cheese and stale biscuit, he surveyed the surrounding landscape, 'a tossed and tumbled region of black and lighter coloured rocks'. The ridge ran directly from the river and at right angles to it. Two miles upriver, narrow and menacing, lay the Shikook Pass, reputedly held by the Mahdists.

When Butler returned to his bivouac later that night, there was a confidential message from Earle: the desert column had managed to get two steamers of troops from Metemma to within sight of Khartoum, only to find that the city had fallen. The steamers had returned downriver without risking entry to the city. Gordon's fate was unconfirmed. The next morning Earle came up to join Butler. Their orders from Korti were unchanged – press on.

As the main body of the river column moved towards the Kerbekan ridge, the Mahdists came down from the Shikook Pass and by 9 February the two forces were facing each other: several thousand Mahdists on the ridge; the river column, numbering 1200, encamped on the rocky ground below it and about 1300 yards from its base. Earle had no option but to fight. He favoured a frontal attack on the ridge. Butler disagreed: casualities would be too high. Instead, he proposed a flanking movement by the west of the ridge which would allow the Mahdist position to be attacked from the rear. Earle was doubtful. It would mean that his force would have to expose its own flank to the enemy as it marched towards, around, and parallel to the rear of the ridge before it would be in position to attack. That night Butler went out with a mounted patrol to reconnoitre, and returned with his mind unchanged. Earle and Brackenbury then accepted his plan. In an army career that had already lasted twenty-seven years, this was Butler's first opportunity to lead men into battle.

By sunrise on 10 February the column was on the move. The manoeuvre took the Mahdists by surprise.The western edge of the ridge was quickly turned and the column advanced parallel to it and towards the Nile before the commands to left-face and attack the ridge were given. While the main thrust of the attack was a direct assault, in which the kilted troops of the Royal Highlanders were piped into battle, Butler led a squadron of eighty hussars in a flanking movement to highly successful effect. He cut off the Mahdists on the ridge from the main body of their forces encamped below it. These forces retreated, defiantly but in some disarray, towards the safety of the Shikook Pass, hotly pursued by Butler and his mounted force. The rocky terrain was used to maximum effect by both sides and Butler almost lost his life:

> I had got to the top of a cluster of high rocks to have a better survey of the masses of rocks surrounding our little party, and I was leaning against a big one for a steadier sweep with the glass of the hills around when a bullet, fired from across the gorge within a hundred yards range flattened itself on the rock six inches above my head. The man was so near that the hit was

simultaneous with the smoke and the report of the rifle. I was down from my perch in a jiffy, and got three men from below; then we went up again to the rocks. I had marked the exact spot on the opposite rock from which my friend had fired; the three carbines were laid upon it; I put my helmet where I had first stood; my friend fired again, and at the same instant three shots went off from our side. He fired no more."

Butler was lucky. Not so Earle. After the ridge had been captured and the battle was over, Earle had the troops drawn up close to a small stone-walled hut. A sudden shot from the hut hit a soldier. Earle ordered the grass roof of the hut to be set alight to smoke out the sniper and a man ran from the fumes on to a waiting bayonet. Earle then walked up towards the hut but was shot in the head by a sniper still inside. He died instantly.

The Mahdists on the ridge had fought to the death. While the river column counted eleven of their own dead and forty-four wounded or missing, Mahdist casualties were estimated variously at between 500 and 2000. Next day, as the column moved up towards the Shikook Pass, the bodies lay everywhere:

> Dead men, they say, tell no tales; but on a battlefield no more eloquent spokesman can call to him who will listen. Here the enemy's unburied dead told the story of their revolt – these old greybeard veterans, these mere boys, these strong men in the flower of their age, as they lay in every attitude of painful death. They had fought to the last cartridge for their homeland. Their 'punishment' at our hands had been severe. The rocks glistened with the leaden splashes of our rifle bullets, where continuous volleys had searched every nook and crevice."

Kerbekan was a critical step in Butler's career progression. At Tel-El-Kebir, as a member of Wolseley's personal staff, he had not taken part in the assault on the Egyptian positions. At Kerbekan he acquitted himself very well. His intelligence-gathering had been excellent and his assault plan successful. During the battle he was decisive in command and courageous in pursuit.

With Earle's death, Brackenbury took command of the river column. He and Butler puzzled over what could have prompted the Mahdists out of their securely held pass to engage in battle on less advantageous ground. They were to find a partial explanation. One of the soldiers engaged in getting the whalers past Kerbekan spotted a saddlebag among the rocks by the shore. In it were papers in Arabic. Literally translated, their message ran:

> 'I inform you that Khartoum was taken on 9 Rabi 1302 [26 January 1885]. The Mahdi prayed his dervishes and his troops to advance against the fortifications and entered Khartoum in a $\frac{1}{4}$ of an hour. They killed the traitor Gordon and captured the steamers and boats."[3]

With no countermanding orders, the column kept on. By 24 February it was close to Abu Hamed, at the tip of the great Nile bend, where there was a despatch waiting from Wolseley. The desert column, which had been taken over by Buller after the fall of Khartoum, had collapsed: any further advance up the Nile would be futile. The river column was ordered back towards Korti. The Gordon Relief Expedition was effectively over. Charles Gordon transmogrified into Gordon of Khartoum, the supreme examplar of heroic virtue for Victorian Britain. Butler, who was among Gordon's biographers, described him as 'the mirror and measure of true knighthood', representing the majority contemporary view of Gordon as a man who combined the Christian ideals of charity and brotherhood with extraordinary courage. The altruism of the rescue, contrasted with military ventures such as the 1882 invasion of Egypt, had caught the public imagination. The professed object of the expedition, to 'rescue and retire' in a phrase of the time, made its failure doubly hard to bear. Britain went into official mourning.

Meanwhile the river column was retiring. Brackenbury stayed with the boats as they turned downriver, giving Butler responsibility for the land force – artillery, and British and Egyptian cavalry. Back at Korti, Wolseley, rundown with overwork and worry, surveyed a campaign which except for the modest success of the river column, was close to a shambles; the leaders of both advance columns, Earle and Stewart, were dead; Khartoum had fallen to the Mahdi, and 4000 of its citizens, a tenth of the population, had been slaughtered. Wolseley, at fifty-one years of age, had received the first critical setback of his career and he found it impossible to come to terms with it. He held the second highest rank in the British army and saw himself as heir to the Duke of Wellington. For someone who described himself in private as 'the jingo of the jingos', the only possible solution to the situation he was in after the fall of Khartoum was to smash the Mahdi. 'If I can only kill him it will be a very happy finale to our expedition up the

Nile',[14] he wrote to his twelve-year-old daughter Frances.

For some weeks Wolseley's view actually got strong support at Westminister. Public opinion, outraged at the failure to rescue Gordon, was reflected in demands at the highest levels of government to avenge Khartoum. On the strength of reports from England, Wolseley lobbied to be made Governor General of the Sudan: he would go downriver to Dongola and spend the coming months building up a new army to take on the Mahdi in September when the Nile was high and the heat a little more bearable.

Halfway back from Kerbekan to Korti, the river column reached the small fortification of Merowe at the village of Abu Doum. It was an attractive spot, sheltered by wild palms. Orders from Wolseley were waiting there. Brackenbury was to continue downriver with the bulk of the column. Butler was to command at Merowe, the extreme British outpost, over the summer. Butler was pleased at this recognition of his martial abilities. He at once prepared for 'six months of blinding heat', glad to be able 'to take off my boots at night, get clean things, and lie down on something besides sand'. It was at Merowe over the next few weeks that he began a first draft of *The Campaign of the Cataracts*. The book put centre stage the endlessly repetitive role of the boats and boatmen on the middle reaches of the Nile. It would be published, with illustrations by Elizabeth, in 1887.

Wolseley came up to inspect Merowe on 18 March, the day after the feast of St Patrick. He had a most convivial reception from his subordinate, and wrote to his wife that Butler was in very good form:

> He is quite happy having created a station, and being in command has restored his equanimity. He is doing it very well. Of course there is the usual didn't I tell you so. No prophetic almanac editor ever professed such powers of prediction as to future events as Butler does. Butler however never gives anyone the benefit of his predictions until after the events have occurred ... He really is a good fellow with all his inaccuracy of statement and other failings for which Irishmen are well known but with all the quick vivid imagination and all those pleasant sympathies with his fellowman, all the quickness and wit and other qualities for which Paddy is celebrated. He has Paddy's faults in an ordinary degree but he has all his good qualities, talents and virtues to overflowing: in fact he is gifted far above ordinary Irishmen and that means that the English and Scotsmen are stupid and uninteresting when placed beside him. He makes me very angry at times but I always like him.[15]

The reference to 'Paddy' in this private letter from a Dubliner to his Cork-born wife vividly illustrates a major divide which ran through Irish society. In the language of the time, this was seen as a racial divide between, on the one hand, Hiberno-Norman and Gael, and on the other the Anglo-Irish. Given Wolseley's distaste for the country of his birth, it is ironic that, among the English upper classes who shaped the higher echelons of the army, 'Paddy' was in colloquial use as a generic term to describe officers from Ireland, irrespective of their backgrounds.

While he prepared to move his headquarters back to Dongola, Wolseley was woken from his dream of smashing the Mahdi. There was no advantage to Britain in attempting to conquer the Sudan – 'that dreadful country', in Gladstone's words. Gordon was dead, the Khartoum garrison massacred. Britain's military responsibility for Egypt stopped with the defence of the Egyptian frontier. A bitterly disappointed and angry Wolseley had to abandon the Sudan. Butler was ordered to evacuate Merowe by 26 May. Unlike Wolseley, Butler was realistic: the Sudan was not a priority and 'we can't keep half the army and all the staff up in this wilderness.'

As the commander of the highest Nile station, Butler had to ensure that every post he passed through on his way downriver to Dongola was cleared of men and supplies. Nothing was to be left for the Mahdists. His own small fort at Merowe was to be razed. He was sorry to leave Abu Doum, 'the Father of Palm Trees ... a place of real Nile beauty', and he had liked the local people, as he recorded in his diary:

> You cannot live much with the Arabs without learning to like them. They are quick, courteous, very brave, good looking. As to their deceit, etc., of which we hear so much, I don't think they are a bit worse than the average acquaintance, I might even say 'friend' one finds in clubs and professions in the daily intercourse of life in England.[16]

Butler did not have sufficient boats to get his entire force downriver. Instead, his 200-mile journey from Merowe to Dongola was an overland one, 'the hottest work that had ever fallen to my lot'.

From Dongola, Butler came down to Egypt in his old boat, number 387, savouring the breeze and the current working in his favour. At Wadi Halfa there was a cable waiting for him from Wolseley, who was already back in England, asking if he would be interested in the command of the Egyptian frontier on the expiry of his home leave. It was more than adequate evidence of the value of his contribution to the expedition.

By the end of June 1885 Butler was home after a ten-month absence. There was an addition to the family, a third son, Martin, who had been born in March. Elizabeth came up to London from Plymouth for Butler's arrival back in England, and, when she had caught her breath, wrote to her mother:

> My dearest Mama,
>
> Will returned on two months leave on the 30th June. I went to town to meet him having but a few hours notice from Brindisi of his blessed coming. I secured nice rooms at the Army and Navy Hotel Westminster and decorated the rooms with roses from Mrs. Collier's. You may be sure I was wide awake at 7 a.m. next morning when he arrived. The sun was shining in through the open window and the air was fresh with flowers. Will is tho' greyer, looking splendid and is nicely slim and sunburnt. Oh how thankful I am for his good health and safety. He is to be a brigadier-general and is to command at Wadi Halfa."

Chapter Ten

ON THE SUDAN FRONTIER

During his leave in the summer of 1885 Butler made time for a short family holiday in Glencar. Politically, Ireland was much changed since the start of the decade. Charles Stewart Parnell had become a respectable political figure supported by the Catholic hierarchy. He was a key player at Westminster, skilfully exploiting the advantages to be gained by tactical alliances. He led a disciplined party which owed little to the large landed interests in Ireland. A general election was due: it would be fought in restructured constituencies and with a greatly increased franchise.

Butler absorbed as much as he could of the atmosphere of change in Ireland before leaving for Egypt with the local rank of brigadier-general. Elizabeth would come out and join him for a time in November if Wadi Halfa proved a routine command. By the end of August he was in Aswan being briefed by Major-General Grenfell, commanding the army of occupation in Upper Egypt. The Mahdi had died and his successor, the Khalifa Abdallahi Ibn Muhammad, had continued the Mahdi's strategy of pushing down the Nile towards Egypt, and had taken Dongola. Grenfell's intelligence reports said the Mahdists would come down below the third cataract while the Nile was high. Butler was instructed to make his headquarters on the frontier at Wadi Halfa, just below the second cataract. He would have three battalions at his disposal, one British, one Egyptian and one Sudanese. His orders were to hold Wadi and to keep open the newly built railway, which ran one hundred miles on the east bank of the Nile, south from the frontier to Akasha. The railway was essential for rapidly moving troops to stop the Mahdists if they advanced towards Egypt.

At Wadi Halfa, Butler found that the battalions at his disposal were weak and poorly supplied. Ominously, there was news that the Khalifa had a 10,000 strong army at Dongola and that this force was already moving to encamp at Kaibar, only seventy miles across the desert from Akasha, a mere two-day camel ride. For Butler, all the signs pointed to an onslaught on Egypt before the year's end. He telegraphed to Grenfell in Aswan for reinforcements, marking the start of what would be an increasingly strident plea for cavalry, infantry and heavy guns. Back at Aswan, Grenfell's intelligence reports from other sources corroborated Butler's view that an attack on Egypt was only a matter of time. On 27 October Grenfell cabled Lieutenant-General Stephenson in Cairo for an extra battalion. However, Stephenson's view was that reinforcements should be held for the defence of Aswan. Sending heavy reinforcements up the Nile beyond Wadi invited the risk of their being by-passed by the mobile desert army of the Khalifa. On the frontier Butler saw things differently: the Mahdists should be stopped as far into the Sudan as possible; the sooner their advance was checked, the better. He also feared for his small force operating at the limit of British control.

The two frustrating months Butler had spent on the 300-mile stretch of river between the second and third Cataracts now paid an unexpected dividend through his knowledge of the river and the harsh topography of its banks. He increased the garrison at the Akasha railhead. Then he put the troops and local labour to work, building a fortified post twenty miles farther south at the village of Kosheh. Situated on a bend on the eastern bank of the Nile, Kosheh was the terminus of the Kaibar desert crossing. The fort, made of sun-baked mud blocks, went up quickly. Into it Butler placed one battalion, the Cameron Highlanders. Directly across the Nile, in the narrow angle of the bend, he built a second fort into which he placed his Sudanese battalion, and in front of it encamped 200 Egyptian cavalry. Meanwhile he kept up a run of supplies to the small posts along the railway. It was a race against time. His plan was to hold the main force of the Mahdists at Kosheh when they advanced downriver, and to deploy his cavalry to strike at any raiding parties which hit the railway.

In mid-November his wife arrived in Egypt with the two eldest children, Elizabeth and Patrick. Contact between husband and wife was confined to letter and cable; Elizabeth came only as far upriver as the Valley of the Kings at Luxor, the limit of tourist travel. Wadi Halfa and the dangerous frontier zone lay 300 miles farther south.

On 28 November Butler was at Wadi when he received a cable from Kosheh. Overnight, a 7000-strong army had swooped out of the desert and encamped at Amara just six miles upriver. Behind them on the Nile was a flotilla of nuggas laden with supplies, ammunition, and seven brass cannon captured at Khartoum. Butler passed the news to Aswan where Grenfell accepted that the Mahdists had to be stopped before they reached Wadi Halfa. The telegraph line between Aswan and Cairo began to hum. On 30 November Butler left Wadi for the front at Kosheh. He had two British and three Egyptian battalions, fifty British cavalry, 'one Krupp gun; one company mounted infantry, and eighty men of the camel corps, with sixty days food and four hundred rounds per man'. A few days later 'the ball opened'.

Twenty-six miles below Akasha, at the railway halting of Ambigol Wells, the lieutenant in command of the military post went out early in the morning, as was his custom, to shoot sand-grouse to supplement rations. There was something unusual about the birds he bagged – their crops were empty; their feeding pattern had been disturbed in the previous twelve hours. He quickly got his thirty-five men inside the post. They were reinforced by thirty more who, as a precautionary measure, had been ordered down by train from Akasha by Butler.

The reinforcements were just in time. A Madhist raiding party, hidden in the rocks around the post, opened fire, pinning the small force inside, while above and below the train, safely out of range of the fort, the tracks were lifted and the sleepers burnt. The Mahdist strategy was to cut off Akasha, and thus Kosheh, from the base at Wadi Halfa by the use of raiding parties, while the main army prepared to lay siege to Butler's force at Kosheh. After the attack on Ambigol Wells, repair gangs got the line open again, only for the Mahdists to return, 900 strong. This time they had a cannon which they had transported undetected across fifty miles of desert from Amara. Half the force were armed with spears and swords, the rest with rifles. Again the railway tracks were ripped up; the telegraph line was also cut. Butler, however, had taken the precaution during November of running a camouflaged wire up the western side of the river to Kosheh, and he used this to send a message downriver to Wadi Halfa for reinforcements.

Large sections of the line between Ambigol and Akasha were by now wrecked. Butler undertook a night march on 5 December to rendezvous with the reinforcements coming up from Wadi and, with a combined force of 400 cavalry and 600 infantry, went to the relief of Ambigol Wells. The

Mahdists melted away, taking their cannon with them. Casualties from Ambigol were light on both sides. Three of the defenders of the post and about twenty Mahdists had died. The next few days saw Butler and his men give of their best to keep the railway open as the Mahdists continued to raid it.

> The work of that week never found outside record or acknowledgement, but I owe it to the brave fellows who freely gave me their toil and sweat to say something about it ... We had literally to do the work of one hundred men with less than fifty. Watched from every side, and with seven or eight thousand Arabs in front and on our flanks for fifty miles, we held our own from Kosheh to Ambigol, repaired every damage as it occurred, and gave back shot for shot on both sides of the Nile.[1]

As December went on, more and more troops came up the line from Wadi Halfa. Early in the month Grenfell had established his field head-quarters at Wadi and he was joined there by Stephenson on 19 December. Stephenson was impressed by what he found:

> To Secretary of State for War. I have the honour to call your attention to the admirable manner in which Major Gen Grenfell and Brig Gen Butler commanding at Wadi Halfa have carried out the arduous and difficult task entrusted to them ... Butler like Grenfell showed great judgment, forethought and vigilance and promptness of action when he had to act on his own responsibility ... [he] has been untiring in his exertions, and by the energy and forethought for which he is remarkable, he placed the whole of his command on such a footing that the enemy has been comparatively harmless and the various posts have held their own with trifling losses.[2]

In Aswan, Elizabeth Butler watched in some trepidation as troop transports passed up the Nile to the front. 'Soldiers' wives in war time have to feel the sickening sensation on waking some morning when news of a fight is expected, of saying to themselves – I may be a widow.'[3]

Meanwhile Butler's intelligence reports told him that the Khalifa was preparing to move his main force from Amara. Five thousand Mahdists advanced downriver to the village of Ginnis, four miles from Butler's position at Kosheh. He sent out patrols to probe the Mahdist deployment patterns. There was the occasional skirmish. Christmas Day itself was busy. When Stephenson arrived with Grenfell and the last of the reinforcements, Butler had everything ready for an attack on Ginnis. The British-led force now totalled 4000. Over 28 and 29 December Stephenson used the artillery he had brought with him to clear the surroundings of Kosheh of small advance companies of the Mahdists. He found Butler impatient, too eager to attack Ginnis: Butler found Stephenson and Grenfell over-cautious. Butler believed that the Mahdists should be pushed back beyond Dongola and the menace of an invasion of Egypt removed for once and for all. Stephenson was satisfied to engage the Mahdists at Ginnis. Besides, his instructions from Cairo precluded any long-term campaigning in the Sudan. On 29 December he finalized his plans with Grenfell for battle on the morrow. The two men relied heavily on Butler's intelligence reports.

The key to victory at Ginnis would be a long, high ridge, some three miles from Kosheh and one mile from Ginnis and the Nile. Butler was given command of the advance brigade with orders to take the ridge, from which an assault could then be launched on the huge Mahdist camp. By 4.45 a.m. on 30 December 1885, in a grey mist from the river, Butler had deployed a force of four battalions – which included a cavalry unit – out-side Kosheh in a hollow square. Inside the square he placed a mobile ar-tillery battery of six guns drawn by camels. He had left little to chance. The previous night he had made alignments in the sand with large stones by which to assemble his brigade for the line of march to the ridge. Six hundred yards to his rear a second brigade was still assembling when But-ler sent back a message to Grenfell requesting permission to advance. He was told to wait until the second brigade was ready. To this he responded with a second message, saying that it was 'imperatively necessary' to move off by 5 a.m. to cover the three miles to the ridge under cover of darkness. There was no response to this from Grenfell and on the basis that silence betokens consent, Butler ordered his brigade forward at 5 a.m. precisely.

By dawn his troops were a quarter of a mile from their objective. They approached on the blind side and Butler, on horseback, led them to the summit as the sun rose. From there he saw the Mahdists streaming to-wards the ridge. Back towards Kosheh he could see the second brigade al-most two miles behind him and off to the east a regiment of cavalry which was being held in reserve. His troops would be on their own for some time. On the summit he deployed his artillery, which pounded the approach from Ginnis to the ridge as the Mahdists advanced. Too late to stop Brit-ish occupation of the summit, they tried to storm the ridge on Butler's left flank. He foiled this movement with his cavalry unit. Meanwhile the mass of his infantry came at the Mahdists hidden in the rocks and gullies at the western foot of the ridge. The weapons of the Mahdists in no way matched those of the British. Half of them were armed only with spears or swords, but for a time they fought fiercely, advancing in strong rushes against the disciplined British fire.

> One or two of them got so close to the line before they fell that one could see every feature of their faces distorted with the delirium of fanatical enthusiasm, ther lips moving in prayer, the eyes rolling, their swords raised in both hands, twirling in a ceaseless circle above their heads. I could not discern any sign of rage in the expression of their faces; it seemed to be the ecstasy of self martyrdom. The battle was soon over; we had it all to ourselves.[4]

From his vantage-point on the ridge, Butler sent word to the second brigade that he was going to advance on Ginnis. Already he could see the camp being broken and the start of what looked like a retreat. He sent an order to the cavalry regiment to ride south of the ridge and place itself across the Mahdists' expected line of retreat. Then he rode for Ginnis, meeting no resistance. The short engagement at the ridge had been decisive and British casualties had been low – seven fatalities and twenty-seven wounded. Ginnis was simply abandoned, leaving behind four cannon and twenty standards. Butler commented later that the only thing *stout* about Ginnis was its name.

Butler was unhappy with the conduct of the cavalry regiment that he had ordered across the Mahdists' line of retreat. His approach to the engagement at Ginnis was to inflict maximum casualties, preventing any formidable regrouping and thus removing any threat to Egypt. The Mahdists had retreated too quickly for the cavalry to block them, but what angered Butler was that the cavalry had not pursued the enemy, as standard tactics required. He left Stephenson and Grenfell in no doubt about what he thought of this. The actual damage inflicted on the Mahdists was still unclear. For the want of completing its operation at minimum risk, the cavalry had endangered the lives of others who would have to finish the job of going upriver to ensure that the Mahdists had been routed.

Butler was basically right, but in the immediate aftermath of Ginnis his outspoken comments antagonized senior cavalry officers. It was pointed out to him that his order had merely told the cavalry to break the line of retreat: he had not specifically ordered them in hot pursuit. The matter would later reach the War Office where, as Butler once observed, 'the absent are always in the wrong'.

That afternoon Butler brought his brigade up to Amara with orders to pursue the enemy and capture what he could of its supplies. Stephenson meanwhile prepared a despatch for the War Office:

> Enemy taken by surprise. All our troops in before aware of our presence. Grenfell commanded division and to him alone is due, with those under his command, the whole credit for all arrangements and operations of frontier force ... Butler commanded his force remarkably well and completely carried out his portion of the plan. He had the brunt of the fight.[5]

The bulk of the Khalifa's army had retreated swiftly across the desert and was estimated to be forty miles south of Ginnis. However, on the river the retreating nuggas, encumbered with wounded and campaign supplies, were making slow progress against the Nile current. On the first day of the new year Butler went upriver to capture as much as he could of the Khalifa's fleet. With 200 mounted infantry and an armed paddle-steamer, he set off in pursuit of the nuggas. It was a three-day operation which resulted in the capture of nine boats laden with arms, food and grain. During the operation it became clear from the number of fresh graves, and from reports at the riverside villages, just how serious the Mahdists' losses had been at Ginnis. The final estimates were 300 wounded and 500 killed. The Khalifa had suffered a severe blow to his prestige as the Mahdi's successor, his army had collapsed and was 'flying through Kaibar to Dongola'.

When Butler got back to Kosheh, Stephenson and Grenfell, well-satisfied with the past few days, had already departed for Egypt. There was a despatch waiting for him from Stephenson:

> The Lieutenant-General desires to express to Br.-General Butler the satisfaction with which he has read the report of his proceeding since the action of 30th ulto., and of his activity and energy in following up the enemy, which has resulted in the important capture of nine laden Nuggers, which it is believed are the remainder of the enemy's river transport north of Kaibar.[6]

Butler came downriver to Wadi Halfa with some 4000 troops. His remit was unchanged – defend the frontier and keep the line to Akasha open.

Elizabeth came up to Wadi Halfa by boat with the children for a six-week stay. The partially reunited family lived on a comfortable houseboat, but their time together was marred by worry over the health of the children. Patrick developed a bad eye infection, and young Elizabeth was prostrate for a time with heat-stroke. By early March the heat was becoming too much to bear and Elizabeth and the children left for England.

Professionally, this was a relaxing time for Butler, in contrast to the previous months, but the cares of command never left him. He grew anxious about the morale and health of his troops. Adequate facilities did not exist for such a large number and medical attention was not comprehensive enough. As early as 12 February he had telegraphed Grenfell at Aswan:

> We are now approaching a very trying season for English troops: we are occupying camping grounds which have been much fouled by previous occupation and from which it is impossible to change. Our sick list is exceptionally high, nearly ten per cent being in hospital; our barrack equipment is nil. We have neither bedsteads, mattresses, tables, nor forms. Three out of my four battalions are in tents, and to build huts for men will be a work of much time, since the district is almost destitute of timber and straw for roofs ... I beg the favour of the transmission of this telegram to Cairo and if necessary to England, so that the fullest effort may be made, while there is time, for the provision of the requisites which will make life endurable during the hot season.[7]

In Cairo, Butler's despatch was seen as unreasonable. The four battalions at the frontier were there as a temporary measure against the possibility of a regrouping of the Khalifa's army. The unlikelihood of this had to be balanced against the expense, time and energy involved in bettering conditions at the front. Butler began to experience the common frustration of the official on the periphery in a period of routine, whose concerns are at odds with those of his superiors at the hub.

His cables became increasingly demanding as the first deaths from heat and fever occurred among his troops. However, Cairo reacted only when enteric fever broke out at Akasha. On 22 March Butler was ordered to retire all British troops to Aswan. They would be replaced by a smaller Egyptian force, more inured to the heat. Withdrawal took weeks and, during it, the full blast of the hot season hit Wadi Halfa. Desperate for shade, the troops lay under canvas by day in temperatures that rose above fifty degrees Celsius, while outside 'a furnace wind' choked the air with grit and dust. Twenty-five men died from heat-stroke during April.

Throughout April Butler assumed that his frontier command would cease with the departure of the last British troops for Aswan. To his surprise, he got no orders to leave as the Egyptian troops arrived to take over from the British. There was no mention from Cairo of a departure date for him. Grenfell at Aswan could tell him nothing. He began to query Cairo as to when he might be relieved of his command. He had been at Wadi Halfa since the previous September; he had held the railway line to Akasha open; fortified it; built advance posts at Kosheh; led the action at Ginnis; gone upriver afterwards and made a significant capture of nuggas; looked after the needs of 4000 troops for two months; evacuated them downriver to Aswan. And for what? To be forsaken and ignored. He found himself re-reading his well-thumbed copy of Barry O'Meara's *Napoleon in Exile*. His weekly letters to Elizabeth through May and June show something of the dejection into which he was sinking:

> *3rd May* I can get no orders from Cairo. They are, I fear, treating me after their old manner, and they now want to detain me here without troops, commissariat or occupation. The weather is as hot as it can be. It is an awful looking place, glaring, burning and baking ...
> *10th May* It looks now as though I should be detained here for perhaps a long while. I do not know why; there is no work for me to do, no troops to command ... You cannot imagine the desolation and loneliness of the place ...
> *23rd May* Unless my health breaks I must stay until August.
> *30th May* I must write you a short letter ... They are too many for me; they are one thousand miles nearer home; and they have the advantage of interior lines, and they can warp words and twist thoughts and actions as they like. But what does it all matter?
> *14th June* I am keeping well thank God, but our poor officers and men are suffering terribly at Aswan. In the twenty four hours ending at 3 p.m. yesterday eleven officers and men died there. More than a hundred and thirty have died in two months, and six hundred sick men have been sent away. More than three months ago I told the authorities what they could expect but I wasn't listened to. Not a word about this mortality gets to England and yet we have not had in this generation such a rate of mortality as this among British soldiers.[8]

Isolated, and ignored by Cairo, Butler wrote to Wolseley at the War Office, detailing the unnecessary trials undergone by his troops, complaining of the unfair treatment meted out to him by Cairo and fulminating against a rumour machine that he felt was slandering him. Wolseley, recently ennobled to a viscountcy, wrote back. The letter shows the strength of the relationship between the two men. And when the disparity in rank between them is considered, Wolseley's sentiments are sensitively expressed.

You take an entirely wrong view of matters here. No one has ever attempted to detract from the good work you have done at the Wadi Halfa frontier nor has anyone attempted in any way whatever to rob you of the credit due to you. You have many good friends and it rests with yourself to keep them ... Now as a great admirer of yours and an old friend and hearty well wisher, I am going to say what you may possibly resent. However we have soldiered too long together for me to remain silent.

Everyone who knows General Stephenson knows him to be a most easy man to get on with, a perfect gentleman all round and the kindest and best hearted of men. Well he cannot get on with you. He has sent home some of the telegraphs you have despatched to him and I confess to thinking them bordering on the insubordinate. Remember that he is your general and you must obey him as you expect others who are junior to you to obey you ... You must learn to work in a team before you can drive one. When the time comes I know how well you will drive your team but in the meantime whether you are follower or leader you must pull with a will and not kick at the others in the team and refuse to answer obediently the call that the chief makes upon you.

You are certainly under a misapprehension if you imagine that there is any plot to rob you of the credit you deserve, or if you fancy that there is any conspiracy against you. You must run straight with your comrades, your equals and your superiors and you will find that all your notions of 'dishonest trickery' are dreams of a brain exhausted by the hardships and the heat and the numerous worries you have been through lately in your well conceived and well executed operation.[9]

In truth, Butler was exhausted. By late May he was dizzy and nauseous and in mid-June he was finally ordered down to Aswan. There his health deteriorated further. Bilious attacks and nausea kept him from eating for days at a time. He had visibly aged. A thinning of the hair on the crown of his head, noticeable for several years, had given way to baldness. His concentration went, he lost even the inclination to continue his diary. He could have asked for leave, but he did not want to lose face. His posting had been a twelve-month one and was not due to end until late August: to ask for leave would be to admit tacitly that he was incapable of routine command. In Cairo the attitude to him was that he needed a lesson in the realities of miltary hierarchy: he was a jumped-up staff officer, an opinionated Wolseleyite who had never been more than a lieutenant in the one unit that had traditionally been the core of the army – the line regiment. Butler sank into 'a condition of lethargic acceptance of his lot'. His health grew worse.

The matter was resolved by the device of having the senior medical officer at Aswan convene a medical board which ordered Butler on four months' sick leave to be spent outside Egypt. By 5 July he was resting in Shepheard's Hotel in Cairo, preparing to go home. From there he wrote briefly to Elizabeth: 'I am only weak and have now no fever; all I want is rest. I am 'played out', that is all ... A week in Glencar would do more for me than all the doctors in Europe.'[10]

On his arrival in London in July 1886, Butler reported to the War Office where his reception was 'cold but cautious'. His letters and despatches from Wadi Halfa had been 'too strong and too many'. He made an unsuccessful attempt to secure promotion for his frontier services. He was told that on the expiry of his sick leave there would be no post immediately available for him and he would have to go on half-pay at his substantive grade of lieutenant-colonel. The prospect was 'not too brilliant ... after close upon 30 years service hot and cold in all parts of the empire'.[11] It was made harder to bear by the continued advancement of several of his old colleagues. Brackenbury, Buller and Wood were at the War Office. Brackenbury was in charge of the rapidly expanding field of military intelligence, while Buller was Deputy Adjutant General.

There was some sympathy for Butler in senior military circles. He did deserve some formal recognition of his work on the Egyptian frontier. Wolseley as Adjutant General felt the matter would be addressed in time – if Butler curbed his impatience.

Butler was approaching his forty-eighth birthday. He was middle-aged, at a stage in life when a realistic appraisal of unfulfilled ambitions should bring an acceptance of one's limitations, a time when what one wants from life should be displaced by what one will settle for. And it was not only his career prospects that engaged Butler in the late summer of 1886, for hanging over him was the impending Campbell divorce case, due for hearing in the coming law term. This was something that forced him to focus on his own marriage and his responsibilities to Elizabeth and their five children. In the autumn of 1886, to protect their privacy, the Butlers rented an old farmhouse outside the medieval walled city of Dinan at the head of the Rance estuary in Brittany. It was far from the noise and gossip of London, yet less than a day's travel by ferry and train from the Royal Courts of Justice.

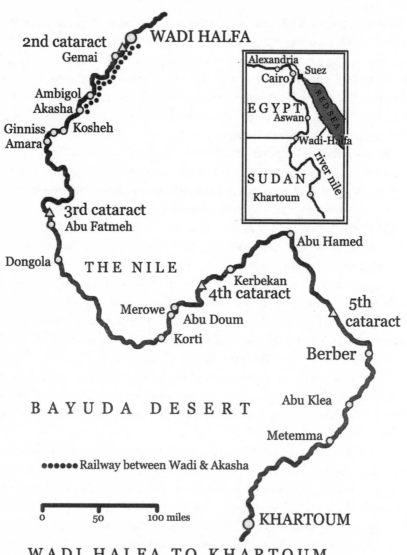

WADI HALFA TO KHARTOUM
From the map illustrating 'The Campaign of the Cataracts' (1887)

Ballyslatteen House, Golden, County Tipperary, where William Francis Butler was born on 31 October 1838. (Courtesy John and Rose Prendergast)

Ensign Butler photographed aged 19 in 1857. (from *An Autobiography*, 1911)

Elizabeth Thompson, *c.* 1875. (Courtesy the Abbot of Downside)

Butler in San Francisco, USA, aged 34 in 1872. (Courtesy Viscount Gormanston)

Butler as aide-de-camp to Queen Victori[a] in 1883. (Courtesy Rupert Butler)

Butler greets Wolseley at the source of the Rainy River, north Ontario, August 1870. (from *The Great Lone Land: A Narrative of Travel and Adventure in the North-West of America*, 1872)

The Dublin-born 'very model' Major-General Garnet Joseph Wolseley in 1873.

Butler in Montreal aged 36 in 1874. (Courtesy the Trustees of the Meynell Archive)

After the Battle: arrival of Lord Wolseley, with Butler centre right, at the bridge of Tel-el-Kebir, Egypt, September 1882. (from a painting by Elizabeth Butler, 1885)

Butler, wearing pith helmet, working up the Nile River in Sudan during the Gordon Relief Expedition in 1884. (from *The Campaign of the Cataracts*, 1887: line-drawing, Elizabeth Butler)

Evicted: an icon painting by Elizabeth Butler, 1890, of a scene she witnessed in Glendalough, County Wicklow, during the Land War. (Courtesy the Department of Irish Folklore, UCD)

Elizabeth Butler in her studio, c. 1893.
(Courtesy Viscount Gormanston)

Butler in South Africa, 1899. (Painting by
Elizabeth Butler, courtesy Rupert Butler)

Lady Colin Campbell, c. 1897. (Painting by
Giovanni Boldini, courtesy NPG, London)

Major-General Sir William Butler KCB,
Dover 1898. (from *An Autobiography*)

Dover Castle, Kent: Butler's official residence as OC South-Eastern District, 1896-8. Elizabeth Butler's studio is over the gate. (Courtesy English Heritage)

Butler aged 66 in 1905, at the time of his report on army contracts in South Africa.

'A Radical General.' (Cartoon by 'Spy' from *Vanity Fair Album*, 1907)

Dublin Commissioners of the Irish Universities Act, 1908. *Front, l-r*: Sir William F. Butler, Dr William Walsh, Catholic Archbishop of Dublin, Chief Baron Palles, Chairman, Sir John Rhys, Dr Henry Jackson. *Back, l-r*: Stephen Gwynn MP, J.P. Boland MP, Dr Alexander Anderson, President UCG, Sir Bertram Windle, President UCC, Dr Dennis Coffey. President UCD.

RED CLOUD,

THE SOLITARY SIOUX.

𝔄 𝔖𝔱𝔬𝔯𝔶 𝔬𝔣 𝔱𝔥𝔢 𝔊𝔯𝔢𝔞𝔱 𝔓𝔯𝔞𝔦𝔯𝔦𝔢.

BY

LIEUT.-COLONEL BUTLER, C.B.

AUTHOR OF "THE GREAT LONE LAND," "THE WILD NORTH LAND,"
ETC., ETC.

"Like a wind, that shrills
All night in a waste land, where no one comes,
Or hath come, since the making of the world."
Tennyson.

BOSTON:
ROBERTS BROTHERS.
1884.

Title-page from Butler's only novel, used as a school text in the Irish Free State.

Red Cloud, eponymous hero, confronts the enemy, bow and arrow against rifle.

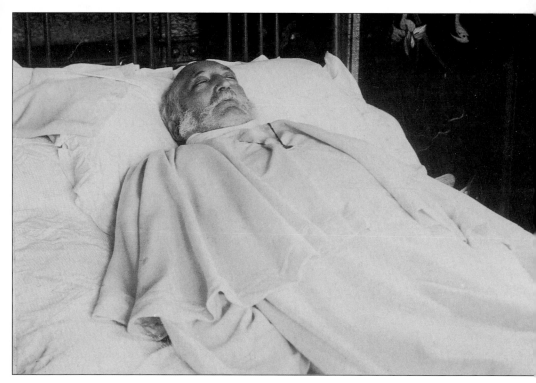

Butler on his deathbed, June 1910. (Courtesy Viscount Gormanston)

Bansha Castle, Bansha, County Tipperary, Butler's Suir Valley home from 1905 until his death. (Courtesy John and Teresa Russell)

Chapter Eleven

THE CAMPBELL DIVORCE CASE

The Campbell divorce scandal of 1886 was one of those judicial cases that are touchstones for their generation. To look back on it from the start of the twenty-first century is to be held as much by the details of evidence in the case as by the picture it gives of polite society and of the clearly separate roles of men and women. This was a world of calling cards and of the sending of notes and letters by a postal service which provided up to fourteen collections and deliveries daily, of an elaborate code of etiquette between the sexes, formal dress, and medical attention in one's own home as a norm. Servants were ubiquitous.

Gertrude Blood's parents, Edmund and Mary, were Irish landed gentry. Edmund Maglin Blood had his family estate at Brickhill, near Quin, County Clare. The Bloods were well-to-do and lived mainly in London. Gertrude was born there in 1857, one of four children and the youngest of three daughters. Nothing was spared on the girls' education, and the Bloods, in common with many of their class, travelled extensively in continental Europe while their children were growing up. Gertrude became multilingual. She was highly talented and, at the age of twenty-one, had published a popular childrens' novel, *Topo*. This was illustrated by Kate Greenaway, Elizabeth Thompson's contemporary at the Kensington Female School of Fine Art. Gertrude herself was a trained artist who exhibited on occasion, and during the late 1870s she periodically visited Elizabeth Thompson's studio.

Gertrude was also a singer of repute, greatly in demand for charitable assignments. She complemented her artistic accomplishments with robust activities such as fencing, horseriding and swimming. Tall, beautiful and vivacious, she was one of the most eligible women in fashionable London society. She had first met Butler when she was thirteen; her father's cousin, Frank Gamble Blood, was a major in Butler's regiment, and during his visit to Paris at the end of 1869 Butler had called on the Bloods who were staying in the city at that time. In the mid-1870s the author of *The Great Lone Land* was among the eligible young men whom the parents of the three Blood sisters made welcome to their London home and included in their social circle.

In July 1881 Gertrude Blood married Lord Colin Campbell, the youngest son of the eighth Duke of Argyll. The couple had met the previous September and had known each other for only three days before they became engaged. It was a rash bethrothal and the marriage itself got off to the shakiest of starts – it remained unconsummated for three months while Lord Campbell was recovering from treatment for syphilis which he had contracted some years previously.

In November 1881 the couple moved to 79 Cadogan Place, Chelsea, a five-storey terraced house. Here they maintained separate bedrooms and Lord Campbell had the services of a personal nurse for his condition. Over the winter of 1881-2 there was little strengthening of the bonds of intimacy between husband and wife. Lord Colin remained semi-invalid, sometimes attending Westminster where he held a safe seat as a Liberal MP. Gertrude continued a social round that included recitals and charity work in the East End of London. Gossip and rumour were potent forces in the world which the Campbells inhabited. There was much sympathy for Lady Campbell, though this was tempered in some quarters by criticism of her. Some indecorum attached to a newly married woman having such a busy social life as Lady Campbell continued to pursue. Her social calendar also kept her in touch with a wide circle of male friends and escorts. One of those was Lord Blandford, George Charles Spencer Churchill, heir to the Duke of Marlborough and uncle of the young Winston Churchill. Blandford was a *bon viveur* and art patron, and a man of some notoriety. In his late thirties and married with three children, his open adultery with another member of the nobility, a Lady Aylesford, had resulted in his being cited in a successful divorce taken by the aggrieved husband in 1878.

Divorce was rare in Victorian England. Until 1857, an act of parliament was necessary to secure a divorce. In 1857 the Matrimonial Causes Act dealt with the issue of marital breakdown by giving the civil courts the

power to grant judicial separations and divorces. The fact that divorce became more easily available did not mean that it was socially acceptable.
Lifelong marriage was the norm as well as the ideal. It was not until 1887
that the innocent party to a divorce could attend a court function in a personal capacity. Society's attitude to divorce was reflected in the annual divorce rate. Four years after the Act there were only 141 divorces, less than
one marriage in every 10,000. This figure increased only marginally over
the next twenty-five years. Furthermore, most petitions were from deserted spouses, almost all wives, or from couples already separated. Grounds
for divorce were different for men and women. A husband could petition
for divorce on the grounds of his wife's adultery. A wife could petition on
the grounds of her husband's adultery plus either cruelty or desertion.

The raffish air adhering to Lord Blandford was thickened by rumours
that his own wife was going to leave him because of his scandalous behaviour. He had first met Lady Campbell in 1880 at a gathering at her parents'
home when she was plain Gertrude Blood. They shared interests in art,
theatre and the world of ideas. Blandford and his wife lived in Cadogan
Square, close to where the Campbells set up house in November 1881. At
Easter 1882 the Campbells were invited to Leigh Court outside Bristol, the
home of Lady Frances Miles, a friend of Lord Campbell and a second
cousin of Lady Campbell. Lord Campbell's state of health prevented his
going, and Lady Campbell went down with her personal maid. Blandford,
unaccompanied by his wife, was also a guest, and he and Lady Campbell
had rooms on the same corridor. Blandford would be the first of the three
co-respondents cited by Lord Campbell in the divorce petition he would
file two and a half years later.

The second co-respondent cited in the petition of 6 November 1884
was Captain Eyre Massey Shaw', head of the London Metropolitan Fire
Brigade. Shaw was Irish, a former army officer in his mid-forties, married
with several children. One of his daughters was a bridesmaid at Gertrude's
wedding. Like Butler, he was a Companion of the Bath. Shaw had a high
socal profile and was in frequent attendance at public functions. Over the
winter of 1881–2 Lady Campbell sometimes visited the Shaw family home
to see his daughters. Shaw himself provided an occasional escort for her.
He also came to Cadogan Place, before the Campbells moved in, to inspect the house with Lady Campbell.

One afternoon during the spring of 1882, Lord Campbell came home
unexpectedly to find both Blandford and Shaw taking tea with his wife. He
was angry and forbade her to have either man in the house again, but Shaw

visited on at least one other occasion when Lord Campbell was absent.

Early in September 1882 the Campbells came down to the seclusion of Leigh Court, where Lord Campbell was to be operated on by William Allingham, England's leading rectal surgeon, and to recuperate over the next six months under the care of Thomas Bird, Professor of Anaesthetics at Guy's Hospital. Bird, an unassuming and stylish forty-year-old bachelor, became friendly with Lady Campbell through their discussions of her husband's prognosis. Lady Campbell herself did not allow her stay at Leigh Court to interrupt her concert engagements in London, and she would travel up by train from Bristol for recitals. When the Campbells finally returned to London in February 1883, Lord Campbell was still ill and Bird visited Cadogan Place as required. At the start of April, Lady Campbell herself was not feeling well. One night she was forced to stop singing halfway through a recital from which she was escorted home by Bird. Six days later Butler entered the story.

On the evening of 11 April 1883 the Campbells attended a banquet at the Mansion House, held to honour the two most senior officers involved in the Egyptian campaign of the previous year: Wolseley, who had commanded the land forces, and Lord Alcester, commander-in-chief of the British fleet in the Mediterranean. The illustrious gathering of military men present included Butler. He had travelled up from Plymouth for the occasion, and he was unaccompanied. He had not met Gertrude Campbell for some time and she invited him to make an afternoon call to Cadogan Place. Two days later he did so. Lord Campbell was not at home when he called and, though he arrived home while Butler was still present, the two men did not see each other.

Shortly after Butler's departure Lady Campbell fell ill with agonizing cramps. Bird attended her over the following days, but there was little improvement in her condition and he called in a leading obstetrician for a second opinion. Over the ensuing weeks, as she made a slow recovery, numerous letters and notes from well-wishers came through Lady Campbell's letterbox. Among her correspondents were Blandford and Butler. Butler's contacts were not confined to correspondence. According to a statement which he later gave to Lady Campbell's solicitors, Butler visited 'five or six times' in total over the early to mid-summer of 1883.

Lady Campbell's illness, and her recovery from it, did nothing to improve her relationship with her husband and, in late July, Lord Campbell confronted his wife and her family in the Blood home at Thurloe Square to complain about his wife's conduct: she had neglected him and had persisted in compromising herself with other men. It was a heated confrontation. Lord Campbell gave as recent examples of her conduct, her entertaining of Butler and her receiving letters from both him and Blandford during her convalescence. Lady Campbell countered with a demand for a written assurance from her husband that he would never again have conjugal relations with her because of the risk to her health. The confrontation brought no resolution and Lady Campbell filed for a judicial separation. Her suit was heard *in camera* in March 1884. She charged her husband with infecting her with 'a venereal disease', and secured her judicial separation on the grounds of cruelty. Lord Campbell appealed the judgment, unsuccessfully. Critically for future events, his counsel had not at any stage argued that Lady Campbell had been promiscuous.

Returning to her parents' home in Thurloe Square, Lady Campbell continued her singing and painting, and began to establish herself as a writer of articles for the *Saturday Review*. Her husband, publicly humiliated, rejected by a beautiful woman who still continued to enjoy the public eye, began an obsessive pursuit of his estranged wife, determined to ruin her. During the summer of 1884 he hired private detectives who spied on her in Paris, where she was seen with Blandford, and he tried to have her arrested there as a prostitute. Further, with a view to obtaining a divorce, Lord Campbell had his agents approach former servants at Cadogan Place to testify against his wife as an adulteress.

All this activity pushed Lady Campbell back on her own solicitors. She was advised to counterfile. After a frenzy of activity, both parties filed for divorce on 6 November 1884. Lord Campbell accused his wife of adultery with Blandford (who had just succeeded to the Dukedom of Marlborough), with Shaw, and with Butler. Lady Campbell accused her husband of adultery with a Mary Watson, who had been a housemaid at Cadogan Place, and of cruelty and neglect. Her solicitors filed her petition a bare half-hour before Lord Campbell's, ensuring that when the case would come to trial, Lady Campbell's counsel would be allowed both opening and closing statements.

Some weeks later, Butler received official notification of having been cited as a co-respondent. During his home leave from Egypt in the summer of 1885 he met Lady Campbell once – at the offices of Lewis and Lewis, her solicitors. There, at her request, he made a statement the starkness of which illustrates the gravity of his predicament: 'I have not been in love with Lady Campbell, nor have I kissed her. Nor have I taken any liberty with her, and there is not the slightest pretence for this charge.'

Meanwhile, Lord Campbell had added a fourth co-respondent to his suit: his physician, Thomas Bird. Bird had not been paid for his medical services and in the spring of 1885 resorted to legal action against Lord Campbell for the recovery of his fees. The addition of his name to make up a quartet of co-respondents introduced an element of farce into what was already promising to be a multi-facetted legal drama.

Campbell v. *Campbell*, and *Campbell* v. *Campbell, Marlborough, Shaw, Butler* and *Bird*, opened before a jury in the Royal Courts of Justice in London on 26 November, and concluded on 20 December, 1886. The court sat for twenty days and established a record for the duration of a British divorce case that was never broken.

The trial itself was a sensation, revealing day after day to a disbelieving public, matters rarely mentioned even in intimate conversations. Twice daily, the newspapers supplied details of the unfolding case to an insatiable readership which was both shocked and titillated by what was brought before it. Into the public domain came Lord Campbell's syphilis; the trauma of first marital intercourse for Lady Campbell; the evidence of two doctors that the maid with whom Lord Campbell had supposedly committed adultery was still *virgo intacta*; an allegation that during Lady Campbell's acute illness in April 1883 her soiled bedsheets showed that she had had a miscarriage – this at a time when she and her husband had not had sexual relations for months; references to Lord Campbell's genital poultices and his need of constant nursing; and mention of Lady Campbell's having 'contraceptive articles' in her bedroom.

These disclosures were complemented by a welter of innuendo from witnesses hostile to Lady Campbell: her ladyship returning home after a concert, from which she had been escorted by Blandford, with the stays of her dress hooked differently to the way her maid had hooked them before she went out; her ladyship observed by her butler through a keyhole, lying dishevelled on her drawing-room floor with Captain Shaw; her ladyship coming out of the drawing-room during Butler's visit with her hair disordered and her face flushed; her ladyship nestling close to Bird in a hansom cab; and Bird, on a later occasion, being found asleep in Lady Campbell's darkened sickroom.

As the trial progressed, it was soon clear that the evidence for Lord Campbell's adultery with the housemaid was negligible. Of the four co-respondents cited as having committed adultery with Lady Campbell, the strongest circumstantial evidence was against Blandford. The evidence against Shaw was weak and capable, without strain, of having an innocuous interpretation put upon it, or of being dismissed in part as a fabrication. The coincidence of Bird having been cited only after he had instituted proceedings to recover his fees worked heavily to exonerate him. The case against Butler was the weakest of the four.

Top counsel had been engaged by all parties. Lady Campbell's legal team was headed by the redoubtable Sir Charles Russell, a future Chief Justice. Lord Campbell had the services of Robert Finlay, a barrister with an awesome reputation. He, in turn, was assisted by Frank Lockwood who, four years later, would represent Katharine O'Shea in the O'Shea–Parnell divorce suit. Each of the four co-respondents was represented by his own counsel. Butler had John Patrick Murphy, an Irish Catholic with thirty years' experience at the bar, as senior counsel.

The case against Butler concerned two visits he had paid to Cadogan Place in 1883, one in April and one in May.

The witnesses against him were two: Annie Duffy, Lord Campbell's nurse, and Ellen Hawkes, a housemaid. Hawkes had worked for just over four months at Cadogan Place before being dismissed by Lady Campbell in early August 1883.

Annie Duffy testified that at about two o'clock on the afternoon of 13 April a gentleman arrived alone in a hansom cab to see her mistress. He gave his name as Colonel Butler and he was shown up to the first-floor drawing-room where Lady Campbell was alone. She continued:

> I showed him into the drawing room where Lady Colin was. Shortly after a lady called. Lady Colin opened the door of the drawing room and, over the bannister, called out 'Helen, Helen [Annie], say "not at home".'
>
> I was downstairs and I said, 'Not at home, my Lady?'
>
> And she said, 'Yes, not at home.' I noticed that her ladyship's hair was disordered and her face flushed. I answered the door and told the lady that Lady Colin was not at home, and she drove away. Shortly afterwards Lord Colin came in. The first word as usual that his lordship said was, 'Is her ladyship in?' I said, 'Yes.' He then enquired, 'Is she alone?' I answered, 'No.' He said, 'I am very tired.' I then advised his lordship to go to bed. I undressed him and put him to bed. He said to me, 'Is it a lady or a gentleman?' I replied, 'A gentleman.' He asked, 'Who is it?' I replied, 'I do not know,' as I always did answer his lordship.' [This produced laughter in court.]
>
> 'I heard General [*sic*] Butler leave. He let himself out.'

Annie Duffy went on to testify that when Lady Campbell was later questioned by her husband about her visitor, she told him, 'He is only an old soldier who has known me since I was a little child.'[4]

Three days after Annie Duffy gave her testimony, Ellen Hawkes took the stand. She was barely audible, and frequently had to be asked to speak up:

> I knew Colonel Butler by sight. He visited at Cadogan Place while I was there. He came the first time about a month after I had entered the service. He saw Lady Colin in the drawing room. A lady called during his visit and was not admitted. Lady Colin called out to Mrs. Duffy to say that she was not at home. I saw Colonel Butler when he left. He was at the foot of the stairs and I waited until he went out. He went out on his toes. [Laughter in court.] He let himself out. His visit had continued for two hours, during which time nobody else was with Lady Colin.[5]

Frank Lockwood, Lord Campbell's junior counsel, then put a question to Ellen Hawkes about photographs:

> Do you remember if there were any photographs of Colonel Butler about the house?
>
> Her ladyship had one in a plush frame, and an old one I found under her pillow one morning. It was after the occasion when I saw Colonel Butler. I found the photograph in making the bed.[6]

When Lady Campbell was examined on events connected with Butler, she was led into her evidence with a question from her second counsel, Frederick Inderwick:

> Had you known the Butler family for some years?
>
> A great many years. I went to a reception in the Mansion House on April 11 1883, and I saw Colonel Butler there. I had not seen him for two years and he said, 'May I come and see you?' and I said, 'Certainly.' And he asked when as he would only be in London for two days. And I said, 'Oh, come tomorrow about two o'clock.'
>
> Colonel Butler came next day and stayed an hour I think. Other visitors came while he was there. That was the occasion of his first visit. I remember his second visit in May 1883. It was at the time I was convalescent. I was lying on the sofa after my long illness. My sister was with me and was present the whole time. He stayed about an hour. I remember the incident

of a lady coming to the house. It was a lady with whom my sister was not on very good terms at the time. She was sitting next to the window and saw who it was. She said, 'Here is so and so, say you are not at home.' I said, 'I can't do that,' and my sister went out herself and called to the servant, 'Not at home.'"

Lady Campbell's sister, Mary Bolton, who had also been at the Blood family home during the explosive meeting in July 1883 between the Campbells, was not available to corroborate this evidence; she had died some time before the divorce suit. Lady Campbell continued her own evidence. Her reference to her five-storey home as 'a mere bird-cage' would have amused sections of the court:

> It is absolutely untrue that I received letters from Colonel Butler every day. I received a letter upon the occasion of my marriage. The house at Cadogan Place was extremely small – a mere birdcage – and had a shelf in my bedroom over the bed where books and photographs were kept. A photograph of Colonel Butler may have fallen from the shelf on to the bed and that may be the origin of the servant's story of Colonel Butler's photograph being found on my pillow.[8]

Under cross-examination Lady Campbell's evidence was not seriously dented. The matter of the photographs was capable of an innocuous explanation. As the author of *The Great Lone Land*, Butler had publicity photographs taken in the early 1870s. It might be expected that copies of these circulated in the Blood household. And, after all, Butler was, in Lady Colin's words, 'an old soldier who had known me since I was a little child'. But those words raised a matter not pursued in cross-examination: the strong probability that Lady Colin found Butler sexually attractive. The giveaway is her use of the phrase *an old soldier*. This was a description that belied Butler, and one clearly chosen for a particular impact. In 1883 Butler was a striking and energetic forty-four-year-old, a decorated hero of the Asante and Egyptian campaigns, the author of one of the most widely-read travel books of the decade, an intelligent conversationalist, and, as an aide-de-camp to the queen, a socialite of some standing.

While all counsel were in court for the opening of the trial, the co-respondents first came to court as observers on different days. Bird was present from the start of the proceedings. Blandford made his appearance on the fourth day, Shaw only on the fifth. By the tenth day of the trial, when counsel for the co-respondents began their opening statements, Butler had still not appeared. There were rumours that he had decamped to Brittany, leaving it to his counsel to put up a fight for him.

On the eleventh day, when Murphy QC rose to speak, his client was still not in court. Murphy opened forcefully on behalf of the absent Butler:

> A more outrageous attempt had never been made to inflict a charge of guilt on an English lady and gentleman than that of the endeavour to bring home the accusation of immoral relations between General [*sic*] Butler and Lady Colin Campbell. He ventured to think that if ever there was an instance of an ordinary visit paid by an English gentleman to an English lady ... which could not create suspicion it was this one. General Butler had been acquainted with the family of Lady Colin and with Lady Colin herself for many years. He drove up to the door in a hansom and rang the bell and gave his name ... During his visit Lord Colin returned home ill and was put to bed by his nurse. General Butler being aware of the fact came down without too much noise, that might have disturbed the sick man ... There was no concealment about his visit, his name was given; and yet because a person who is over 6 feet high went downstairs with as little noise as possible and let himself out, that was to be called a surreptitious visit, and that was the evidence on which he was placed in the position of a co-respondent.[9]

Murphy's defence of Butler masked an increasing anxiety that his client was not going to appear in court to defend himself: frantic behind-the-scenes efforts had been going on, without success, to get Butler back from Dinan. These efforts were not confined to Butler's legal team: Lady Campbell's legal team thought it vital to have Butler attend to deny the charge against him. Just before the start of the trial, on 15 November, Lady Campbell herself had written directly to Butler in Dinan. She addressed him as 'a friend a gentleman and a soldier', and reminded him that in the previous year when he had met her at her solicitors he had said that he would attend when the case was heard. Butler had replied briefly on 23 November, saying that he was resolved not to appear in person and giving no explanation for this stance.[10]

On the fourteenth day of the trial, Blandford and Shaw went into the witness box, denied under oath the charges of adultery and submitted to cross-examination. The court rose at the end of the day awash with speculation as to whether Butler would be in court the following morning. He was not, and Murphy told a hushed court that his client would not be appearing in his own defence. Proceedings moved on to the examination and cross-examination of Bird, who, like Blandford and Shaw, denied the charge of adultery.

The non-appearance of Butler provided the greatest excitement of a sensational case. Murphy's oratorical skills were tested to the limit as he made his closing statement on what he called 'a rag of a case' against his client:

> Though his client had not gone into the witness box there really was no substantial evidence against him ... [his] absence would doubtless be explained on the ground that Butler was a guilty man, but an honourable man who would not deny the charge against him and tell an untruth. But those that gave that explanation must know that if Butler was a man who would not tell an untruth of that kind, *a fortiori*, he was not a man who would commit the offence with which he was charged. He had no right to tell the jury what were the views of General [sic] Butler which had induced him to absent himself but if it were held that one inference were alone possible, he would remind the court that there were some men who held that all divorce proceedings were wrong and contrary to God's laws and that an accusation of this kind made against a man of honour was sure to fail because of its own inherent weakness ... He concluded by asking the jury to bear in mind that a man ought not to be called upon to answer an accusation until some ground was shown for believing it to be true."

In his closing address to the jury, Robert Finlay, for Lord Campbell, tore into Butler's counsel and Butler himself:

> All that heavy artillery of his learned friend was only meant to cover the retreat of the gallant general. For the last three weeks he by his two counsel and a solicitor had been entering with gusto into the case, but when the time came for his appearance in person he was not here, though it had never been suggested since the trial began that he was further away from London than Dinan. They had learned that Sir [*sic*] William Butler was an honourable man and a gallant soldier, well he believed that Sir William was that; but he might be an honourable and gallant soldier without being a Joseph ... From evidence given days ago General Butler must have known that if he had not committed adultery with Lady Colin Campbell his evidence that he had not would be vital to clear an innocent woman. That being so could the jury believe that such a man as General Butler would

remain away, if without committing perjury, he could enter the witness box and deny Lady Campbell's adultery with him? The absence of General Butler was decisive of this – that he knew he would be committing perjury if he swore that Lady Colin had not with him been guilty of the immorality with which she was charged, and that, though he had been guilty of adultery, he declined to be guilty of perjury.[12]

The judge, Sir Charles Parker Butt, in his summing up was ambivalent about Butler. The evidence against him was 'not great', and the judge 'could not quite agree' with Finlay's argument. He pointed out to the jury that offences against all four co-respondents 'are brought home to them not by suspicion but by proof'. However, Butler's presumed innocence still left his character impugned. Butt addressed this matter directly:

> If he is innocent of this charge it is difficult to exaggerate the meanness of this man – this fine upstanding soldier as he has been called – from appearing before you. Just consider the position, on the assumption that he is innocent. For fear of some personal inconvenience to himself, for fear of some possible discredit that may attach to his evidence, he leaves this woman, whom he prejudges by his absence, to be falsely accused and prosecuted in this court on a charge of this kind. Whatever may have been his views with regard to his duty to himself, what excuse can he give for his neglect of his duty to her?[13]

Butt's exhaustive summary of the case lasted three hours. It was 6.45 p.m. on 20 December when the jury retired to consider its verdicts. After three and a half hours the jury reported itself decided on the first suit, the charge of adultery against Lord Campbell, but divided on the second suit, the alleged adultery of Lady Campbell with each of the co-respondents. The judge urged them to deliberate further. They again retired, and at 10.15 p.m. returned to the packed courtroom with their verdicts.

Six questions were formally put to the foreman. He was first asked if the jury found that Lord Colin Campbell had committed adultery with Mary Watson. His answer to this was no. He was next asked if the jury had found that Lady Colin Campbell had committed adultery with the Duke of Marlborough. Again the answer was no, and this time it was greeted with applause. With regard to adultery with Shaw, Butler and Bird, the answers were also no. Finally the foreman was asked if the jury had found that Lady Colin Campbell had committed adultery with a person or persons unknown. Again the answer was no. On each count the jury verdict was unanimous. With those verdicts Lord and Lady Campbell would remain married to each other.

The jury was concerned to make public its reason for the long deliberations. The foreman was permitted to add a rider to its verdict, and he was applauded when he read it out: 'The jury desire to express their opinion that in not coming forward in the interests of justice, General [*sic*] Butler acted in a manner unworthy of an English officer and gentleman and is responsible for the jury's difficulties in coming to a decision.'[14]

In the aftermath of the case there was public judgment of all the principals. Butler was the one for whom the strongest criticism was reserved. *The Times* singled him out in an editorial on 21 December. Acknowledging that the case against him was weak, it found his refusal to go into the witness box inexplicable:

> It is extremely dificult to form any theory consistent with the consciousness of innocence to account for his conduct. The reputation of a woman was at stake, the reputations of other men were likely to be to some extent injuriously affected by his silence. Every motive that can be supposed to weigh with a gentleman dictated a frank and positive denial of the charge, if denial was possible, yet General [*sic*] Butler did not appear.[15]

And there was more. The day following the trial, Gertrude Campbell made an excoriating statement to her solicitors as to why Butler had not attended court:

> He has been making pilgrimages I hear to the shrine of St. Martin and other warrior saints of olden times, deriving much spiritual ecstasy therefrom.[16]

The Times editorial judgment on Butler was echoed by the rest of the press, with the one exception of *The Tablet*, England's leading Catholic weekly. It was controlled by Cardinal Manning, who had officiated at Butler's wedding. Its editor was John Snead, who had a wide circle of Irish and Catholic friends. The Christmas Day issue carried a 1600-word editorial headed 'The Court of Shame'. It opened with a reference to Lady Colin as a 'wronged and hunted woman', beset by 'a little army of discharged servants and hired spies'. Then it moved quickly to 'the distinguished Catholic soldier whose name since this trial has been so sadly dragged in the mud, and upon whose stainless honour every warrior in Grub Street now feels himself permitted to spit'.[7]

The Tablet's explanation of Butler's absence was an expansion of Murphy's: the divorce court was 'a well of defilement', which in the Campbell case had 'flooded all the land with filth and, as we verily believe, tainted the whole moral atmosphere of our time'. The editorial went on to say that Catholic instincts and Catholic ideals could be alien to Protestant instincts and ideals; a Catholic might in conscience avoid appearing in a divorce court because of its intrinsic immorality. And in Butler's case the evidence against him was so weak that his appearance would give a moral respectability to an immoral law. This argument of *The Tablet* is vitiated, however, by the fact that Butler engaged counsel in his own defence, and that his senior counsel was a Catholic.

Edward McCourt in his biography of Butler dismissed as facile the explanation, attributed to Wilfrid Meynell, that Butler did not appear in court because, 'although innocent himself, he was afraid that truthful testimony under cross-examination might implicate others and convict Lady Colin. In order therefore to protect Lady Colin's reputation he gallantly risked his own and in so doing almost destroyed both.'[18] McCourt suggested that Butler's refusal to appear in court was 'in fact a refusal to lend himself to the making of a Mayfair circus; and that he was untouched by the charge of having washed his hands because he knew he had not soiled them'.[19]

There is another explanation. Butler's non-appearance in court may be indicative not only of his gallantry but of something else – his sexual interest in Gertrude Campbell. Contemporary accounts of the trial, and all published references to it since, have treated Butler as if he was *sui generis*. He was not. He was a married man, whose wife was expecting their fourth child. He was also restless and, after the challenge of the invasion of Egypt, stifled with the routine of Devonport.

Why did Butler call, alone, on Gertrude Campbell on 'five or six' occasions during the late spring and early summer of 1883? Of course, he was solicitous for her welfare, he would have heard the rumours sweeping London about the state of her marriage. When he met Gertrude Campbell at the Mansion House on 11 April, he was flattered to be invited to call to Cadogan Place. Ostensibly, he went there as an old friend of herself and her family: he also went in the role of a wooer.

On this interpretation, Butler would have had two separate reasons for not appearing in court. The first would concern himself alone. The probability is that Butler did not commit adultery with Gertrude Campbell. However, he may still have had something to hide. Once he was cited, he had no option but to protect his reputation by contesting the charge of adultery. He engaged the services of a highly experienced senior counsel for his defence. The next obvious step for him was to appear in court and deny under oath the charge against him. Yet he did not do this. He was satisfied to leave his defence in the hands of his counsel. If he took the stand, he would be cross-examined, and he could expect a range of probing questions about his afternoons with Gertrude Campbell. What did they talk about for up to two hours? Was he aware of Lady Campbell's marital difficulties before he visited? Where did he sit while in the drawing-room? Was Lady Campbell at any time distressed? Did he comfort her?

This line of enquiry could have lead very easily to Butler's 'possible discredit', to use the words of the trial judge. Butler was not a prevaricator. He would be unable under oath to trim the truth. His personal testimony therefore, while it might clear him of adultery, would not clear him of suspicion about his motives in visiting Gertrude Campbell. Whether he attended court or stayed away, the outcome for him would be much the same – most unsatisfactory. His absence would at least have the merit of saving him acute embarrassment. In the circumstances, he left it to his counsel to rebut the charge against him.

The other reason for his absence would be related to his wife. If his visits to Gertrude Campbell were motivated by sexual interest, these visits may have been ones he did not reveal at the time to Elizabeth. Their eventual disclosure could have been as early as July 1883, at the time of Lord Campbell's confrontation with the Blood family. Elizabeth certainly knew of the visits before Butler left on the Gordon Relief expedition.[20] In any event, Butler's contacts with Lady Colin were something that required explaining to Elizabeth and something that she would be justifiably aggrieved about. It would not ease matters that at the time Butler's comfortable material circumstances were partly due to Elizabeth's accumulated capital from her paintings.

The passing of this marital milestone would then have been on the private understanding between the spouses that Butler would get personally involved no further. This understanding would probably have been reached during Butler's home leave in the summer of 1885 – after he made his formal statement to Gertrude Campbell's solicitors denying ever having been in love with her.

The divorce case profoundly marked on the one side Gertrude Campbell and on the other William and Elizabeth Butler. The Butlers' friendship with Gertrude Campbell and the Blood family was destroyed by Butler's refusal to appear in court. During the course of the trial there was a short exchange of correspondence between Gertrude Campbell and Elizabeth Butler which shows why. The two letters, reproduced below, illustrate both Gertrude Campbell's desperation at the prospect of being branded an adulteress, and Elizabeth Butler's cool resolve to protect the citadel of her own marriage. Gertrude Campbell's appeals to womanhood and friendship wither before Elizabeth Butler's glacial response.

Gertrude Campbell to Elizabeth Butler

13 December 1886

My dear Lady [*sic*] Butler

I do not know if you are aware of all the efforts I have made to induce your husband to return to his original intention of appearing in person at the present trial, but as those efforts and all of the many others I have caused to be made on all sides have failed utterly in producing any effect, I write now to you to make a last appeal to your womanhood to try and persuade your husband to come forward and repeat the denial which he has already made in his statement and in his letter to Mr. Lewis of a year ago. It is simply my life as well as my honour that are at stake for if your husband does not appear the case must surely go against him, and to lose this case would be my death blow.

Will you therefore stand by and see another woman done to death before your eyes when you can so easily prevent it? I pray and beseech you to help me in this the darkest hour of my life and get your husband to reconsider his last decision and appear in court. What harm can it possibly do him to deny a fact which is already disproved – namely about his two visits to me. I have been and am fighting a battle as hard as any woman ever had to fight. Have you then as a woman, let alone as a friend who has known you and yours for so long, no pity or sorrow for me? If you have you will induce your husband to come forward and do what he can as any honourable man would to help me in the battle which, remember, I am fighting as much for his honour as for my own.

As you hope for mercy on the last day show mercy to me now and lighten the load which is almost past endurance to bear, by persuading your husband to appear –

I remain very sincerely yours
Gertrude Elizabeth Campbell.

Elizabeth Butler to Gertrude Campbell.

15 Dec 1886

Dear Lady Colin Campbell
In answer to your letter received this morning I beg to say that I am fully aware of all the efforts you have made and have caused to be made to induce my husband to appear at your trial. Your appeal to me touches me deeply. I would I could help you, but I believe this case to have passed out of our hands and to have gone before a tribunal where human aid is impossible –

I remain sincerely yours
Elizabeth Butler."

Chapter Twelve

RETRENCHMENT AND RENEWAL

The events of Butler's adult life show two critical turning points, each of which pressed him into an examination of himself and of his values. The first of these was the shock of the Asante War of 1873–4 when he was thirty-five years old. At that time he faced not only the stigma of personal failure, but death. The second, when he was sixty, was the blow to his professional reputation when he resigned his command in South Africa in 1899. Between these two crises, one private, one public, there was another development in Butler's life, less sudden and distinct but no less crucial. This was the deepening of his relationship with his wife. It was triggered by the Campbell scandal.

Following their marriage in June 1877, the Butlers were together for less than twenty-one months before the upheaval of Butler's year long assignment in Natal. Subsequently, he continued to hanker after Canada. There was his attempt in 1881 to join a civil expedition to the Mackenzie River, and his seven-week trip to Saskatchewan at the end of 1883, followed by a two-month military assignment in Ottawa. In addition to the two months of the Egyptian campaign in 1882, he was away from home on the Nile from September 1884 to July 1886, except for two months leave during the summer of 1885. This pattern of absence from the domestic hearth was not conducive to a strengthening of matrimonial ties.

As the Campbell scandal swept London in 1884 Butler was forced to rethink his priorities and his responsibilities. Elizabeth's trip to Egypt in late 1885 with the two eldest children, and her subsequent stay in Wadi Halfa, are the clearest outward sign of the support she was prepared to give him in the upcoming divorce case. The family move to Dinan in late 1886, as it drew Butler heavily into his role as paterfamilias, sent the strongest social signal of the deepening of the relationship between husband and wife.

The Butlers spent eighteen months in Dinan where there was much sunshine,

> and even the lessening balance at the banker's did not lessen the sunshine beaming from the eyes of the growing group of children who used to romp and play in the terrain between the old house and the railway...'

From those days there exists a pen sketch of the Butler ménage by Gertrude Sweetman who would become one of Elizabeth Butler's closest friends. The Sweetmans were related by marriage to Butler; two of his sisters, Mary and Alice, had married into the Sweetman family of Longtown, County Kildare. Gertrude Sweetman was on holiday near Dinan with her mother and sister when they received a visiting-card inviting them to call for afternoon tea:

> We found Lady Butler alone in the drawing room. Her hair, as I remember, was divided at the side, looped in two plaits and tied across with a large black bow. She wore a blue and white striped cotton [*sic*] as it was then very hot weather, and she captivated us all by her simplicity and charm of manner. Looking from one to the other of our party – which consisted of my mother my sister and myself – she exclaimed enthusiastically, 'At last we have met!' ... Sir William, full of vitality, came in just as the conversation was beginning to flag and began enquiries about our mutual relations. Later their two little girls appeared: the eldest about eight and the youngest, Eileen some years younger. I remember an amusing incident of the afternoon. Coos, the elder child, suddenly with her eyes shooting fire, attacked her little sister, exclaiming, 'You've got my dress on,' and furiously seized the garment in question, – which must have been lying for some time in a drawer as it showed evident marks of tucks, having been let down even for this small creature. In revenge for this outrage she proceeded to snatch a bright coloured handkerchief which the little Eileen was clasping with much affection to her breast. She held on to it like grim death, crimson in the face; her father laughing and approving the fierce struggle which ensued, whilst her mother, characteristically placid, only remarked at intervals, 'Don't, dears'.²

Gertrude Sweetman's reference to *Lady* Butler and *Sir* William marks Butler's new status. In April 1887 he had been invested at Windsor Castle as a Knight Commander of the Bath, for his services on the Egyptian frontier. The honour was all the more valuable to him for being conferred in the golden jubilee year of Victoria's accession to the throne of the United Kingdom of Great Britain and Ireland.

Elizabeth continued her painting at Dinan. Butler himself spent much of his time writing. The next decade would be his most sustained period of publication. In 1887 his *The Campaign of the Cataracts*, the account of the Gordon Relief Expedition which he had begun at Merowe in March 1885, was published with illustrations by Elizabeth. It was well received. Its detailed descriptions of working through the cataracts, of ferrying men and supplies up the Nile, were complemented by reflective passages which placed modern human endeavour against aeons of time.

Butler now turned to biography, taking as his subjects military heroes. His first subject was Gordon. *Charles George Gordon*, published in 1889 in the Macmillan *English Men of Action* series was described by the *Annual Register* as 'perhaps the best life' of Gordon, and is still a very readable volume. There is an immediacy and vigour in the writing which is fuelled by Butler's involvement in the relief expedition of 1884-5, and by the strong impact that Gordon had made upon him over their club dinner in 1877. Butler's achievement in *Gordon* was to present his subject convincingly as an extraordinary man, without distorting the facts of his career setbacks or ignoring his eccentricity and his unsettlingly introspective nature. Gordon emerges from the biography as an exemplary Christian. 'Bigotry, that common weakness of even great minds, he was absolutely devoid of.'[3]

Gordon has the customary Butler subtext – the faults of empire: its greed and rapacity; its blindness to cultural values other than its own; its siding with the strong against the weak. Occasionally, the undisguised voice of Butler's own experience breaks into the narrative, as when he remarks of Gordon's time in Equatoria during the mid-1870s that

> 'The man who works at the Nile frontier must expect to have his work and his motives by the time they reach Cairo, rent and twisted and tortured out of shape as though they had in concrete and bodily form been sent down the windings and cataracts and whirlpools of the great river.'[4]

Into *Gordon*, Butler also brought Ireland. Gordon had spent part of his childhood at the Pigeon House Fort on Dublin Bay while his father, an artillery officer, was stationed there. He had returned to Ireland in 1880 for a month's tour of the west and south-west to see for himself the state of the land question and the plight of the poor. He subsequently wrote a long letter to Gladstone critical of establishment policy. Butler quoted this letter in its entirety on the grounds that

> The question of Ireland is still an open one ... the warning voice of this great soldier is raised in vain. He is listened to when he speaks in the cause of some distant race in Central Africa; and he has legions of admiring readers when he points the road to right and justice for some nameless tribe in the remote Soudan; but he is ridiculed and told he knows nothing of his subject when he tells the people of England that within twelve hours of the capital there exists a deeper misery and a more unnatural injustice.[5]

Butler's second biography, a life of General Sir Charles Napier, also had an Irish dimension. Napier was the officer who, according to *Punch*, had put his classical education to practical use by coining a Latin pun – *Peccavi* – to report his conquest of Sind in north-west India in 1843. *Sir Charles Napier* was published in the *English Men of Action* series in 1890. It had a mixed reception. Wolseley read the book during a rough crossing of the Irish Sea and wrote about it to his wife:

> It is good and it is bad. Some parts very good, but it aggravates me occasionally when he [Butler] magnifies France to depreciate England. Anything that can be twisted into a glorification of the Celtic race is made to perform on his stage and lauded by a magniloquent chorus. He writes very well and often most touchingly and sympathetically, but there is always too much straining after word effect, too great a conscious [*sic*] of superior skill.[6]

Charles Napier was born in England in 1782, but when he was four years old his family came to live in Ireland, at Celbridge, County Kildare. Napier's personal qualities did not endear him to others. He was a social misfit from his earliest days, hot-tempered and arrogant. Compromise did not come easily to him. As a young ensign he joined the Limerick-based 22nd Regiment of Foot, most of whose rank and file were Tipperary men. What drew Butler to him as a subject were Napier's sense of justice and political sympathies. Napier was a radical who during his life castigated corrupt electoral practices, the restricted franchise, and vested interests that

blocked reform, and supported minority causes such as the rights of aboriginal Australians.

Butler's biography of Napier, like his biography of Gordon, is a highly
sympathetic portrait of its subject. Gordon and Napier were soldiers distinguished by reckless courage, uninhibited outspokenness, and deeply
held personal beliefs that had led them to reject much of the world around
them. For Butler they were heroic and inspirational figures who sacrificed
their comfort, their career prospects and, in Gordon's case, life itself, for
the betterment of mankind. His choice of these two men as biographical
subjects during his middle years is indicative of the value he himself put on
courage, compassion and the ideal of service. It is instructive to contrast
Butler with Gordon and Napier, against whom he appears almost staid.
Like them, he was a career soldier, but though he was outspoken, it was
usually within limits acceptable to the military establishment. He was neither a maverick nor a fanatic; his contemplative qualities manifested
themselves in his writings and in a love of the out-of-doors, rather than in
withdrawal and isolation.

Wolseley had carped at *Napier*. He did not like what he saw as Butler's
'glorification of the Celtic race'. This referred in part to Butler's gripping
account of the battle of Miani in 1843, where Napier's force included 400
Irishmen from his old Limerick regiment:

> The leading line – the Twenty-Second Regiment – is only one hundred
> yards from the enemy. The moment had come for the chief skirmishers to
> fall back and give place to the chief combatants now so near each other.
> Napier puts himself in front of the Irish soldiers whose serried line of steel
> and scarlet extends two hundred yards from right to left, and then the com-
> mand to charge rings out as three and thirty years earlier it had sounded
> above the strife of Corunna. Until this moment the fire of the skirmishers
> has partly hidden the movement of formations behind, but when the magic
> word that flings the soldier upon his enemy was heard, there came out of
> this veiling smoke a sight that no Beloochee had ever seen before, for bend-
> ing with the forward surge of a mighty movement, the red wall of the 22nd
> fronted with steel is coming on at the charge.[7]

The pull of Ireland had been becoming stronger for Butler since the
mid-1880s. On his short visit to Ireland in 1885 he had become keenly interested in the new nationalist politics, and during his time at Wadi Halfa
had kept abreast of Irish developments. These had acquired a new mo-

mentum after the general election of November 1885 which had led to a result pregnant with possibilities for Ireland. The Nationalist Party under Parnell held a power balance. In January 1886 Parnell voted the Liberals into government and Gladstone embarked on a policy of Home Rule for Ireland.

About this time Butler took a tentative and abortive step into political lobbying by writing from Wadi Halfa to one of Gladstone's cabinet, probably John Morley, the Chief Secretary for Ireland. The subject of his correspondence is lost, but news of it caused a brief flutter in the War Office, addding to Butler's woes on the frontier. Wolseley referred to this correspondence in his homily of May 1886 when he had taxed Butler with conduct verging on the insubordinate:

> As I am on the fault-finding-tack, I shall wind up with a piece of advice about political matters. You and I as soldiers have nothing to do with political questions such as Home Rule. And as we are both Irishmen we should be very guarded as long as we wear the Queen's uniform to say nothing that any hearer can in any way construe into disloyalty to the Queen or to the United Kingdom over which she rules.
>
> May I venture to say that you have no right to open a correspondence with any of Her Majesty's ministers on public matters and your doing so is as foolish as it is unwarrantable ... I am most anxious to serve you but I cannot do so if you become a politician. We don't want politics in the army. We belong to a great empire. Let us all strive to add to its renown and strength.[8]

Wolseley was a convinced Unionist. He believed that Home Rule would hand Ireland over to the wrong people and would lead, first, to the break up of the United Kingdom, and then to the dismemberment of the Empire. Butler, in contrast, believed that Home Rule would make for a more equitable distribution of power in Ireland; it would curb violence and induce respect for law; it would strengthen, not weaken, the United Kingdom and the Empire.

In April 1888 Butler left Brittany and moved with his family to Delgany, 'a little nook among the beautiful Wicklow hills'. The move was a substantial upheaval. Trying to settle into their new home Elizabeth wrote to her sister Alice:

> We arrived here at 9.30 a.m. last Friday having left Dinan at 3 p.m. on Wednesday and I must say that I was tired! But I think that the journey

was worthy of record as one of the great forced marches of history with three small children, two raw Breton maids and some 27 packages. Delgany is a very clean thatched whitewashed hamlet with none of that feeling of dilapidation and pigs which one has so resolutely to master while enjoying the grand scenery around and beyond the villages of Clare and Kerry ...'

'Monavoe', the Butlers' new rented home, was a spacious detached country house just outside the village. A couple of hours drive away, at Avondale, was the family estate of Parnell. Parnell had a hunting lodge at Augavanagh on the southern slopes of Lugnaquilla, Wicklow's highest mountain. Parnell himself had assumed heroic stature in Ireland. Gladstone's first Home Rule Bill had failed and the Conservatives under Lord Salisbury were in power. The Irish land question was again causing major tension, and another destructive cycle of agrarian outrage-reprisal-outrage was in motion. When in 1887 *The Times* published letters implicating Parnell in the 1882 assassinations of Chief Secretary Cavendish and Under Secretary Burke in the Phoenix Park, nationalist Ireland rallied to him as the victim of forgeries.

In August 1888 at the start of the grouse season, Butler was invited over from the ordered landscape of Delgany to join Parnell and a group of nationalist MPs in the heart of the mountain massif. Butler studied Parnell over the next few days:

> ... one of the most remarkable men then living in the Empire ... Tall and strikingly handsome there was in him something beyond definition or description. It was power, utterly careless of its possession, seemingly unconscious of its own strength, unaggressive in its mastery, unstudied, impassive, without one touch of haughtiness ... The quality in Parnell that most impressed me was the entire absence of sense or thought of superiority. Even in the most trifling details of life this was apparent. When he opened his gun-case the gun was found rusty; but he would take no help in the cleaning of it; he did it himself. He did not seem to be self-conscious in anything.[10]

At the end of August 1888, shortly after his visit to Augavanagh, Butler received a commission to undertake an examination of army ordnance. During the previous two years he had not lost touch with developments at the War Office. A restructuring of the top military posts had taken place over 1887–8. This had left Wolseley *in situ* as Adjutant General, next in standing to the Commander-in-Chief, the Duke of Cambridge, who was now in his seventies. The restructuring had created the post of Quarter-master General and Redvers Buller was promoted to fill it. His responsibilities included food, quarters and troop movements. However, it was the civil arm of the War Office that looked after ordnance – supplies and munitions. This was an inefficient system and, from the point of view of the military, a most unsatisfactory one. It was agreed that the Ordnance Department should be examined. Wolseley's choice for the exercise was Butler, to be assisted by a Colonel Henry McGregor.

The choice of Butler was no accident. He could be relied on to produce a detailed and provocative report. To allow him maximum flexibility during the four months he worked on the report, he was not brought back on staff until its completion. He was given access to 'Piles of Blue Books and Reports ... dead liturgies of the preceding fifty years'. The finished report ran to twenty pages, incorporating fifty-five clauses and four extensive appendices. It was lucid and well-written and its conclusion was measured and emphatic. Within the Ordnance Store Department there was

> ... not so much a fault of system as a want of system. Want of a higher stronger determining influence acting upon a lower fixed executive. The great trade test of profit and loss cannot be applied to government establishments but the proof of efficiency can always be demanded and if the absence of that proof has been made more palpable year by year in our Ordnance Department it is only because the ill-set foundations of the past have had year by year a heavier weight imposed upon them."

If that image of a fundamental flaw was certain to annoy the civil arm of the War Office, it was the report's appendices, with their specific proposals for change, which outraged a sizeable element in the military, for whom anything to do with trade was too vulgar a process for a gentleman to engage in. The report was not formally presented to the Secretary of State until 25 February 1889. It was shelved as too radical, though most of its proposals would eventually be accepted.

Butler meanwhile was back on staff since 17 December 1888. He had resumed duty as an assistant adjutant general attached to the War Office and been promoted to the substantive grade of full colonel. Delgany remained his home and he became a frequent traveller on the Kingstown–Holyhead ferry where his travelling companions were often nationalist MPs with whom he socialized. He followed Irish issues at Westminster closely. The

Parnell forgeries investigation was nearing its climax and on the afternoon of 22 February 1889 Butler came down to the Law Courts for the cross-examination of the forger Richard Pigott. He was unable to get into the public gallery, so he sent in his card to Parnell who came out personally and brought him into the well of the courtroom where he sat at the table of Parnell's solicitor.

The collapse of Pigott has passed into Irish folklore. Parnell's counsel, Sir Charles Russell – who had defended Lady Colin Campbell – asked Pigott to write down certain words that had been misspelt in the original letters. Butler watched fascinated:

> There was the historic scene set in cramped and clammy compass. The three judges to my left, the narrow round table [at] which the rival counsel were seated, the commanding figure of Sir Charles Russell on the right and above all, full in front, at the further side of the table, the small witness box, with the short bloated figure of Pigott in it, his toad-like face and bull neck streaming with perspiration, as he tried to answer in some shape the merciless questions which, in deep and ringing tones, the great counsel rapidly put to him. The climax had come. 'Take these, sir,' thundered the lawyer, as he handed up to the witness pen and paper, 'and write.' Then came three or four words in rapid command, and the trembling wretch in the box scribbled as the lesson was dictated. Then the words 'hesitancy' and 'likelihood' were spoken, and again the witness scribbled ... As the man wrote, the attention of the crowded court became so wrapt that one could hear the scrape of the pen upon the paper. 'Give me the paper, sir.' The fatal words were on it, misspelt again, as they had been misspelt in the forged letter.[12]

The vindication of Parnell was a severe embarrassment to the government of Salisbury. Parnell was at the acme of his power and appeared unassailable. Yet before the year's end he would be cited as the sole co-respondent in the *O'Shea* v *O'Shea* divorce suit. The outcome of this case would split the nationalists and wreck Parnell's career.

Butler's Irishness was becoming central to his view of himself. In Elizabeth he had a confidante with reciprocal views on Ireland. It was at this time, while living in Delgany, that Elizabeth embarked on her most famous Irish painting, *Evicted*. This canvas shows a barefoot peasant woman, her strong, upraised face bathed in light as she stands before the gable walls of her razed cottage, her strength and solidity emphasized by the grandeur of

the surrounding mountain landscape. In the distance are the receding figures of a police patrol and 'the crowbar brigade' – to use Butler's own
phrase about the eviction he had witnessed as a child.

The painting was exhibited at the Royal Academy in 1890 where its
subject caused some discomfiture.[13] At the Academy dinner, not attended
by the Butlers, who were in Egypt, Prime Minister Salisbury was the guest
of honour. His comment on *Evicted* was a calculated and crass down-play-
ing of the painting's subject matter: 'I will only say with respect to it there
is such an air of breezy cheerfulness and beauty about the landscape which
is painted, that it makes me long to take part in an eviction myself.'[14]

Following his return to the War Office at the end of 1888, Butler had in-
dicated that he would be interested in a posting abroad. At the end of 1889
he was offered postings to either Alexandria or Singapore. He had no hesitation in choosing Alexandria. He had liked Egypt with its wide skies and
its great river. Alexandria, on the Mediterranean shore of the Nile delta,
had the further advantage of being easily accessible by train and steamer
from England. He would have annual home leave, and Elizabeth could visit
during the lengthy cool season. It would be his fourth tour of service in
Egypt and a more leisured one than any of the preceding three. He left
London in late February 1890 and on 7 March, with the local rank of brigadier-general, took up his post as commanding officer of the garrison of
the army of occupation in Alexandria.

The British occupation of Egypt was in its eighth year. The country
was quiet, with Khedive Tawfiq still in Cairo, and Sir Evelyn Baring still
Consul General. There was no talk of British withdrawal. The realities of
power were evident in a number of ways, not least militarily. There were
two armies in Egypt: the Egyptian army and the British army of occupation. The titular head of the Egyptian army was the khedive, but control
rested with the British sirdar. The British army of occupation had its headquarters in Cairo and Alexandria held its second garrison, which consisted
of two regiments. The city was cosmopolitan: 40,000 of its 300,000 in-
habitants were foreigners and ninety per cent of all Egyptian trade passed
through the port.

By early April 1890 Elizabeth, unaccompanied by any of the children
because of the risk to their health, had joined Butler for a ten-week visit.
Butler's quarters were a spacious flat in Government House which overlooked the sea on the Boulevard de Ramleh. He had numerous public
functions to perform. Elizabeth was obliged to co-host several receptions

for visiting dignitaries, something which with her shyness and lack of small-talk she found an ordeal, in contrast to her sociable and eloquent spouse. This routine was to be part of her sojourns during the next three winter seasons.

Butler's material needs were well catered for. He had a good wine cellar and the services of an excellent majordomo, a Maltese named Magro. During Elizabeth's time in Alexandria Magro would be very attentive to her:

> A good honest Maltese, his devotion to 'Sair William' was really touching. I was only as the moon is to the sun, and to serve the sun he would, I am convinced, have risked his life. I came in for his devotion to myself by reason of my reflected glory. One morning he came hurtling towards me through the rooms, waving aloft what at first looked like a red republican flag, but it proved to be a sirloin or other portion of bovine anatomy which he had the luck to purchase in the market (good beef being so rare). 'Look miladi, you will not often meet such beef walking in the street!' ... This is the way he used to ask me for the daily orders: 'What will miladi command for dinner? Cutlets? (patting his ribs); 'a loin?' (indications of lumbago); 'or a leg?' (advancing that limb); 'or, for a delicate entree, brains' (laying a finger on his perspiring forehead).[5]

While in Egypt, Elizabeth made the most of her opportunities to sketch and watercolour. While she was in Ireland, Butler used much of his leisure time to steep himself in the Egyptian campaign of Napoleon. He visited many of the historic sites associated with 'the Great Captain' and his other outdoor pursuits included horseriding in the desert and wild-fowl-shooting in the swamps of the delta.

Butler made full use of his opportunities to travel outside Egypt. In June 1891, with Elizabeth, he visited Arcole, Marengo and Austerlitz, and other Napoleonic battle sites. However, Butler's most outstanding journey during these years was the pilgrimage he and Elizabeth made in Palestine at Easter 1891. Elizabeth called it 'the most memorable journey of our lives'. Palestine, like Egypt, was part of the Ottoman empire. It was a country still without railways, though that did not deter the heavy traffic that passed through the port of Jaffa to visit the most sacred sites of Christendom. The Butlers embarked from sleazy Port Said, 'a hideosity in a coconut shell', on a pilgrim ferry where Butler was not impressed by his fellow passengers: 'pilgrims – mostly grim pilgrims – man-eyed English and

Scottish women in helmets and great puggarees with husbands of a more feminine type; clergymen of many persuasions; hopeless-nosed men'.[16]

Butler had been adamant about not being part of an organized tour. He and Elizabeth had their own horses and a couple of servants with pack animals. While they availed of lodgings in the main towns, they also camped as they rode north from Jerusalem to Galilee. As they travelled, they found it an overwhelming experience to see the places hitherto known only as names from the Bible. Butler was fascinated by Jerusalem's smallness of scale and its redolence of a unique past. At Nazareth he found the environs powerfully evocative:

> It was here, on these grassy hills, that those wonderful Eyes drank in, through three and twenty years, all that imagery of fruit and flower, of seed and harvest time, all the secrets of the trees which afterwards became the theme of similitudes and parables. It was here that the Master prepared to manifest all that infinite knowledge of soul and sense, the pale reflection of which, as it is found in the Evangelists, has come as a moonbeam over the troubled river of the lives of men.[17]

Butler commanded at Alexandria for over three and a half years, during which Egypt continued on the road being mapped out for it by Baring who, in 1892, was elevated to the peerage as Lord Cromer. In December of that year, Butler was promoted to the substantive rank of major-general.

The consolidation of British power in Egypt had been paralleled by increased British involvement in other parts of the continent, and by the early 1890s the political map of Africa had seen huge changes. Already, for those who dreamed of the Union Jack fluttering from a thousand flagpoles between the Cape of Good Hope and Cairo, the dream was becoming feasible. In the late autumn of 1893 Butler's Alexandria command came to a close and he returned to England for a home posting. Everyday life had not stood still during his absence abroad. London had its first tube train; there was a telephone line between London and Paris; electricity for domestic and public lighting was coming into general use; bicycles with equal-sized wheels and pneumatic tyres were revolutionizing leisure activities for the young, while from across the Atlantic there was news that a Henry Ford had designed a gasoline buggy.

At the War Office there had also been changes. Wolseley was no longer there. His old post as Adjutant General had gone to Buller, while he himself was in charge of the armed forces in – of all places – Ireland. He had taken up this post six months after Butler had gone to Alexandria. In Dublin his official residence was the Royal Hospital at Kilmainham, not far from his birthplace in Goldenbridge. He hated being back in 'dirty Paddyland', and on a tour of inspection of Munster wrote to his wife from Bandon: 'I hope when our ship comes in, our lines may be cast elsewhere than in squalid Ireland. Decay meets you on all sides: decay without any of those associations that make it lovable and interesting; decay joined to dirt, untidyness [*sic*] and squalor.'[18]

The ensuing years did not soften Wolseley's attitude, his only solace being that nationalist Ireland was in disarray, traumatised by the death of Parnell and a deep rift in the Irish Parliamentary Party. In November 1890 Parnell had been found guilty of adultery with Katharine O'Shea and within a year, at the age of forty-five, he was dead. The party was lacerated by internal dissent and would remain split until 1900. Gladstone, back in government for a fourth term in 1892, had again tried unsuccessfully to get Home Rule on to the statute book. In March 1894 he would resign as Prime Minister to be replaced by his Foreign Secretary, the strongly imperialist Lord Rosebery.

Butler had hoped to secure a command of his own in England, but there were no immediate vacancies and on 11 November 1893 he took up a post in Aldershot, in charge of the Second Infantry Brigade. The camp was under the command of Arthur Duke of Connaught. Butler found Aldershot a congenial posting, and under his command the 2nd Brigade became the camp's most efficient unit.

At Aldershot, Butler lived *en famille* in a brick-and-timber bungalow. Dogs and horses were a big part of family life and the children went for frequent gallops on the downs. Butler had an old courts-martial hut converted into a studio for Elizabeth. During Butler's time their distinguished visitors included Queen Victoria, whom Elizabeth found 'shrunken into a tinier woman than ever she was'.

The most stimulating part of Butler's social life at Aldershot centred on Farnborough. There, the widowed Empress Eugenie, whose son had fallen to Zulu assegais in 1879, spent six months of each year. She had a small estate with its own chapel and a mausoleum to her son and husband. Butler was soon a welcome visitor at Farnborough. He and Elizabeth became quite close to the Empress who took a strong liking to their younger daughter Eileen. The family often rode over to mass at the Farnborough chapel. Butler's untiring interest in Napoleon was further stimulated at Farnborough where 'I seemed to live again in the atmosphere of the Great

Captain ... and it now seemed more than the mere accident of chance that I should have found near Aldershot, a centre of so many gathered Napoleonic interests, such a mass of memorials of that vanished time – portraits, busts, names and recollections of an unmatched epoch."⁹ The Empress as keeper of the Napoleonic legacy had a distinguished guest-list. Among others, Butler met the Princes Murat, Ney and Massena – scions of Napoleon's generals.

His contact with the empress stimulated Butler to attempt to write about Napoleon. Napoleon's last years fascinated him, but he was unable to find a suitable frame of reference for them. He had a working title, 'The Prisoner of St Helena', but he was never to get beyond a preliminary un-published essay. Napoleon remained elusive, an irruption into history, the means by which such terms as citizenship and democracy came to be the common political coin of Europe. What Butler saw as the promethean symbolism of his final years on St Helena remained too difficult for him to translate into a standard biographical framework.

From Aldershot, social events for the Butlers extended to London. There was the annual Queen's Ball at Buckingham Palace, and in June 1895 the Butlers were present for the laying of the foundation stone of West-minster Cathedral. There was also a trip to Italy in January 1896, during which they went to Rome and attended mass celebrated by Pope Leo XIII in the Sistine Chapel. This Italian journey was partly a celebration of But-ler's having secured promotion. On 24 February 1896 he became com-manding officer of the south-eastern district of England, an area that in-cluded the Cinque ports which he had first become familiar with some twenty-two years earlier while stationed at Hythe as a lieutenant. As his aide-de-camp he appointed his nephew, Captain Michael Sweetman, son of his sister Mary.

Butler moved with his family into the historic Dover Castle, superbly sited on a hill above the port. Contrasted with Aldershot, Dover Castle was sumptuous, though it shared one feature with the Aldershot bungalow – it was draughty. The Butler family quarters in the Constable's Tower, 'the best quarters in England', contained a full library and spacious rooms for entertaining. Elizabeth's retreat was a studio that overlooked the moat.

Family life was not without the normal strains between parents and adolescent children. As a father Butler conformed to Victorian stereotype. His younger daughter Eileen, twelve years old when the Butlers moved to Dover, was to look back on her adolescence with some vivid memories:

What is surprising is that one who in public life invariably championed the under-dog, should in his own home have been a complete autocrat. No one there ever dared dispute my father's will – least of all my mother, in whom loyalty was an outstanding quality, who detested rows, and who, fortunately had her studio into which to retreat ... To me as a child, he was an idol; but an idol to be worshipped from afar. My love for him was one of the strongest emotions of my life; but I was too shy of him ever to be able to demonstrate it to him. All I could do was – unknown to him – to half kill myself with work at school, so as to please him by bringing home all the prizes possible. Once when, with nervously thumping heart, I brought him the pile of books, and he beamed down at me, quoting:

> *And still he [sic] gazed and still the wonder grew*
> *That one small head could carry all she [sic] knew.*

I longed for him to know that the one small head had worked itself almost into a brain fever to achieve this result, and that it was the wish to give him pleasure that had been the driving force. But I could no more have told him that than I could have jumped over the moon. This was a pity, because beneath his stern exterior was a very tender heart which craved affection and it would have comforted him greatly had he known of the flame he had lit in the heart of his small daughter ...

With my brothers my father was overstrict. He would summon them to his study to receive what they called a 'jaw' for the most minor misdemeanours, and the atmosphere of the meals which followed was nerve-racking. While my heart ached for the boys – they were such *good* boys, I thought – I would laugh consumedly at the most trifling joke, (generally addressed to me) which my father, now relenting, would make; and I would look from under my eyelashes at my brothers' downcast faces, hoping to see some slight glimmer of a smile in response to my forced hilarity.[20]

This picture of a censorious father is softened by the reference to the 'very tender heart', and the image of the loquacious Butler doing his best to retrieve situations which he has created through an excess of paternal zeal.

Butler was rarely betrayed by his tongue in social situations. The contrary was usually the case. It is apparently from his time at Dover that the following story dates:

Once when a militant Protestant lady asked whether there was any truth in the report that an unhappy lady whose mysterious disappearance had intrigued the whole of England, had as alleged been abducted by the Jesuits, his answer came with crushing effect and without a moment's hesitation; 'No madam. I am in a position to positively contradict that rumour. Perhaps you are not aware that we Roman Catholics maintain a religious order especially for such services. We call them the Trappists.'[21]

Eighteen ninety-seven was the year of Victoria's diamond jubilee. The summer was heavy with imperial pageantry, in which Butler played his part. Ten years on from his quiet life in Dinan as a lieutenant-colonel on half-pay, he was in London for Jubilee Day. His ceremonial duties had him on a grey charger before the statue of Queen Anne outside St Paul's Cathedral.

During his time at Dover, Butler kept up his informal contacts with the War Office where recent developments had created much ill feeling. At the end of 1895 Wolseley, by then a field marshal, had achieved his ambition to become Commander-in-Chief, but the prize was dross. The government had used the retirement of the Duke of Cambridge to reorganize the War Office into five military departments, thus creating five top army posts: Commander-in-Chief, Adjutant General, Quarter Master General, Inspector General of Fortifications, and Inspector General of Ordnance. While the Commander-in-Chief remained chief military adviser to the Secretary of State for War, each of the other departmental heads was given direct access to the Secretary. Wolseley was reduced to being, in his own words 'the fifth wheel on the coach'. The metaphor was accurate. The post would disappear within eight years to be replaced by the post of Chief of Staff.

Wolseley himself was seriously ill during 1897 and his recuperation was slow. He was frail and had memory lapses. Butler, anxious about his welfare, visited him several times at his home in Glynde on the South Downs. In February 1898 he was happy to be able to write to Louisa Wolseley:

how more than pleasant it was to see my old chief and true friend of so many years looking so well happy and active. Most of the scenes of life upon which my memory dwells are associated with him in some way or another and to see and hear him last Sunday afternoon during our walk across the Downs was like a breath from some old scene bygone in South Africa or Canada.[22]

At Dover, Butler continued to research biography, working on a life of his old colleague George Colley. Following his death at the hands of the Boers at Majuba in 1881, Colley's reputation had not been a high one. Even Wolseley, his mentor, acknowledged that in the military sphere Colley had 'a tendency to attempt too much with too little'. Following the success of his lives of Gordon and Napier, several approaches were made to Butler to give Colley a memorial in print. He spent almost two and a half years on the work, examining blue books and despatches. Colley's private correspondence was also made available to him by his widow Edith. His research was to have an unexpected benefit: he would be well briefed for the South African commission that would be offered him at the end of 1898.

Butler's *The Life of George Pomeroy Colley*, published in 1899, was much less partisan than his biographies of Gordon and Napier. Running to over four hundred pages, it traced its gifted and insecure subject from his birth in 1835 through a career that allowed him to make extensive use of his considerable intellectual ability before precipitating him to an untimely death through his inexperience as a field commander. Almost one-third of *The Life of Colley* was given to the last month of his life which ended with the rout of the British force at Majuba Hill on the Natal–Transvaal border. Butler closed the biography with a typically graphic piece of descriptive writing, detailing the engagement at Majuba, where almost 600 British troops, holding an apparently impregnable position on the summit of the precipitous hill, were routed from it by less than 400 Boers who, in broad daylight, used stealth and marksmanship to achieve the summit and scatter the defenders. Colley, deserted by his panic-stricken men, 'found a soldier's death on the field he would not leave'.

Butler flatly acknowledged that Colley's decision not to entrench his men on Majuba was 'an omission' and he gave full recognition to the superiority of the Boers who stormed the summit:

> The men composing this leading attack although few in numbers, were admirably handled, or perhaps it would be more correct to describe the method of their advance not as being due to the will of one acting upon the many so much as the instinct of each individual unit acting on the whole body and producing without order or command the best result attainable. This indeed had been the secret of all the successes the Boers had hitherto gained. Their methods of fighting, their fire tactics and knowledge of the ground, were instincts imbibed from early youth upwards in the exercise of daily life amid the storm and sunshine of this wild land. Ours were

the dogmatic teachings of the barrack square, the acquired lessons on un-reasoned drill, the accepted formulas of collective movement, subordinat-ing action to one mind and one command and liable to produce inertness and helplessness whenever circumstances became such as previous precept had not contemplated.[23]

This passage was written in 1898. The date is important. During the course of the South African War, Butler was to be accused, among other things, of being wise after the event, of not having foreseen the military capability of the Boers. His 1898 tribute to Nicholas Smit's commando is proof of the contrary. *The Life of Colley* was well received. Wolseley was de-lighted with it: 'The book on Colley is quite excellent. It could not be done better and the expert cleverness with which you skate over dangerous and thin parts of the ice is incomparable ... The style is perfect; so easy and so natural and yet pregnant with thought and imaginative inspirations.'[24]

In February 1899 *The Times* gave the biography a 1500-word review, de-scribing it as 'an admirable book' with the story of Majuba 'admirably told'. It was recognized as being the work of a man who understood the Boers. Butler was fortunate in his publication date. It is impossible that such a lengthy and complimentary review could have appeared in *The Times* much later in the year, for by then his behaviour in South Africa was unleashing hostile comment in the London press.

Chapter Thirteen

THE NEW SOUTH AFRICA

Following the Boer War of 1880–1 the Transvaal had succeeded in securing internal autonomy from Britain. South Africa seemed set for a period of calm. The two British colonies, Cape and Natal, lived, if not quite in harmony, at least in some accord with the two Boer Republics, the Orange Free State and the Transvaal. The word *Afrikaaners* came into common use in the two colonies to describe Europeans of Dutch descent who, particularly in Cape Colony, formed a substantial portion of the white population. This state of affairs was ineradicably altered in 1886 when gold was discovered in the Transvaal, on the Witswatersrand – the rand – not far from Pretoria. It quickly became clear that here, not in some mythical South American El Dorado or in the Canadian Rockies, was the greatest source of gold in the world. This vast mineral wealth in a traditional farming community brought staggering developmental problems, as the Transvaal was transformed into the richest country in southern Africa and the Babylonian city of Johannesburg took sprawling shape on the veldt. Thousands of *uitlanders* or aliens, mainly Britons, swarmed into the Transvaal to work in mining and a myriad of ancillary activies.

Two figures dominated South Africa at this time, Paul Kruger and Cecil Rhodes. Kruger was president of the Transvaal, and while gold transformed his country he kept tight control of the mining industry. This caused resentment among the large entrepreneurs, many of whom had already made fortunes in the diamond mines of Kimberley and were well-established in Cape Colony. They came to be known as the 'randlords' and they included a strong group of Jewish financiers of German or British birth. Rhodes, an Englishman, was one of the wealthiest men in Cape Colony. His dream was to see the British empire expand in a continuous series of colonies from Cape to Cairo, and in 1887 he had founded the British South Africa Company (the BSAC) to exploit the high veldt north of the Transvaal. Rhodes came to believe that the only thing that would save South Africa for the empire was a British-dominated Transvaal. Political power would have to be wrested from Kruger and the instrument for this would be the *uitlanders* who were denied voting rights in the Transvaal. By 1895 Rhodes, now Prime Minister of Cape Colony, was secretly working with the major randlords of the Transvaal to get the *uitlanders* to revolt.

At first political events in Britain assisted him. Joseph Chamberlain, the radical Birmingham industrialist, was Conservative Colonial Secretary. Chamberlain was determined to restore British hegemony in the Transvaal. He covertly encouraged Rhodes in his attempts to topple Kruger. Rhodes had conceived an audacious plan: if the *uitlanders* raised the flag of revolt in Johannesburg, he would send across the western border of the Transvaal a mounted force led by Dr Leander Starr Jameson of the BSAC. However, the *uitlanders* continually balked and the revolt was postponed on several occasions. Jameson, who had assembled a small force of 470 men for an incursion, decided to raise the standard of revolt himself. On the night of 29 December 1895 he invaded the Transvaal on what became known as the Jameson Raid. Within four days this lunatic venture had put him behind bars in Pretoria.

The raid had immense repercussions. At the level of great power politics, it introduced a new tension into Anglo-German affairs. The Kaiser sent a congratulatory telegram to Kruger on his deft handling of the crisis. In London the Colonial Office came under scrutiny, and a parliamentary committee of enquiry sat early in 1897 to look into the origins of the raid. Chamberlain succeeded in having himself appointed to the committee and its conclusions were largely a whitewash. Rhodes was seriously weakened as a power-broker, but little was elicited that damaged Chamberlain. The committee became known as the Lying-in-State Committee, an epithet that reflected the cynicism with which its main findings were greeted.

It was in South Africa that the repercussions of the raid were most sustained. Butler wrote of the raid that 'it was the point of cleavage, social and political, in the entire fabric of life and politics in South Africa'. For the Boers there was a revival of all the old suspicion and distrust that had marked relations with Britain following the ill-judged annexation of the Transvaal in 1877, and Kruger embarked on a new armament policy. Rhodes was forced to resign as Prime Minister of Cape Colony, while in Cape and Natal loyal Afrikaaner subjects became unsettled.

In Britain, the late 1890s were years of increased imperial stridency. Chamberlain became convinced that if the Transvaal was not made amenable to imperial control, the whole of South Africa would be lost and a United States of South Africa, dominated by the Transvaal, would replicate the events which had occurred in the American colonies during the reign of George III. In spring 1897, to forestall such an eventuality, he appointed Sir Alfred Milner to the joint posts of High Commissioner to South Africa and Governor of Cape Colony.

Milner was a gifted intellectual, a former Oxford academic. He had worked in Cairo on Egyptian finances between 1889 and 1892, when he had occasionally met Butler at social functions and enjoyed his conversation. From Egypt, Milner had returned to England to take up the post of Head of the Inland Revenue Board. He was a convinced imperialist, in his own words 'a British race patriot'. In appointing him to South Africa, Chamberlain was happy about Milner's views. However, there was one imponderable: Milner had up to this time been in close proximity to those for whom he worked. How he would fare when he was 6000 miles from his superiors was not known.

Once in South Africa, Milner moved cautiously on the Transvaal question, studying various options and making strong contacts with various anti-Boer interest groups. However, in February 1898 a general election in the Transvaal overwhelmingly returned the seventy-two-year-old Kruger to the presidency for a five-year term, and any hopes that Milner had entertained of an easy end to 'Krugerism' evaporated. He came to the conclusion that the best solution to the Transvaal problem was war. Nothing as bald as this could be articulated either in South Africa or Britain. Indeed, Milner was running way ahead of what Chamberlain would countenance.' He began, as he put it, 'to work up to a crisis'. His chosen instrument was, as it had been for Rhodes, the lack of the franchise for the *uitlanders.*

The franchise issue was the constitutional key to the control of the Transvaal. Some 30,000 Boer burghers had the vote; some 50,000 *uitlanders* did not. Kruger was fully alert to the implications of these numbers. He insisted on long-term residency, and other conditions, for enfranchisement. The interests of the *uitlanders* were by this time being pushed by the South African League (SAL), represented throughout South Africa, but most actively in the Transvaal where it had the backing of the English-speaking press. Many of its most important figures had close links with the randlords.

By October 1898 Milner had been out of England for over eighteen months. He was keen to get back on leave; it would allow him to tête-à-tête with Chamberlain and other senior officials to assess current thinking on South Africa. The Colonial Office approved his leave but this in turn created a problem. The commander of the imperial forces in South Africa, who would normally deputize in the absence of the High Commissioner, had fallen sick. Milner wrote to Chamberlain:

> General Goodenough who would administer in my absence is so seriously ill that I doubt whether he would be fit for work for many months ... It would be really disastrous if, because things are quiet at the moment, the War Office thought they could use the opportunity to provide for some worn out lieutenant-general for whom they were anxious to find a billet. No doubt that is not even the worst that can befall us.[2]

Five days later, on 24 October, with Milner's letter still *en route* by steamer to England, Lieutenant-General Sir Henry Howley Goodenough was dead. Milner sent an urgent cable to Chamberlain stressing the importance of a suitable replacement. Chamberlain was unable to move fast enough to influence his cabinet colleague Lord Lansdowne, the Secretary of State for War. Lansdowne had already accepted Wolseley's recommendation for the position of General Officer Commanding in South Africa and the nominee's name had been sent to the queen for ratification. Milner had, indeed, not got a 'worn-out general'. He had got Butler.

The Secretary of State for War, Henry Charles Petty-Fitzmaurice, fifth Marquis of Lansdowne knew and liked Butler. Seven years Butler's junior, Lansdowne had been Governor General of Canada during Butler's six-week assignment to Ottawa in 1884, and the two men had socialized together. County Kerry would have featured in small talk between them: Lansdowne had extensive landholdings there, while Butler's honeymoon sojourn in Kerry had been in the Glencar Hotel – formerly a Lansdowne shooting lodge. From the point of view of the War Office, Butler was a good choice. He was familiar with South Africa, had solid, if limited, credentials as a field commander and a substantial experience of garrison and district command. He could be relied on to do a thorough and intelligent job. Under him, he would have a force of 8500 men, the combined total of the imperial troops in Natal and Cape Colony.

For the Colonial Office, Butler's appointment was a setback to Chamberlain's policy. Butler's views on South Africa were no secret. He had disagreed with the annexation of the Transvaal in 1877; he did not see the British defeat at Majuba as a national humiliation which had to be avenged; and, in common with most liberal opinion in England, he viewed the Jameson Raid as the product of unbridled capitalism. In South Africa, Butler would be subordinate to Milner, but he would have his own direct line to the War Office. Milner would have to handle him carefully.

Chamberlain had a more immediate problem: with Milner coming home on leave, Butler would be the most senior British official in South Africa for anything up to three months. He would be Acting High Commissioner as well as Acting Governor of Cape Colony, reporting in these capacities directly to Chamberlain. Chamberlain asked the War Office to arrange for Butler to come to see him so that he could assess for himself what kind of man he was getting. Butler found the subsequent interview a puzzling one. It lasted less than half an hour:

> The Secretary of State passed in review many South African subjects ... so barren was the short interview of any expression of policy or plan, so negative in any indication of intention, any warning of possible trouble, any necessity for preparation or caution – the homecoming of Sir Alfred Milner not even mentioned so far as its cause, objects or duration were concerned – that when I came to think over it all afterwards I could only conclude that the object of the interview was solely for the purpose of inspecting and taking stock of the new Acting Governor and High Commissioner.[3]

Butler's departure was hurried. He left for South Africa on 12 November 1898 with the temporary rank of lieutenant-general. It was arranged that Elizabeth and three of the children would join him before the following Easter. On arrival at Capetown, he was greeted by the recently elected Prime Minister of the Cape, W.P. Schreiner. Schreiner was a moderate Afrikaaner, loyal to the queen and eager to harmonize relations between British and Dutch throughout South Africa. The two men took an immediate liking to each other. Later Schreiner introduced Butler to his elder sister Olive, famous in England as the author of the novel *The Diary of an African Farm*. Olive Schreiner was a relentless critic of the rapaciousness of the randlords and of the designs of Rhodes.

Rhodes was in Capetown for the first month of Butler's tenure. Neither man made any formal approach to the other and, notwithstanding the opportunities afforded by the Christmas season in a compact British community, there was no informal social encounter between them. Their only contact took place at the end of December when Rhodes, with some colleagues, was embarking for England. Butler had come down to the pier to see off some acquaintances and the two men passed each other near the gangway to the steamer. Their eyes met and Butler noted that the expression on Rhodes's face 'struck me as one of peculiar mental pain'. Rhodes's pain was not without cause. Butler, in less than a month, had made a substantial personal contribution to the South African situation which was completely at variance with what the SAL and what Butler called 'the Party of the Raid' – Rhodes and his colleagues – were pursuing.

To look with hindsight at Butler's actions in December 1898 and early 1899 is to distort their context. The enormity of what Milner was moving towards – war as a solution to the Transvaal question – was, and would remain for many months, a secret. Even Chamberlain was prepared to go no further than endorsing the exertion of peaceful *uitlander* pressure on Kruger, provided that this pressure was seen to come from South Africa and not from London, where official government policy was for a peaceful resolution and establishment of a *modus vivendi* between 'the two races' within the Transvaal. Butler was thus astonished to find on his arrival in Capetown that the English-language press was virulently anti-Transvaal, publishing at length every possible instance of Boer heavy-handedness towards the *uitlanders*, and generating huge publicity around the mistreatment of Cape Coloureds – British subjects – working in Johannesburg. This reportage was also flowing to London since the editors of the leading papers were special correspondents for sections of the British press.

The English-language press in South Africa was 'almost wholly in the hands of men who are bent upon one persistent policy, that which is vulgarly known as getting the fat in the fire'. As Acting High Commissioner, Butler saw it as his responsibility to give the strongest possible message that Her Majesty's Government desired a solution to the tensions in South Africa through an equitable accommodation between both sides. He soon found an opportunity to speak his mind when asked to open a colonial exhibition at Grahamstown. There, on 17 December, at a public lunch hosted by the city's lord mayor, he told a distinguished audience that what South Africa needed was not surgical intervention but rest. His strong speech ended with an emotional appeal:

Perhaps Mr. Mayor I ought to offer you an apology for what may be deemed this short excursion into the borderland of politics. But I venture to regard this question from another, and I hope, a higher standpoint; and I do not think it is inconsistent with the season we are now approaching, which for more than eighteen hundred years has repeated to men its first message of goodwill ... if I now lift my glass and drink with all my heart to the peace, the brotherhood, as well as the progress and prosperity of this country.[4]

Butler's speech was widely reported. It sent a frisson throughout South Africa, signalling to the SAL and its supporters a reversal of the support they had hitherto enjoyed from the High Comissioner's office. However, the value of the speech was unproven. Perhaps in the week before Christmas nothing else could be expected of an appointee fresh from London except platitudes about goodwill. What happened next, however, left no doubts about where Butler stood on *uitlander* grievances.

Thomas Edgar was an Englishman working as a boiler-maker in Johannesburg. On the night of 18 December he seriously assaulted a fellow Englishman – who subsequently died from his injuries – in a drunken brawl. The police were called and in the resulting fracas Edgar was killed by a single shot from the pistol of a Boer constable. The constable was arrested on a charge of murder but released on bail on the lesser charge of manslaughter. *Uitlander* feelings were unleashed in an illegal demonstration on Christmas Eve, during which a crowd of 5000 pushed to the office of the British vice-consul in Johannesburg. Their leaders handed in a petition calling on Queen Victoria for protection and asking her to ensure that the constable be subjected to the full rigour of the law. The vice-consul cabled Butler in Capetown about the petition.

Butler refused to accept it on two grounds. The first was a technicality: the petition had been published in the Transvaal press before being presented, a breach of procedure. The second was substantial: the case was *sub judice*. The bail of the constable had also been revoked on the orders of the Transvaal attorney general, the young Jan Smuts. In Butler's view there was no reason to believe that the Boer government was not taking Edgar's killing with due seriousness.

In the events which followed – the arrest of the leaders of the Christmas Eve demonstration, the delay in putting the constable on trial – every nuance of sympathy for the position of the *uitlanders* was exploited by the SAL. Butler kept the Colonial Office informed of the situation. On 15 January 1899 he wired that 'Present agitation in Johannesburg is a prepared business. Machinery is fully visible here and only clumsily concealed. Objects sought are, first political and financial effect in London; second, to make government in Johannesburg impossible; third, to cast discredit upon the ministry now in office here [Cape Colony]. Needless to indicate the original train layers: they are nearer to you than to me.'[5] The train layers were Rhodes and his party who had sailed for England at the year's end.

It would be difficult to exaggerate Butler's detestation of the unaccountable world of international finance: its working had been visible behind the Egyptian campaign of 1882; its influence could be clearly seen behind the Jameson Raid of 1895. Now in South Africa, Butler got a very close view of it engaged in a crude exercise of power.

Chamberlain's worst fears about Butler were confirmed. The sooner that Milner got back to South Africa and relieved him of his civil responsibilities, the better it would be. The Colonial Office cabled Butler, curtly telling him to substantiate what he was claiming. He did so on 25 January in a lengthy letter, in which he discussed the Edgar case and went on to make some general observations:

> I do not think I err when I say that it is easy to discern in many directions in this country the trace of influences which are being steadily directed, I will not say to the promotion of racial antagonism, but certainly to the evolution of aims which cannot fail to evolve that end. This policy, in my opinion can only end, if it is persisted in, in producing a war of races, – a conflict, the ultimate consequences of which no one could adequately estimate. I do not believe that such a conflict is necessary to our interests here. On the contrary, I believe that these interests can be best advanced by the steadily applied forces of peace and progress acting upon two races which are not in their institutions or beliefs naturally antagonistic to each other.[6]

By this time Milner was on his way back to South Africa. His stay in England had had mixed results. He had found no strong public feeling about the situation of the *uitlanders*, and Chamberlain had been unable to give him anything more definite than to continue pressuring Kruger to effect peaceful change in the Transvaal. However, Milner's determination to 'work up to a crisis' was not a whit lessened by what he had seen and heard in London. His return voyage to South Africa was broken by a stopover at Madeira where he found a cable from the Colonial Office outlining the gist of Butler's letter of 25 January which had just been received in London.

Milner cabled a reply to Under Secretary Selborne, one of his closest confidants and son-in-law of Prime Minister Salisbury:

> With me, amusement at Butler's idiotic proceedings overcomes annoyance ... the Gilbertian flavour of a two and a half months' High Commissioner out-Krugering Kruger appeals to me. And perhaps if I have got if possible to get on with our friend somehow, it is just as well that I do not land in a bad temper.[7]

Selborne responded to Milner's well-turned phraseology with a plodding caricature of his own:

> *My name is High Commissioner Butler*
> *The World has ne'er seen a ruler subtler.*
> *I had not landed at Capetown a day,*
> *When I saw that Milner had gone astray...*
> *In the Transvaal the Briton is the blight,*
> *For the Boer is sweetness and Kruger light.*[8]

Milner reached Capetown on 14 February and Butler was relieved of his civil responsibilities. Milner at once set to turn about the reversals of policy that Butler had been making. He assured his confidants that Butler's tenure of the High Commissionership had been an aberration. To the Governor of Natal, Sir Walter Hely-Hutchinson, he wrote:

> my distinguished locum tenens, having in his impulsive way contrived – in less than three months – to fall foul of all his subordinates as HC and of his only colleague as Governor – all of them being perfectly easy to get on with – it is not unnatural that a period of slightly diminished tension should now be desired ... P.S. Don't think that Butler is a bad fellow. He is hasty and rhetorical, fearfully deficient in judgment. But he is well meaning enough and a most agreeable companion.[9]

Butler meanwhile had gone upcountry on a 3000 mile journey to reconnoitre the Natal–Transvaal frontier. He had received a despatch from the War Office in mid-January, dated 21 December 1898, asking him to submit a plan for *defensive* operations in the event of the Transvaal initiating hostilities against either Natal or Cape Colony. In view of later interpretations put on Butler's response, or lack of, to this instruction, its salient features are worth quoting. The despatch was routine. Its opening sentence stated that 'Her Majesty's Government have no special reason to apprehend hostilities with the republics in the immediate future but as a matter of military precaution it is essential that the possibility of such hostilities should be borne in mind.'[10] It went on to say that, in the event of war, no serious incursion into Natal or Cape Colony was expected but that 'Raids, however, of 2000 to 3000 men may be expected and it is against such raids that careful preparation on your part is necessary.' Under-pinning these instructions was that section of the Queen's Regulations which said that the defence schemes of the general officer commanding in any dependency 'should deal only with men and material actually available'.

The top military post in Natal Colony, that of General Officer Commanding (GOC), was directly subordinate to Butler as the South Africa GOC. However, the post was vacant for five months from January 1899, and Butler was directly responsible for imperial troops in both colonies. It is a strong indication of the vacillating attitude of the War Office to the military situation in South Africa during the first half of the year that the post was vacant for so long.

Butler's reconnaissance of the Natal frontier was thorough. Among the sites he visited was Majuba Hill. Mindful of Colley's defeat and death, he climbed to the summit. Conventional military intelligence held that Natal would be best secured against raids by establishing forward troop positions. Butler assessed that to do this would be foolish and dangerous, an evaluation which would later be accepted as sound. He worked out an alternative strategy based on the concept of ordered retreat, and he used what he had learnt during his command at Wadi Halfa in 1885–6 to safeguard the new railway which wound up into the Transvaal through northern Natal. He resolved to keep his plans to himself as long as possible, that is until he was asked for them by London – knowing that they would probably be rubbished at the War Office, 'that terrible congeries of confused opinion and congested clerkship'.

Chapter Fourteen

'THE CENTRAL STORM SPOT OF THE WORLD'

Butler was back in Capetown for the arrival on 7 March 1899 of Elizabeth and three of the children. As their ship docked, he was on the quayside to take them to their new home, 'Erinville', with its panoramic views of Table Mountain.

The next two months were outwardly calm; relations between Butler and Milner were cautious. While Butler was punctilious in the discharge of his military duties, there was between the two men little of the informality of good working relationships. During Butler's absence on the frontier, Milner had let it be known that a second *uitlander* petition would be well received. The Transvaal government handed the SAL its opportunity when the trial of the Boer constable who had killed Edgar resulted in an acquittal. At the end of March, Milner accepted 21,000 signatures which he forwarded to London to rouse public opinion in Britain. Tension was noticeably increasing in South Africa. Kruger's government was constructing a highly visible defence system around Johannesburg, and arms imports took on a new spurt.

Throughout March and April Butler sought to represent himself and the imperial forces under his command as being removed from the intrigues of the SAL and of the financial and industrial interests behind it. He avoided having anything to do with local volunteer colonial forces, and confined his troop movements largely to barrack squares and to ceremonial parades, calculating that long-distance deployment in the two colonies would be interpreted by each side to suit its own purposes. He also made early and elaborate preparations for military participation in the celebration of the queen's birthday on 24 May to demonstrate that imperial policy towards South Africa remained supportive of racial harmony between Dutch and British. This approach set him increasingly at variance with the anti-Boer faction in Cape Colony and Natal, and pushed him closer to the moderate Afrikaaners who were loyal to the empire and to the concept of equality between 'the two white races'. His conduct as GOC was admirable. He was walking a tightrope and he was doing so with skill and confidence.

It was otherwise with his relationship with the War Office. Following the Colonial Office rebuff of his views in January, Butler began writing privately to Wolseley and others, expressing his views on the situation in South Africa with his customary force. The unofficial political observations of any commanding officer in a dependency would normally be treated with some seriousness, but for several reasons this did not happen with Butler. The War Office was riven by factionalism between the civil and military wings. The Military Intelligence Department had little in the way of resources. The 1895 restructuring had produced muddled lines of communication, and the various departments vied with each other for precedence with their political masters. Further, the military wing of the War Office had no indication from the Colonial Office that there was a powerful clique in South Africa actively working towards a crisis. Finally, and critically, Butler was a man with a reputation for over-reacting: there had been the matter of Urabi Pasha in 1882 (see Chapter Eight), and in 1886 his vehement correspondence from Wadi Halfa (see Chapter Ten).

No action was taken on foot of Butler's observations on the situation in South Africa. Had any other man in his position said what Butler was saying, London would have listened; yet no other man in Butler's position would have said what he was saying. South Africa continued to slip towards catastrophe.

Milner was having his own problems throughout late April. The petition forwarded to London had failed to rouse public opinion in support of the *uitlanders*, and something more drastic was needed. Milner unilaterally decided to break cover, and abandon all pretence of not fully supporting the *uitlander* cause. He sent the Colonial Office what became known as 'the Helot Despatch', an impassioned and rhetorical plea which compared the *uitlanders* to the serfs of Sparta in ancient Greece. The despatch was a gamble to force Chamberlain to seek the Cabinet's public backing of the *uitlanders*, and it presented London with a hard choice: decline to back its High Commissioner and thus concede that Britain's claims to suzerainty over the Transvaal were meaningless; or back its High Commissioner and accept that the consequences, if diplomacy failed, could lead to war.

Within a week Chamberlain had convinced the Cabinet that, once Kruger realized that the imperial government was backing the *uitlanders* on the franchise issue, he would start to compromise. Reluctantly, the cabinet decided to stand by Milner, and their decision was cabled to him. Chamberlain also mailed him a letter advising him to meet Kruger and be conciliatory towards him on 9 May. There was now an open race in South Africa between those who believed that the differences between the Transvaal and Britain should be solved by negotiation and those who believed that force was the better solution. Milner, still secretly, was determined on war.

The day after Milner received news of the Cabinet's decision, he had a long discussion with Butler without disclosing to him either the existence of the Helot Despatch or the reply he had received to it. He wondered aloud if the existing forces in Natal could be used to pressure the Boers by being deployed at the frontier. Butler 'laughed openly at the idea' and said that for such an operation 40,000 men, over four times the number at his command, would be needed. Four days later Milner called to see Butler who noted in his diary that Milner looked 'worried and in need of sleep and rest'. Milner was embarked on a perilous course, trying to assess how far he could go towards war without destroying his own career and ending up like Bartle Frere, his predecessor of the late 1870s.

Milner probed Butler about the possibility of Boer raids into Natal and the Cape. He conveyed that while he himself wanted a peaceful resolution of the Transvaal question, Chamberlain's association with the Jameson Raid presented a problem. Milner needed a show of military support from Butler that could be construed by Kruger as putting pressure on the Transvaal. He suggested that Kimberley, the diamond city in the north of Cape Colony near the border with the Orange Free State, was exposed and in need of reinforcement. Butler disagreed: sending reinforcements to Kimberley would only inflame Boer suspicions. Milner back-tracked – so successfully that Butler, writing to Wolseley a few days later, stated:

> if he [Milner] had a clear unhampered hand, I believe he could settle the
> Uitlander difficulty as it stands in a few days and I have reason to believe

that he thinks so himself. But will he be allowed that free hand or will the fatal habit of Home interference which has so often in the past fifty years dashed the cup of peace from the lips of unfortunate South Africa, again mar the situation?'

Milner's view of Butler at this time is summed up in a confidential despatch he sent to Colonial Under Secretary Selborne on 24 May which concluded:

> – about the General. This is of course a disagreeable subject to touch upon, but I am bound to do it. *He has behaved perfectly well towards me since my return.* He does not meddle in political affairs in any way. On the other hand he keeps me absolutely at arm's length over military matters. I do not mean that he refuses to answer questions or to give effect to any wishes I express. He answers what I absolutely request. But there is no feeling of communication between him and me ... he will, of course, loyally do his duty and he is an able man. *The last thing I should think of would be his removal at this juncture* for he has got hold of the threads and, if the worst came to the worst, I have no doubt there would be absolute co-operation between him and me.'

Over the following days Butler remained impervious to Milner's attempts to change his attitude to troop deployment. Milner grew nervous and, on 28 May, cabled the Colonial Office with some urgency: 'I hear ugly rumours from many quarters of the attitude of Boers in the Transvaal, which are too numerous to be wholly groundless though they may be exaggerated. It would be well if the War Office could give the General Officer Commanding Sth Africa, who regards me as a brawler, a hint to be on the lookout.' The handling in London of this secret cable is significant as an example of what Butler was up against: Its contents were passed in writing to the War Office, but not before the phrase *who regards me as a brawler* had been deleted; Milner's supporters at the Colonial Office were doing everything to protect him.

Butler meantime had antagonized Chamberlain directly. To help bring parliamentary and public opinion behind his policy, Chamberlain had ordered the Colonial Office to prepare a bluebook on the background to the Transvaal issue. The Office of the High Commissioner in South Africa would supply much of the material for this bluebook. However, Butler had occupied the post for two and a half months, and his cables and despatches from this period could not be published in full without jeopardizing

Chamberlain's version of events in South Africa. When Butler resisted any editing, Chamberlain's reaction was to let him hang. The bluebook appeared in June, it omitted several of Butler's despatches; but carried in full his strong letter of 25 January 1899, which by its lack of any criticism of the Boers – something not relevant to its substantive subject – could convey the idea that Butler was not sound.

The publication in late May of London's decision to back the *uitlanders* had spurred a round of intense diplomatic activity. President Steyn of the Orange Free State offered Bloomfontein as the venue for a conference between Kruger and Milner. From Cape Colony, the Afrikaaner ministry of W.P. Schreiner quietly urged Kruger to settle the matter of the franchise. Kruger's own government was largely in favour of a conciliatory approach to the British.

The Bloomfontein conference opened on 31 May 1899. Kruger came to it prepared to make substantial concessions, offering the franchise after seven years' residence. Milner demanded five years' residence as the qualification. Most observers of the conference thought the gap was bridgeable. There was therefore shocked disbelief on 5 June when Milner abruptly announced that the negotiations were over, and the conference failed. Kruger responded: 'It is our country you want.'

In his autobiography Butler remarks that he went out blindfold to South Africa in 1898, but that the bandages soon fell off. If the bandages fell off when he realized the extent of the propaganda war being waged against the Transvaal, it was after the collapse of the Bloomfontein conference that the scales fell from his eyes: Milner, her majesty's most senior representative in South Africa, was leading the war party.

For some time Schreiner and other members of the government at the Cape had suspected that representations they had been making to Milner for forwarding to London were not being passed on. The Cape government's observance of procedure in communicating with London was working to its disadvantage because of Milner's lack of scruple. Butler now took the unprecedented step of forwarding to the queen a private letter sent to him by Schreiner which set out the position of moderate Afrikaaners. He sent the letter to her son, Arthur Duke of Connaught, asking him to show it privately to the queen. The Duke replied to Butler, though not as he had hoped:

Windsor Castle
1st July 1899

My dear Butler, many thanks for your letter of the 21st enclosing one from the Prime Minister of the Cape which I have read with much interest. In accordance with your request I showed it to the Queen who has taken full note of it. I don't know what may be the upshot of this Transvaal question but it is a very serious and important one for the welfare of South Africa and especially the maintenance of British supremacy in that part of the African continent. Sir Alfred Milner's position is a very difficult and responsible one but I am glad for his sake that he has got a capable first officer like yourself who come what may will not fail to support whatever action may be deemed necessary.[4]

However, the collapse of the Bloomfontein conference had highlighted the gravity of the situation for the British establishment. Prime Minister Salisbury pressed Chamberlain for a diplomatic solution. The War Office was slowly beginning to stir. On 6 June Butler was cabled for the scheme of defence he had been asked to provide the previous December. He completed it within a week and mailed it to London. Separately, on 12 June, he cabled George Wyndham, Under Secretary at the War Office, on his own initiative:

Am of opinion that situation of [affairs] here not understood in England. In the event of crisis arrived situation would be more that of civil war than regular military operations free from complications. South African Dutch community form very suspicious views as to intentions of British govt ... Consider it my duty to inform you, in view of possible final decision on basis of information in your possession, which is, in my belief, incomplete.[5]

With a flash of his old exuberance, Butler used the code name 'Fertil-is-er' to sign this cable. He was further cabled from Lansdowne's office on 21 June to make various purchases including mules and wagons. That cable concluded:

Main object of these steps is to increase efficiency of existing force; apart from question of re-inforcements which is not now raised. Do you desire to make any observations?[6]

Meanwhile Milner, guided from the Colonial Office by Selborne, was kept informed of the mood in Cabinet, told of the impact his increasingly nervy communications were making, and advised to guard himself 'most carefully against any appearance of jumpiness' in his cables to London.

Milner and Butler were in daily contact at this stage. Still unsure how far London would back him, Milner needed Butler's co-operation to provoke the Transvaal by the deployment of imperial troops. Butler agreed to carry out any instructions Milner gave him, but only if they were in writing. This was of no use to Milner: if he did this and things went askew, he would be blamed for usurping the function of the Secretary of State for War. On 22 June he made one final attempt to get Butler's co-operation: showing him a letter (written four months previously) which confirmed that the SAL was working for an invasion of the Transvaal, he hoped to push Butler into moving imperial troops out along the Natal–Transvaal frontier and approving the deployment of colonial forces along the border, ostensibly to prevent raiding by the irregulars of the SAL, but signifying to Kruger that her majesty's forces were mobilizing against the Transvaal.

Butler again declined Milner's bait and returned to military headquarters deeply dejected. The cable of 21 June, which he had just received from London, had asked in conclusion for any observations he might wish to make. He now replied to Lansdowne, holding little back: 'You ask for my observations. Present condition of opinion here is highly excited ... Believe war between the races coming as sequel to the Jameson Raid and the subsequent events of the last three years, would be greatest calamity that ever occurred in South Africa.'[7]

Butler expanded on his cable in a mailed letter and passed copies of cable and letter to Milner. It marked the end phase of their working relationship. The key entry in Milner's diary for that day was 'Butler or I will have to go'. Not confining himself to a private written observation, he also cabled Chamberlain asking that Butler be replaced. Chamberlain prodded the War Office from which in turn a cable was despatched to Butler from the Secretary of State's office:

> You were invited to offer observations as to suitability for War Office proposals for securing object in view, viz. increased efficiency in existing forces, not as to general merits of policy adopted by H.M. Government. You cannot understand too clearly that, whatever your private opinions, it is your duty to be guided in all questions of policy by HC who is fully aware of our views, and whom you will of course loyally support.[8]

On 3 July Butler received a private letter from Wolseley. Wolseley told him that there were unsubstantiated reports circulating in London that Butler had 'caused it to be generally felt in South Africa that my [Butler's] sympathies are with England's possible enemies' and that he (Butler) considered 'the claims of the British subjects upon the Transvaal Boers for equal political rights to be unjustifiable, and the resistance of the Boers to those claims for political rights to be fair and right'. Wolseley advised him that, if the reports were true, he should resign his command.

Butler went directly to see Milner and bluntly asked him if he had ever been 'a hindrance or an embarrassment' to him. Milner, equally bluntly, told him he had, and gave him three specific instances, all from the preceding three weeks and one of which was his cable and letter of 23 June to London. Butler's professional isolation was complete. He had no heart left for resistance. He cabled his resignation to Lansdowne the following day. He also replied to Wolseley's letter, saying among other things:

> I do not know who has spread these reports about me and my opinions. It is true that I have, and long have had, sympathy with the people of the Dutch race of South Africa. Long ago I studied their history and formed my opinions about them, and these opinions I have openly stated in my writings for years past; but I have never held the opinion that the claims of British subjects upon the Transvaal Boers were unjustifiable, nor that resistance of the Boers to those claims was fair and right.
>
> I have written very openly to you during the last three or four months, but I think you will look in vain for any such statement. I have held all along since my arrival here the view that powerful agencies were at work in England and in South Africa to inflame racial differences and to provoke or produce strife with the Transvaal.[9]

Butler's resignation was not at first accepted. At a time when the Cabinet was committed to a peaceful solution of the Transvaal crisis, Butler's departure from South Africa would send the wrong signal. Milner was reined in by Chamberlain, and diplomatic efforts to end the crisis were renewed.

While public opinion in Britain was moving towards the view that it might be necessary to teach the Boers a sharp lesson, the government was pressed to find a peaceful solution to the crisis. The Cape ministry had contacts in London and the view of loyal Afrikaaners was circulated to the Liberal opposition. The government was also irritated by a small number of Irish nationalist MPs who articulated a pro-Boer position: the Boers were serious about negotiaton, they were offering striking concessions, why were they being threatened with war? Almost eight years after the death of Parnell, the Home Rule Party was still divided, but moving towards reunification. In particular John Dillon, leader of the anti-Parnellites, had an interest in imperial affairs. Butler's acquaintanceship with the Nationalist Party, which went back to the 1880s, paid an unexpected dividend for him after the publication of Chamberlain's bluebook on South Africa when Dillon pressed Chamberlain in the House of Commons as to whether the Colonial Office had suppressed any material from Butler. Chamberlain avoided a direct answer to Dillon's questioning.

By late July the government believed that war had been averted. Lansdowne, however, was prevailed upon to accept Butler's resignation – just in case matters took a turn for the worse, the High Commissioner was entitled to have a GOC in whom he had total confidence. The timing could not have been more pointed. Butler was cabled on 8 August, the day before parliament adjourned for the summer recess: no awkward questions could be raised in the Commons. To ensure minimum public attention, nothing was released to the press. It took seven days before any English papers carried the news and even then it had been cabled from Capetown.

At the War Office, Wolseley, in ill health and with noticeable memory lapses, was furious with Butler for once again letting him down by his intemperance. Butler had seriously embarrassed him, yet it was he who had recommended Butler for the South African command. He therefore accepted that the neatest solution as to what to do with Butler was to have him switch posts with the man chosen to succeed him, a Lieutenant-General Forestier Walker commanding the Western District at Devonport, where Butler had previously served following his return from Egypt in 1882. The decision pained Wolseley, and his pent-up anger found some release in a letter to his brother George:

> Between you and me strictly Butler, whom I selected for the Cape as the ablest man we have, has made an ass of himself. At heart he is an Irish rebel and took Arabi's part and the part of every enemy England has had in my time. I have let him down easy for reasons I cannot put down on paper vice Forestier Walker who takes his place at the Cape.[10]

There was another view in the War Office about Butler: that he was an upright and capable man who had done his best in circumstances where he had been getting no direction from his military or civil superiors.

In Capetown on 9 August Butler had received the secret cable accepting his resignation, and informing him that Wolseley had recommended him for the command of the Western District. Butler replied asking permission 'respectfully to decline, not desiring to be the cause of possible embarrassment to the government'. In the plethora of communications sent by Butler from Capetown to London during his time in South Africa, that one message stands out. It catches perfectly one of his strongest character traits, a scrupulous decency. Lansdowne himself replied generously to it:

> You need have no misgivings as to possible embarrassment here. Commander-in-Chief and I discussed the question in all its aspects before making proposal which represented our opinion carefully arrived at. Please tell me, under these circumstances, if you adhere to your resolve as to Western District. I shall take no steps until I hear from you again but an early decision is necessary..."

Butler accepted the posting to Devonport. He sailed with his family from Capetown on 23 August. It was a quiet departure. He left letters for several people he had got to know during his nine months in South Africa. Among them was Olive Schreiner to whom he revealed something of his pessimism: 'How often in our youth do we imagine that we might have made the world better – happier? – it is only a vain dream which age dispels. Death is as necessary to man as life, it is more merciful."² There was a shipboard farewell for himself, Elizabeth and the children, attended by his personal staff and their families and 'almost all my English friends'. There were no Afrikaaners present. Those goodbyes had been private, for men like W.P. Schreiner believed that their presence on board would be misinterpreted by their enemies as disloyalty to the queen, especially since the common view in South Africa was that Butler had been *recalled*, not that he had resigned. With the small reception over and the well-wishers ashore, the ship cast off into a grey sea.

In London, the prospect of war grew ever closer. Conventional thinking was that a short sharp military shock in the autumn would settle the Transvaal issue before Christmas, at a cost of less than £10 million. Following precedent, the conduct of such a war would be given over to a military supremo who would go out from England as leader of an expeditionary force. It would be a plum posting, an opportunity for a senior army man to add lustre to a military career, as the century and the reign of the age-ing Victoria drew to a close. Wolseley wistfully accepted that he could not go himself; his health and his status as Commander-in-Chief were against it. The old rivalry between himself and F.S. Roberts, now a field marshal, was still sharp. Roberts had replaced Wolseley in Ireland and Wolseley was happy to leave him there. Nor was he enamoured of any of Roberts's pro-tégés at the War Office. Of the old Wolseley Ring, Wood was Adjutant General, having succeeded Redvers Buller in 1897. Henry Brackenbury was Director of Ordnance; and Buller, a full general since 1896, was comman-ding at Aldershot. Wood was seen by many as the man for South Africa, but Wolseley had never forgiven him for selling out to the Boers by nego-tiating an end to hostilities after Majuba. Besides, Wood was now deaf. The choice fell on Buller as the man for South Africa if war was declared. Meantime khaki-clad troops began to move out in substantial numbers from Britain and Ireland. By the end of September, imperial forces in South Africa would have more than doubled to 22,000.

Butler reached England in the second week in September and went di-rectly to Devonport to take up his new post. A few days later he came up to London where he saw Buller and Wolseley at the War Office. It was an unsatisfactory meeting, with little in the way of relaxed interchange be-tween old comrades reunited. He then had a short private meeting with Lansdowne, who kept matters on a formal level. In the charged atmos-phere of the War Office, the rights and wrongs of the South African situ-ation, which were weighing heavily on Butler, were not of major topical in-terest. His views were not required in London. He returned to Devonport dispirited, with the small consolation that he had been allowed to retain his temporary rank of lieutenant-general.

It was difficult to settle into the command of the Western District. Press comment about Butler's return was decidedly cool. *The Illustrated London News* carried a half-page photograph of Butler's final inspection of his troops at Capetown with the double-edged comment 'Sir William But-ler during his few months of the command has put exceptional activity into the exercises on the parade ground'.[13] This was a mild foretaste of what Butler would endure during the opening months of the war.

On 9 October the Transvaal gave Britain a forty-eight hour ultimatum to withdraw imperial troops from the Natal border and recall all recent re-inforcements from South Africa. This was seen in London as a ludicrous demand. The Great Boer War, or the South African War, began on 11 October 1899. Three days later Redvers Buller left Southampton for Cape-town. Britain was not prepared for war, and reverses were swift and spec-tacular. By the end of the month, over 1700 officers and men were dead, wounded or missing. At home, developments in photography meant that formal photos of individual soldiers were available to a press which had the technology to reproduce them. The British weeklies carried row upon row of fresh-faced casualties of the Boer guns. A wave of public incomprehen-sion turned to one of anger that things could be going so wrong. On 30 October at Ladysmith near the Natal border, 1000 British troops surren-dered to the Boers. Many of those who surrendered were men of the Gloucestershire Regiment from Butler's Western District. Rumours began to circulate in the West country about Butler. He was scapegoated, as if by not having prepared for hostilities during his time in South Africa he was responsible for the strategic and tactical errors that were leading to such disasters. The jingoistic *Daily Mail*, with a circulation figure of a million, wrote 'a vast number of people believe that General Butler neglected his duty in not preparing Cape Colony against invasion from the Transvaal'.[14]

Butler tried to carry on as if he was not the focus of innuendo and mal-ice. On 6 November he addressed 1000 men of the Duke of Cornwall's Light Infantry battalion before they left for the front. His speech was car-ried by the press:

> He appealed to them, no matter what might be their difficulties or dangers to remember the word duty ... Soldiers were not merely intended for the fine weather of peaceful civil life. It was their duty to face the storm and he impressed upon them that what they had read of recent events, increased and magnified by the excitement of public rumour, was nothing but the or-dinary work of war, and he was sure that they would face it in a warlike, sol-dierlike, Briton-like manner.[15]

Such manifestations of Butler's acceptance of the military code by which he had lived for forty-one years did little to ease his position as a public figure. The full measure of feeling against him became evident when he was ordered by the War Office not to attend a huge civic recep-tion in Bristol for Queen Victoria on 16 November, during which 8000 of the troops he commanded would line the six-mile processional route. The Bristol city fathers were afraid of demonstrations against 'the pro-Boer general' if Butler were in attendance on the day. It was a hard blow for one who had been an aide-de-camp to Victoria and whose personal regard for the monarchy was high. Making it no easier to bear was the fact that the queen would be accompanied to Bristol by the Duke of Connaught, Butler's former comrade and commanding officer. Butler accepted the prohibition of the War Office but he was stung to make a formal protest about what was happening to him:

> In view of recent circumstances connected with the command of the troops at Bristol ... I beg to bring to the notice of the Secretary of State for War the fact that for some time past persistent attacks have been made by a section of the London press upon my character as an officer and upon my conduct of miltary affairs while in command of Her Majesty's troops in South Africa. These attacks began at the time of the publication of the Blue Book in June last, in which a despatch addressed by me as Acting High Commissioner to the Secretary of State for the Colonies appeared. They have increased in violence since the opening of hostilities in South Africa. In conforming with the rules of the Service, I have taken no notice of these libellous accusations, but I now find that in the immunity which my silence gives my libellers, I am more and more pointed out to the people as being responsible for the existing state of affairs in South Africa ... I respectfully submit that the time has come for some action by my military superiors in the matter of these continued attacks – either that, or I should be given the opportunity of meeting some specific charge in relation to my late command in South Africa, or that they (my military superiors) should do something to vindicate my character.
>
> In suggesting either course I would beg, however to add that if there should exist any reasons of public expediency or state policy why no steps should be taken at present to put a stop to these libellous attacks, I shall deem it my duty to bear them in silence.[16]

With that final sentence Butler showed that, in spite of his intense upset, he had not lost sight of military priorities. He was realistic enough to see that, with hostilities raging in South Africa, he might get nothing by way of comfort from the War Office. He was therefore not altogether surprised to get a response which merely told him to continue to take no notice of press comment.

Abuse continued to pour in on him. Elizabeth found herself having to deflect some of it. Writing of this period in her autobiography, she said that 'The Press was letting loose all the poison with which it was being supplied, and I consequently went through, at first, the bitter pain of daily trying to intercept the vilest anonymous letters, many of them beer-stained missives couched in ill-spelt language from the slums'.[17]

The War Office staggered from blow after blow. Cables continued to stream in from South Africa: Mafeking and Kimberley under siege, defeats at Magersfontein, and at Colenso – where Buller himself had commanded. The projected short, painful lesson for the Boers had turned into something very different. Wolseley was forced to concede the unthinkable, and Roberts was summoned from Ireland. A week before Christmas he sailed for Capetown to take over as commanding officer from Buller. He was confidently expected to bring matters to a swift and victorious conclusion, but the war would go on for another two years and five months, costing Britain £200 million. The number of imperial troops committed reached 45,000, of whom 22,000 died; the Boers commited 88,000 men, of whom 7000 died. An estimated 100,000 Africans[18] were coerced into supporting the two factions; it is not known how many of these died. On the British side 10,000 African conscripts bore arms in what Butler described as 'the central storm spot of the world'.

Chapter Fifteen

NEW HORIZONS

As the last month of 1899 drew to its close Butler, with a self-restraint that must have surprised many of his military colleagues, set himself to the wheel of routine. Rigidly adhering to protocol, he offered his services for the South African campaign and was not surprised that they were declined. Privately he spoke often of his abhorrence of the war and those who had brought it about. Butler's wide circle of civilian friends shared his disgust at what had been allowed to happen to him, and among the military there were many who commiserated with him because of the invidious position he was in through the lack of coherent policy at the War Office.

Among the Liberal opposition in parliament there was some sympathy for him; in February 1900 several MPs raised the matter of the Butler despatches omitted from the bluebook of the previous June. This was done in an attempt to embarrass the government which was having to admit that the war showed no signs of being brought to a satisfactory and speedy conclusion. Of much more importance for Butler's reputation, though he knew nothing of it, was the notice taken of him by one of the most astute and authoritative figures in British public life, Reginald Balliol Brett, 2nd Viscount Esher. Formerly one of Gladstone's bright young men, Esher had been an MP for five years before breaking with Gladstone and leaving the House of Commons. Under Conservative patronage, he had held a succession of influential civil service posts. His change of political allegiance did not hinder continuing political contact with his former Liberal friends. In December 1899 he wrote to Lord Harcourt: 'what a national fiasco so far. The series of horrors culminating with the yielding of the government to the pressure of those who insisted on the holding and relief of Kimberley ... And what a justification of the unfortunate Butler."

The first public manifestation of support for Butler was not military or political, but literary. It came from his sister-in-law Alice Meynell. In July 1900 her biography of the recently dead Ruskin was published. The title page bore the inscription 'Dedicated to Sir W.F. Butler', and carried a quotation about Butler from Ruskin's *Bible of Amiens*: 'A British officer who is singularly of one mind with me on matters regarding the nation's honour.' Butler's gratitude to Alice Meynell was fervent: 'what can I say about the words you have put on the dedication page. I am altogether unable to speak or write my thanks to you ... my name on that page setting it on the dome of the temple you have built to his memory'.²

Two months later, in September, there was a positive signal from Wolseley at the War Office. Butler, while continuing to hold the senior post in the Western District, was asked to take over temporarily at Aldershot where, during Buller's prolonged absence, standards had slipped. Aldershot was the home of the first army corps and vital to the defence of Britain. Butler's commission was to raise training and morale. At Aldershot military etiquette permitted him to live in Buller's official residence. He declined to do so, since Buller's wife had stayed on there in her husband's absence, and Butler did not want to inconvenience her by having her move out. Instead, he and Elizabeth moved into a bungalow near Farnborough where the Empress Eugenie was still living.

During these months, much of Butler's attention was focused on the political situation. In October there was a general election, the 'khaki' election – so called because of the pivotal importance of the war to it. The South African conflict had already lasted a year. The government set out to convince the public that the war was almost over and that the integrity of the empire was assured. The Liberals were unable to stir up anti-war feeling without leaving themselves open to the charge that they were unpatriotic, though individual candidates like the young Lloyd George were unrestrained in their criticisms of the government. The Conservatives held on to power and in the ensuing Cabinet reshuffle St John Brodrick, a contemporary and friend of Milner, became the new Secretary of State for War. One of his first acts was to retire Wolseley and give the post of Commander-in-Chief to Roberts. Roberts returned from South Africa in December to take up the post, leaving General Herbert Horatio Kitchener behind to find ways of counteracting the guerrilla tactics of the Boers. Unable to defeat the Boers in combat, Kitchener adopted a scorched-earth policy, burning their homesteads and crops, and set up huge concentration camps, into which over 120,000 Boer women and children and African labourers were forced. Malnutrition and disease in the camps led to some 25,000 deaths during 1901 and caused an outcry in Britain over what Butler privately described as 'infamous things done'.

In January 1901 Redvers Buller resumed command at Aldershot. He had returned to England the previous November, having fallen foul of Roberts in South Africa. Butler returned to the fogs of a Devonport winter. On 22 January Queen Victoria died. She had reigned for 63 years and 216 days, occupying the throne longer than any other British monarch. The Victorian Age came to a formal close with Britain enmeshed in an imperial war in Africa which for duration, ferocity and suffering eclipsed all other nineteenth-century ventures on that continent. Albert Edward, the Prince of Wales, succeeded to the throne as Edward VII, with Alexandra as his queen.

South Africa continued to ruin military reputations. Wolseley's retirement had no grace to it. Coming when it did, it was a public slight on him. He was bitter at his treatment and envious of Roberts, who had been made an earl, an order of nobility higher than Wolseley's own viscountcy. In the House of Lords in March 1901 Wolseley spoke at length, blaming the defects of the War Office on its political masters. Misguidedly, he proposed a motion to oblige the government to disclose all papers that might vindicate his own actions or lack of them. His peers decisively rejected his appeal. It was a humiliating end to a glittering career and, in the words of his biographer, Joseph Lehmann, this 'little old man' – not yet sixty-eight years of age – 'retired into silence and obscurity'. He also retired into intensifying periods of memory loss and disorientation.

Butler's independence of mind and outspokenness, which had always kept him at a professional remove from Wolseley, unexpectedly began to work in his favour at the War Office. Roberts was concerned to place his own protégés in senior positions, but he was not vindictive, and he was satisfied to utilize the best talents available for specific projects connected with the war effort. Early in September 1901 he came down to Devonport to inspect Butler's troops on night manouevres as they defended Plymouth from a mock seaborne attack. The display impressed him: Butler's methodical deployment of troops and artillery showed imaginative, detailed planning. Six weeks later Butler was asked to head an internal enquiry into the operation of the Remount Department at the War Office. This was the first tangible evidence for Butler since Wolseley's retirement that he would not be consigned to oblivion for the remainder of his career.

The Remount Department was responsible for the supply of horses and mules for the South African war, and it had ceased to function effectively with the demands made upon it. Those demands were unprecedented: in 1901 alone, 129,000 horses were shipped to South Africa. British officers scoured places as diverse as Hungary and the United States, buying poor-quality animals at inflated prices. Between October 1901 and February 1902 Butler commuted frequently to London by train to complete an investigation which, as Elizabeth reported to her sister, was 'a staggering revelation of jobbery and robbery in all directions. And incapacity. Incredible."

Grateful as he was to be given this commission, Butler was still very much his own man. Early that month he had heard with dismay the news that another of his old colleagues was following Wolseley down the road of ignominy. Redvers Buller, whom he had known for over thirty years, and from whom he had taken over as look-out officer on the Canadian frontier in those halcyon days of the late 1860s, was in disgrace. The war had already lasted for two years and there was no sign of it ending. Buller, back in England, was an easy target for hostile armchair theorists. This hot-tempered man found it almost impossible to cope with persistently negative press comment on his role in South Africa. Things were made no easier for him by the knowledge that much of this comment was politically inspired by Brodrick at the War Office.

At a public function on 10 October Buller finally snapped, lashing out at his tormentors in what was described by the *Annual Register* as 'an act of absolutely astounding indiscretion'. Within twelve days he was sacked from Aldershot and his army career was over. Unlike Wolseley, he attracted a great deal of private sympathy, for he had been manifestly provoked into giving the War Office an excuse for dumping him.

It was into these murky waters that Butler plunged at the end of October after a disciplined two-year silence following the Bristol incident. In the very week of Buller's disgrace, the same week in which he accepted the Remount enquiry – and partly motivated by anger at the War Office's treatment of veterans like Wolseley and Buller, who in their time had contributed so much to the army – Butler drafted a letter to the Secretary of State for War to complain about Chamberlain, whom he was privately calling 'the Artful Dodger'.

The occasion of Butler's letter to Brodrick was a speech given by Chamberlain on 25 October 1901 in Edinburgh, before an invited audience of 8000 members of the Liberal Unionist Association of Scotland. Most of Chamberlain's speech was a defence of government policy on the South African war (during which he attacked the 80-strong Irish Parliamentary Party as 'avowed enemies of the empire'). He made a bold attempt to defend the government's miscalculations about the duration of a war, which had already lasted two years instead of three months. He went on:

> I say that as far as I know there was not one single man who was entitled to the slightest confidence or even pretended to be an authority upon the subject, who anticipated the prolonged resistance which we have incurred. That was the case. [Cries of 'Butler'] There's another fable. A distinguished general is to be quoted, not on his own authority, without his leave, by some person who perhaps has never seen him, as having predicted all that has happened. I wish I knew that general myself. It seems to me that we stand very much in need of men who can predict the future and turn out afterwards not to be false prophets: but we did not meet with him at the time [laughter], and even later it was the same thing.[4]

Chamberlain's remarks were widely reported in the national press. Butler had had enough. Undeterred by any repercussions which might affect his chairing of the Remount enquiry, he began an exchange of correspondence with the War Office. He wrote directly to Brodrick:

> ... the Secretary of State for the Colonies [has] thought fit to denigrate as *another fable* the idea that my despatches, written from South Africa before the War, had in any respect differed in opinion or forecast from the general belief held by the servants and advisers of the Government regarding war with the Dutch Republics in South Africa. In consequence it has become my duty to break the rule of silence which I have observed for more than two years ... I affirm that ... I pointed out in numerous telegrams and despatches, and in unmistakable language, the effects that certain parties were then making to produce and enflame racial feeling in South Africa and to bring about racial strife at all costs.[5]

Brodrick did not deign to reply to this, but delegated the matter to an underling. Butler found that the 'minute guns' of bureaucracy were turned on him with full force:

In your despatches you undoubtedly warned the Government, that for reasons which you stated, the outbreak of hostilities between Great Britain
and the Dutch Republics in South Africa might in the existing state of feeling produce a racial war which, you pointed out would be 'the greatest
calamity that ever occured in South Africa' ... Your warning to the Government was directed to the political effects likely to occur, whereas the
Colonial Secretary spoke of the nature and extent of the military resistance
likely to be offered.[6]

Butler ripped into this piece of civil service artifice in his riposte:

In one sense no doubt, my despatches dwell upon the political aspects of
the matter, but not in the sense which your letter seems to assume. It is the
soldier's duty, as a rule, to ignore politics, but it is equally imperatively his
duty to recognise and to draw to the attention of those in authority any political conditions which affect the military situation.[7]

This reply of Butler's drew down on him at the start of the new year a
further bureaucratic barrage; now the dispute widened to include Butler's
delay in supplying the defence scheme for which he had been asked early
in 1899. He was told that the civilian side of the War Office had no more
to say to him, and that if he wished to continue his correspondence it
should be with the Adjutant General, a rebuff which Butler turned to his
own advantage by doing just that. Evelyn Wood had recently vacated the
post and gone to India. Butler sent his successor, General Sir Thomas
Kelly-Kenny, a 2500-word account of his defensive preparations, ensuring
entry into official files of a comprehensive record of the circumstances
prevailing at the time.

The Adjutant General, a Clare man and a Catholic, privately sympathetic to Butler, brought the correspondence to a firm close with a speedy
response which concluded:

The Commander-in-Chief considers it unnecessary and inexpedient further to discuss this subject. His Lordship has no reason to doubt that you
acted to the best of your judgment and ability during the period in question and he observes that your recall from South Africa was not due to any
neglect of duty on your part but to your resignation on the ground that
your presence at Capetown was likely to be a source of embarrassment to
Her Majesty's Commissioner.[8]

During this lengthy exchange, Butler was coming to and from the War Office for the Remount enquiry where his every appearance occasioned informal comment about his pursuit of the 'fable' incident. The consensus was that he was following the matter with an obsessiveness out of all proportion to its importance. Chamberlain's comments had, after all, not been scripted but were an extempore response to a heckler at a mass meeting. For Butler, however, nothing could be more important for his professional integrity than to set the record straight, though his doggedness about this never pushed him over the brink as it had Wolseley and Buller.

In early March 1902 he was heavily involved in preparations for the royal visit to Devonport of Edward and Alexandra for the launch of the battleship *Queen*. This was primarily a naval occasion but the army had its part to play and Butler was to the fore of the ceremonial display which greeted the king and queen on their arrival at Plymouth on 7 March. The Butlers both knew the royal couple. Butler himself had made their acquaintance during his time as an aide-de-camp in the 1880s. Elizabeth's acquaintanceship with Edward went back to 1874, the time of 'The Roll Call'. Alexandra was an admirer of her watercolours.

During a lull in the ceremonial review of troops, Edward came over to Elizabeth 'and said with considerable emphasis; "Your husband is a very fine soldier, Lady Butler, but it is a pity he takes so much part in politics." The royal steps retreated a few paces and then approached again and the one emphatic word *"Pity"* was repeated.'[9] That night there was a relaxed dinner on the royal yacht. Unlike what Elizabeth described as the 'painfully solemn, whispered dinners of dear old Queen Victoria', Edward preferred popular music and animated conversation as ingredients of such ocassions. After the meal the king chatted privately to Butler about the ongoing war. He then had a tête-à-tête with Elizabeth: 'in a confidential tone [he] began about Will. I think he is fond of him. What he said was kind and I knew he wanted me to repeat his sympathetic words to my husband afterwards. He spoke of him as a "splendid soldier".'[10] Some weeks later Butler had his temporary rank of lieutenant-general made substantive and backdated to October 1900.

Family life for the Butlers was undergoing changes. A week after the royal visit to Devonport, their daughter Elizabeth was presented at court. She would shortly cause her parents deep anguish by marrying a divorcee, Lieutenant-Colonel Randolf Kingscote from County Mayo. Patrick, their eldest son, was set on a military career and passed his army entrance examination with excellent results in April 1902. Richard, the second son, entered the Benedictine novitiate at Downside in Somerset. Eileen, just finishing in convent school, was looking forward to her coming-out ball. Martin, the youngest, was already showing a strain of capriciousness which, after Butler's death, would lead to his estrangement from the rest of the family. Elizabeth was still painting, though her income from her work had become negligible. Butler himself was noticeably slowing down physically. He was beginning to suffer from sciatica, and lumbago was making it increasingly difficult for him to mount a horse. He was also developing a bronchial chest. However, his mental vigour was undiminished and, with retirement on the horizon, he was turning more of his attention to Ireland. Since the outbreak of the war in South Africa he had, as a serving officer, avoided any overt association with politics, and he was careful to keep a formal distance between himself and the Irish nationalist MPs at Westminster.

In January 1900 the nationalists had buried their differences and united under John Redmond, who had led the minority wing which had remained loyal to Parnell at the time of the disastrous split. Nationalist opposition to the war was genuine and representative of majority opinion in Ireland. A week after the reunion of the Irish Parliamentary Party, Redmond had proposed to the House of Commons that the war should be brought to a close and the independence of the two Boer republics recognized.

Butler's interest in Ireland became more active when he joined the Irish Literary Society in London. Founded in 1891, with the young William Butler Yeats as one of its principal originators, the society was one of several established in the years of the Celtic Revival. Besides affecting popular culture – dancing, games and sports – the Celtic Revival gave an emotional depth to the Irish past by its exploration of myth and legend. This led to a sympathetic examination of Ireland's 'golden age' of sainthood and scholarship, while the study of Ireland's subjugation to the English Crown reclaimed and dignified those centuries for the nationalist majority.

Disillusioned now by the way the dream of Empire had become dissipated by greed and the pursuit of power and profit, Butler gave much of his free time to Ireland. He was in demand as a speaker and one memorable night in March 1902, while in London for the Remount enquiry, he spoke on Cromwell to a packed meeting of the Irish Literary Society. Among the audience, which included a number of nationalist MPs, was Wilfrid Blunt, the champion of Urabi Pasha during the Egyptian campaign. Blunt found the lecture 'a most able and brilliant performance'. The young Stephen Gwynn, later a noted literary critic and author, was also present. He wrote of Butler: 'nobody I think ever possessed more perfectly the gift of writing prose intended to be spoken: and the tall superb Tipperary man had a voice that could have carried easily across any barrack square yet was pleasantly modulated.'[11]

Butler's lecture on Cromwell survives in print.[12] It is strongly partisan. The Lord Protector is described variously as a 'bankrupt brewer' (a reference to his family business); a man of 'matchless hypocrisy'; and 'the greatest dissembler of whom history holds record'. Butler viewed Cromwell as a disaster, not only for Ireland, where he had campaigned in 1649 and 1650, but for England where 'while raving of liberty he subverted in turn every liberty which Englishmen had ever known'.

It was probably through the Irish Literary Society that Butler became friendly with Alice Stopford Green. Alice Stopford had been born in Kells, County Meath, in 1847, the daughter of a Church of Ireland minister. She had married an English historian, John Richard Green, and come to live in England. When he died in 1883, she took up his pen, turning to Ireland's past for her subject matter. By the turn of the century she had become the best-known Irish society hostess in London. Stopford Green was working on her magnum opus, *The Making of Ireland and its Undoing*, and among those to whom she circulated draft chapters was Butler, though he protested that he was no historian: 'You credit me with a lot of knowledge of history which I do not possess. Mine has been such "foraging" reading, never study in its true sense but enough to make further travel always pleasant.'[13] Stopford Green's Irish interests were not confined to writing. She was involved with the economic development of her home area along the Leinster Blackwater, and through her connections Butler began to write to the wealthy nationalist MP James McCann, whose range of projects for the region included a canal, a timber mill and a bacon factory. Butler believed strongly that small scale economic self-sufficiency was the key to twentieth-century progress for Ireland.

Living and working in Devonport did not deter Butler from keeping himself well-informed of contemporary Irish developments. He followed Kuno Meyer's discoveries in Old Irish, and took an informed interest in the setting up of the Irish School of Learning in Dublin. He was enthusiastic about the efforts of Sir Horace Plunkett to bring about development on the land, and applauded the aims of the newly established Department of Agriculture and Technical Instruction, of which Plunkett was vice-president. He watched, initially with some suspicion, as the Chief Secretary for Ireland, George Wyndham, worked towards what would become known as the Wyndham Land Act; in 1903 this Act would broadly settle the Irish land question on the basis of peasant proprietorship by allowing extensive tenant purchase at affordable rates. Butler also became actively interested in the question of primary education: he disapproved of what he termed the '*so-called* National Schools', which he believed were responsible for 'the taking out of the heart of the people' by excluding much of the Irish past from the curriculum; and he corresponded on the issue of denominational education in England with his brother-in-law Wilfrid Meynell, holding strongly that denominational education was a civic right.

The South African War had ended in May 1902 with the defeat of the Boer Republics, and now serving army officers could articulate their political leanings with more freedom. On his trips to London, where he would stay at the Junior United Services Club in the West End, Butler occasionally visited the House of Commons and became friendly with John Redmond whom he had first met in the 1880s. Acquaintances on the Liberal benches always greeted him cordially and it caused no surprise when Butler volunteered himself as a witness before the royal commission which was set up in the autumn of 1902 to look into the conduct of the war. The commission sat for fifty-five days between October and February and examined 114 witnesses. Chamberlain did not appear before it. He was, conveniently, on a lengthy tour of South Africa where Milner, now Viscount Milner, was Governor General. The commission was chaired by the Liberal Unionist Earl of Elgin, a former Viceroy of India. Viscount Esher sat on it and also Lord Strathcona and Mount Royal who, in 1871 as Donald Smith, a governor of the Hudson's Bay Company, had been impressed by Butler's report on the Saskatchewan.

Butler appeared before the commission on 11 February 1903. He had two aims. First he hoped that the commission would flush out of the Colonial Office files all his despatches from his time as Acting High Commissioner, thus putting them on the public record. In this he was unsuccessful: the commission's enquiries into the preparations for war were confined to military preparations. However, Butler succeeded in his second aim which was to get on to the public record his protracted correspondence with the War Office over the winter of 1901–2 on the 'fable' incident. By presenting all this correspondence to the commission, he ensured its inclusion in the final report, bringing into the public domain his version of events in South Africa in 1899.

Butler's reception by the commission was mixed. He was pushed on the matter of troop numbers – 400,000 imperial troops had been deployed during the course of the war. How could Butler, as late as May 1899, have so miscalculated what would be needed as to tell Milner that 40,000 men would be required if hostilities broke out. Butler flatly refused to accept that this question had any merit; without an actual strategy, estimates of numbers would be only guesswork: 'There is no such rot in the world as the forecasting of numbers. Excuse me for using the word "rot" but there is no other word to describe it. It is evident that what would take the German army to Paris would not take it to the Pyrenees for instance.'[4] He also clung tenaciously to his original assertions that the Boers had not wanted a war, and he capably defended his decision not to move troops to the frontier. He was on shakier ground with regard to his delay in forwarding a defence scheme to London. He had sent it in June only when he had been asked a second time for it. His spirited reply to questioning on this was that the delay was not inordinate.

Butler was an eloquent and witty witness. At one stage, Elgin asked if extra staff supplied to him would have been used 'in advance of the force you had'. Butler, deliberately obtuse, answered 'No. Not in advance – behind at the base.' This provoked from Elgin a terse, 'I meant in addition.' On another occasion, discussing the machinations of the members of the South Africa League, Butler suddenly pulled from his papers a photograph of a rough and brutish individual. 'Is that', he was asked, 'a fair sample of the SAL?' To which he retorted, 'It's a fair sample of the upcountry chairman of the time.'

The evening after Butler's appearance, Esher, who was privately keeping the king informed of events at the commission, wrote to him:

> In view of the accusation made against Sir Wm. Butler in the winter of 1899, a full opportunity was given to that officer to state his case, of which he availed himself. It is clear that he held strong military and political views of the situation then obtaining, which were not in accord with those of His Majesty's advisers, and Sir Wm. met the usual fate of those who give unpalatable advice. That much of the advice he gave has since proved correct, is not possibly of advantage to him in certain quarters. There is no doubt that he is among the ablest of Your Majesty's servants, and possesses an intellect capable of grasping large problems and of dealing with them in a practical manner. His Irish blood may possibly influence his temper and political judgment, but leaves his military capacity untouched ... Upon a highly controversial political question [the Edgar petition] – in which as

Acting High Commissioner he became involved – his judgment was possibly faulty, and that is all that can reasonably be urged against him. Intellectually he stands (as he does physically) head and shoulders above the majority of his comrades ... His evidence upon the preparations for war only proved once more that uncertain counsels prevailed throughout the summer of 1899 ...'[5]

The eventual findings of the commission were a blow to the War Office and its political masters: as late as October 1899, no plan of campaign had existed for the conduct of a war in South Africa. Wolseley and Lansdowne were both censured. Esher added a personal statement to the report recommending that the post of Commander-in-Chief should be abolished. This would happen in 1904 with the creation of the post of Chief-of-Staff.

For Butler, as the commission drew to a close in February 1903, there was, fleetingly, the prospect of a promotion to the War Office. His conduct of the Remount enquiry had made a positive impression on Secretary of State Brodrick. The post of Quarter Master General was vacant, its previous incumbent having gone as governor to Malta. Brodrick sounded out Esher about Butler. He was concerned that Butler's outspokenness and political leanings would be hindrances in the post. Esher was happy to reassure Brodrick on this, and, as he told the king,

> [I] pointed out that no political question entered into the duties found in Your Majesty's forces; and were Lord Esher in Mr. Brodrick's place, he would prefer a capable administrator, like Sir Wm. Butler, in the office of Q.M.G., to a less able man whose amiable qualities might be more assured. Managed with tact, Lord Esher believes that Sir Wm. B. would not be the *mauvais coucheur* which he is represented to be.[6]

However, Butler's chances of securing this post were never more than slender, for reasons which had nothing to do with his personal qualities. The decisive factor was that he was identified with the wrong military camp. He was a Wolseleyite. Roberts as Commander-in-Chief was supplanting Wolseley's colleagues with his own men. Butler, sixty-four years old, stayed on at Devonport in what he called the 'oakum picking' of routine command.

Chapter Sixteen

HOME

The demands on Butler's time were plentiful. Through the Meynells, both he and Elizabeth kept in close contact with intellectual Catholic life in London. From Devonport he had, some years before, donated to Downside Abbey the medieval-style altar of the Lady Chapel with its magnificent reredos. He was a member of the Catholic Truth Society and his home was open to Catholic activists, lay and religious. In July 1903, a letter which he sent to Alice Stopford Green was black-bordered because, as he explained, Pope Leo XIII had just died, 'the 258th Bishop of Rome. How small beside that wonderful line look all other Kingdoms and Empires." This letter has a particular poignancy as an indirect affirmation of Butler's professed faith and of his acceptance of its rules. Two days after it was written, on 23 July, his daughter Elizabeth married the divorced Randolph Kingscote. Her wedding was without benefit of a Catholic blessing and her parents, obeying precept, did not attend it.

That summer Butler's chest gave him some trouble and his doctor advised a trip to a continental spa. However, he decided that the air of Ireland would do more for him. Early in September he and Elizabeth crossed to Dublin and made a five-hour train journey to the west, to Clew Bay in County Mayo. They stayed at Mulrany at the newly opened Mullaraney [*sic*] Railway Hotel, set on a wooded hillside with a panoramic view across the great bay towards Ireland's holiest mountain, the isolated quartzite cone of Croagh Patrick.

Mulrany, sheltered from the excess of the Atlantic by the island of

Achill, and with a profusion of greenery reminiscent of south Kerry, delighted them. Elizabeth found that its cloud patterns and colourings gave endless opportunities for watercolouring and sketching. Butler's bronchitis cleared up under a regime of 'the best air in Europe, splendid views and a fair table'. He returned to Devonport ready to face into the winter.

There was no decrease in the demands on his time. From the Jesuit college of Clongowes Wood in County Kildare, where his son Patrick had boarded, came an invitation to address the students; he was nominated to be one of the governors of Kuno Meyer's Irish School. He continued to correspond with James McCann about economic schemes along the Leinster Blackwater, and, on occasional trips to London, saw both nationalist MPs and civil servants in connection with them. There was an unexpected outcome to this when, with the sudden death of McCann in mid-February 1904, the tantalizing prospect of entering politics opened up before Butler.

McCann had held the seat for the St Stephen's Green Division of Dublin City as an 'independent' nationalist – before the reunification of the Parliamentary Party in 1900 he had been an anti-Parnellite, not a Redmondite. Redmond, casting round for a candidate who would hold the seat against strong unionist opposition, calculated that his best hope was to run a compromise candidate free of any taint of faction. He was conscious that waverers in the electorate who were nervous of Home Rule stridency would be reassured by seeing a nationalist candidate with such obvious establishment connections as had Butler, the soldier of empire.

Butler pointed out to Redmond that he could not just leave the army overnight, but was assured that the by-election would probably not be held for six months. In a flurry of half-thought-out possibilities, Butler went to Dublin for McCann's funeral and met several influential nationalist activists.

It was Butler's first experience of mainstream political lobbying and he did not take to it. It angered him that some of those to whom he spoke did not level with him about their own intentions, either to enter the race themselves or support the nominations of others. From a hectic few days, he came back to Devonport assuming, incorrectly, that Redmond had been two-timing him. The truth was that Redmond was not secure enough to impose his own candidate. Pressing a perceived advantage, the government issued the by-election writ at the beginning of March and put their candidate in the field. Redmond acceded to the selection of another 'independent' nationalist, Laurence Waldron, a stockbroker, who secured the seat with almost twice the votes of his rival. Butler, bruised, remained in Devonport, 'very tired', and with a recurrence of his bronchitis which took months to shake off. As the spring of 1904 quickened into summer, the lure of 'that land of pure air and green grass' proved irresistible, and at the end of May he and Elizabeth came back to Mulrany.

There, moving towards his twilight years, he reflected on his life. On three sheets of hotel notepaper he penned some verses which are a vivid mark of his emotional attachment to the land of his birth and to its common people.

> *Give me six foot three*
> *(One inch to spare.)*
> *Of Irish Earth and dig it anywhere*
> *And for the poor soul*
> *Say an Irish prayer.*
> *Above the spot.*
>
> *Let it be hill where cloud and mountain meet.*
> *Or glen amid the tufted meadow-sweet.*
> *Or 'borreen' trod by peasants' shoeless feet.*
> *It matters not.*
> *I loved them all_*
> *The valley and the hill*
> *The moaning shore, the flagged lined rill*
> *The yellow furze.*
> *The lakelet lone and still*
> *The wild bird's song.*
> *But more than hill or valley, bird or moor*
> *More than the green fields of my own dear Suir.*
> *I loved those hapless things – the Irish poor –*
> *All my life long.*
> *Little did I for them of outward deed*
> *I fought far off 'gainst lust and selfish greed.*
> *What good I did for strangers*
> *Theirs the mead.*
> *I learnt it there*
>
> *So give me an Irish grave*
> *And let the grass grow green above it*

When the peasants pass
On Sundays p'haps they'll say
On the road to Holy Mass
For me a prayer.[2]

Butler was not due to retire from the army until his sixty-seventh birthday in October 1905, although his command at Devonport could be terminated before then. When in September 1904 he was officially advised
that his tenure at Devonport would cease at the year's end, he began actively looking for a home in Ireland. He appeared to be easing down to retirement when he was, in the new year, precipitated into the public eye on
two fronts, military and political.

On the military front it was the apparently never-ending repercussions
of the South African war that led to the Butler Report. Following the
Esher reforms of early 1904, the Public Accounts Committee of the
House of Commons asked the War Office to investigate how some 6.5 million pounds had been squandered by the Army Stores Department in the
wake of the war. The stores division in South Africa had sold off stocks at
huge losses to civilian contractors while simultaneously inviting civilian
contractors to submit tenders to supply the army in South Africa. Mindful of Butler's work on the Remount enquiry, and in what Elizabeth Butler
described as 'an act of poetical justice', the Secretary of State for War, now
Arnold Foster, was satisfied to approve the recommendation of the newly
instituted Army Council that Butler be assigned as chairman of a four-man
committee to look into what was being commonly referred to as the army
stores scandal. The committee's remit was limited. The six specific cases
it was asked to examine involved lower ranking officers. This hampered its
freedom 'to report upon the responsibility of those concerned'. For Butler, this was a challenge to be accepted with relish. Throughout his army
career he had consistently resisted the easy path of letting those on the
lower rungs of the ladder carry most of the blame when things went badly
wrong.

The comprehensive Butler Report of 1905[3] pushed the responsibility
for the scandal far above luckless individual officers 'for whom mitigating
circumstances may probably be found'. Collective responsibility lay with
the entire Office of Supplies, which had in turn been subject to higher
powers. It followed that 'responsibility for policy and administration in
South Africa must reach beyond the Office of Director of Supplies'. The
inference was clear: it was the highest levels of the War Office which had

been to blame for the scandal. The report reserved its most scathing attacks for the civilian contractors who had fattened on British taxpayers through corrupt practices.

Butler, with his love of alliteration and penchant for sonorous phraseology, wrote up the conclusions with an eye to their stylistic impact. It helped that he was only months from retirement and relieved of his Devonport command. He personalized the report's attacks on civilian contractors and radically altered phrases from the draft stage. One contractor, who is originally described only as 'a hard drinker', becomes 'decidedly addicted to drink' in the final report. 'A family concern' becomes 'a mushroom firm' because of the numbers of members who suddenly appear to take advantage of army generosity. Famously, in phrases which would enter War Office folklore, Butler referred to the fact that the nebulous personalities behind contractor fraud were never prosecuted. Instead, punishment was meted out occasionally to 'some clumsy pantaloon in puttees,' or 'some agile harlequin in a helmet'.

Butler was pleased with the reception of his report when it was published in June 1905. *The Times* criticized 'the extravagant and tasteless rhetoric in which much of the report is clothed,' though it conceded that 'It remains a paper which must cause a profound impression ... amongst all those who have at heart the welfare of the Army and the Empire'. The *Daily Mail* hailed it as 'one of the most outstanding documents ever issued to the public'. Butler had the melancholy satisfaction of seeing parliament react to his report by setting up a royal commisssion which would effectively bury the scandal.

Butler was adjusting to life after Devonport, which he left at the end of January 1905. He had been approached by the Liberal Party to stand as its candidate for East Leeds in the next general election, due to be held before the year's end. Butler had perfectly understood the liberal stance during the Boer War. Liberal opposition to the policy which had led to war had taken a secondary position to the need to back Britain at a time of crisis. Yet even after the war, the liberals were not strongly critical of the government, and Butler privately described them as 'a very tame pack – poodles most of them'.

He was reluctant to let his name go forward – the imminence of retirement in Ireland where he could combine writing with an active involvement in the educational and cultural life of the country was very appealing. Besides, after his experience in Dublin, he was dubious about entering politics. For the liberals Butler seemed a certain candidate to wrest a seat from the conservatives in East Leeds: he had a high public profile, was an excellent speaker, and would have credibility on the hustings. He would also attract the Catholic vote in East Leeds. Elizabeth recorded the Liberal wooing of Butler in her diary:

> *January 31st 1905.* Will is to stand for East Leeds. It is all very sudden. Liberals so eager that he has almost been (courteously) hustled into the great enterprise. Herbert Gladstone, Campbell-Bannerman and other leaders have written almost irresistible letters to him, pleading. When he goes to the election at Leeds he is to be *put to no expense whatever* and they are confident of a *handsome majority.* We shall see!
>
> *February 13th.* We went to a very brilliant and (to me) novel gathering at the Campbell-Bannermans. All the leaders of the Liberal party there. An interesting if not a noble study. All so cordial to Will. Tremendous crush ... Winston Churchill, a ruddy young man with a roguish twinkle in his eye ... All these MPs seem to relish their life. I suppose it has a great fascination, this working to get your side in as at a football match.[4]

Once having accepted the nomination, Butler applied himself wholeheartedly to studying the various planks in the Liberal platform. Primary education was one such, and he spent a hectic few days in March 'mastering the knotty points' of the debate on state versus denominational schools. In the following months Yorkshire became the main battleground in England for control of voluntary schooling. In mid-summer Butler, on the advice of the Catholic Education Council, stood down as a Liberal candidate. When the general election was held in January 1906 the Liberals surged to victory with an eighty-four seat majority – though the East Leeds seat was won by the Labour candidate.

Throughout the early part of 1905, Butler's work for the War Office and the Liberals had not impeded his search for a retirement home in Ireland. He bought Bansha Castle, an imposing eighteenth-century residence at the foot of the Glen of Aherlow, on the edge of the Suir Valley. The house stood on a low eminence just outside the village of Bansha on the main Tipperary-Cahir road. Close by was the ancestral Butler home at Ballycarron, and a little farther east across the Suir was the place of his birth, Ballyslatteen House, while directly south of his new home rose the Galtee mountains of his childhood. The seclusion of Bansha was offset by the railway line to Dublin which ran by the village, providing easy access to the wider world.

The Butlers moved to Tipperary in July 1905. For Butler himself, it was to be his last domestic upheaval, after a lifetime of movement which had started when he was three years old, with a journey to stay with his aunt and uncle in Dublin. Bansha Castle was in some disrepair and unfurnished, which added to the settling-in problems. In August he wrote to Alice Stopford Green:

> Since we came here just a month ago I have been on the lowest level of non-conformity with the recognised rules of correspondence. We had to begin at the beginning and it is only now that the writing table comes in. All the other tables go before it – kitchen tables, dining tables etc. My books and papers still lie in unpacked cases. Nevertheless we are emerging into better phases of home life. The roof gives little trouble – perhaps due to absence of rain – and the floors undulate less menacingly.[5]

The formal termination of Butler's army career, a career that had lasted forty-seven years, was his sixty-seventh birthday, 31 October 1905. He was retired on a pension of £850 per year. He had not made the rank of full general. At the time of his return from South Africa he had realized that such a possibility was a remote one for him. His handling of the Remount enquiry, his evidence before the commission into the war, and his conduct of the investigation into the army stores scandal had ensured the continuation of an ambivalent attitude towards him at the highest levels of the War Office, particularly the civil level. However, his lieutenant-generalship should be seen in perspective. In 1905 he was one of only twenty-five senior officers in the entire army to hold that rank. The army had only twenty full generals, several of whom were continental nobility holding honorary rank.

Butler had barely settled into life at Bansha when the London *Tribune* asked him to undertake a tour of South Africa and write a series of articles on what he found there. He accepted, leaving Southampton on 6 January 1906 for what would be a five-month assignment, and travelling unaccompanied. He found South Africa greatly altered. Milner was back in England; his ambitious reconstruction schemes had failed to regenerate the ravaged Orange Free State – now the Orange River Colony – and the Transvaal.

There were many old faces in Cape Colony to greet Butler, but too much had changed. Many of the leading warmongers had not only survived secure in public or commercial life, but had thrived, profiting handsomely from the war. In the former Boer republics the evidence of ruin and suffering was pervasive. Butler found it depressing, and the seven years which had passed since his South African command had taken their toll of his energies. He found it difficult to write to order for the *Tribune* and he missed Elizabeth, and Bansha, and his books and papers. His *Tribune* articles were published in book form in 1906, under a title of his own careful choice, *From Naboth's Vineyard*. A Bible-educated, reading public in Britain could not miss the allusion: Naboth had lost both his vineyard and his life because of the covetousness of his neighbour Ahab. The volume was dedicated to 'Some future South Africa (I pray not distant) when the *Good Hope* of the old navigator shall have been realised'.

Returning from South Africa, Butler chose to travel on a steamer calling at St Helena, taking what he knew would be his last opportunity to see the promethean rock of the Great Captain. He arrived back in England to find that on the first honours list drawn up by the new Liberal administration, he was to be invested as a Knight Grand Cross of the Bath. It was an honour whose bestowal personally pleased the king. Butler did not delay in England but hastened to Bansha 'more tired than I have ever been for years'. His travelling days were at last over. In Bansha, reading and writing, he was, in his daughter Eileen's words, 'at leisure for the first time in his life'.

It was typical of Butler that a fair proportion of that leisure activity was spent in public life. His formal army connections were not completely broken, for he became a governor of the Royal Hibernian Military Academy. He also found much to speak out about in his homeland. His value system had been shaped by a lifetime of discipline and an ideal of service, and he was critical of certain aspects of what he found around him in Ireland. There was a fecklessness and 'a wild waste of individualism' in too many of his countrymen. He noted among the newly propertied rural class an aversion to making the most of their good fortune by land improvement and productive farming. He thought that Irishmen in general were squandering their best resource – themselves – in their mania for sport and their over-indulgence in drink and gambling. Too many people were 'going to the devil on the backs of horses and in betting booths'. He was also critical of an Irish nationalism that excluded unionism.

In October 1907 Butler gave the inaugural address at the fifth annual conference of the Irish Catholic Truth Society, held in the Rotunda Rooms in Dublin. He spoke before a distinguished audience of clergy and laity. The conference was formally opened by Cardinal Logue, archbishop of

Armagh, who introduced Butler as 'an Irishman of European renown'. Butler spoke with fluency and power. The following day the *Irish Independent* devoted its main editorial to commenting on his speech: 'Few of the soft nothings of flattery fell from the lips of Sir William Butler in the brilliant address he delivered last night ... An Irishman filled with an intense love of his native land, he spoke with candour of the weaknesses of his countrymen.'[6]

Indeed, although much of what Butler said was the familiar soothing platitudes of contemporary nationalist orations – that the island of Ireland was a unique spot blessed by Heaven with a proud past and a special people – there was more:

> The difficulty with the Irish race is not a matter of joining hands across the sea – we do that readily enough – the trouble is much more local than that. It is a matter of joining hands across the Boyne or across the Bann or over some paltry streamlet across whose waters the feeblest butterfly could flutter. It has sometimes seemed to me that if we were a little less like each other in Ireland we could get on better together – each party knows the other so well that they are never at a loss where to find the exact spot to hit the other man. The weak place in the armour is always visible. If the Boyne or the Bann were as wide as the Mississippi or the St. Lawrence the rival champions would not be able to see each other's eyes. As things are, they can go one better than that, for they can discern the green and the orange tints in them ...
>
> Ireland has now to go into business on her own account, and it will be no use for her to plead in the future the black statutes of a past injustice. The thing that is of vital importance to her is that she should rub her eyes, see where she is standing, study whither she is going and tackle the problems, social, sanitary, economic and educational, that are lying immediately before her. For the solution of these problems everybody can join hands – priest, parson, physician, patriot and policeman – can all come together, and from the field of common labour no man or woman need be absent.[7]

This speech, later printed as a pamphlet by the Catholic Truth Society, struck what would be the consistent public note of Butler's occasional public addresses in the last years of his life. His view that Irish people must shake off much of the past was shared by Elizabeth, as her daughter Eileen attested:

Her English commonsense was often irritated by the Irishman's habit of blaming present-day ineptitude on bygone injustice, and also by his perverseness. 'I suppose this is all Oliver Cromwell's fault,' – I heard my mother mutter, as with a face puckered with disgust, she entered a filthy Dublin cab whose harness was held together with string and whose floor was carpetted with straw.[8]

Elizabeth loved the serenity of the Tipperary countryside. Her artist's eye feasted on the surroundings of Bansha and on the cloud formations over the Galtees. Of the Butler children, only one, Eileen, came to live with her parents. For a young woman of twenty-two, fond of socializing and used to the bustle of Plymouth, Bansha could be lonely, and it was as much for Eileen's sake as for any desire to be sociable that the Butlers joined the Irish social round – Horse Show Week, the Castle Season and occasional weekends in the homes of the Catholic nobility. In 1911 Eileen would marry Jenico Edward Preston, 15th Viscount Gormanston.

Butler did not lose touch with English public issues. He joined the recurrent debate on the construction of a channel tunnel between England and France. In 1907 proposals to build a tunnel were brought further than ever before. A joint Anglo-French commercial concern, the Channel Tunnel Company, produced a comprehensive collection of essays on different aspects of the project. Butler's contribution was an essay entitled 'The Channel Tunnel and National Defence'. It made a vigorous and prescient case for an imaginative leap forward by Britain. He appealed for an exhaustive examination of the project, while accepting that there might be 'cogent reasons' for turning it down. A rational veto based on all the arguments was one he would have little problem with. What he could not accept was the abandonment of the project 'because of old-world fears and prejudices ... begotten in the days when the cocked hat and grey riding coat of Napoleon, stuck upon a stick on the coast of France, were deemed sufficient to frighten all Europe from its propriety'.[9]

The Channel Tunnel Company fell victim to British concerns about national security. Wolseley had vehemently opposed an earlier similar scheme. When visiting him around this time Butler had the upsetting experience of finding Wolseley temporarily incoherent and unable to recognize him. Other old comrades were slipping away. Buller died in 1908.

Butler remained actively involved in Irish education. He was on the governing board of Clongowes, and was a commissioner of the National Education Board. He was also on the statutory commission for the setting up of a national university and became a senator of the new National University of Ireland following the enabling legislation of August 1908. It was in this capacity that he gave his heaviest commitment to education. He was a capable ally of William Delany S.J., the president of University College Dublin. Delany was his near contemporary and a former rector of Tullabeg. Both men were opposed to the idea of a national university being narrowly nationalistic in its orientation.

Butler had strong reservations about the influence of the Gaelic League in third-level education. Through the latter part of 1909 there was much argument about the allocation of professorships. Butler's patience was tried. He wrote to Alice Stopford Green that work on the commission was 'a thankless job like many other things in this land of clamour'. His main concern regarding the professorships were the chairs of History and Celtic Archaeology. As he explained to Stopford Green:

> I take a greater interest in the teaching of these two subjects to the coming race of Irishmen than I do in regard to any other items of instruction. I feel very strongly about the whole matter and I want to see the best man in these chairs irrespective of other considerations ... A proper school of History we must have – an all round school. That is the particular in which the Gaelic League fails. It is narrow, one-sided and largely ignorant of the outside world.[10]

Butler also supported William Delany's unsuccessful attempts to resist the introduction of Irish as a compulsory matriculation subject. Butler's involvement in public life was formally recognized in 1909 when, in the king's birthday honours list that June, he was made a Privy Councillor for Ireland.

While educational matters occupied Butler to some extent, it was in the seclusion of Bansha, among his books and papers, that he spent most of his time. Daily routine saw Elizabeth in her studio in the paddock and Butler in his study. He wrote a preface for a new edition of *The Wild North Land*, and collected miscellaneous essays representing over forty years of his writing, published under the title *The Light of the West* in 1909. Butler had previously written about St Patrick, to whom the title referred, in 1880 for the Catholic periodical, *Merry England*.

Much of Butler's attention was given over to his autobiography, for the most part, a leisured and anecdotal journey through his life. He worked chronologically and at the time of his death was tackling South Africa in

1899: the tone and content of this section show how deeply he still felt, eleven years on, about events at that time.

The North American West was never far from his thoughts. For years his memories of those days had been a staple of his imagination – sometimes in the unlikeliest of situations:

> 'If you have once tasted well of that wild fruit, you have got an antidote forever against being bored. My friends sometimes say to me, 'How can you listen so patiently to that old bore General Pounce?' or, 'I saw you today in the morning-room with that stupid old Major de Trop, and you seemed to be hanging on every word he said,' at which I smile, but say nothing for it would destroy my happiness if the secret were known. As he ripples along I launch my canoe on the stream of his story, merely on the sound of it and I sail away into the lone spaces.'[11]

In a coincidental affirmation of the value of his North American experiences, he received in May 1910 a message relayed from former President Theodore Roosevelt who was visiting Britain. Roosevelt, who had spent two of the formative years of his life as a ranch hand on the prairies, wanted to meet the author of *The Great Lone Land*, one of his favourite books. From Bansha, Butler sent a telegram: 'Regret extremely. Unable to leave room owing to chill. Please express to Mr. Roosevelt honour I feel at his kind message, and reference which I shall always prize, to my little book of nearly forty years ago.'[12]

Butler's death was unexpected. The chill which confined him to bed at the time of Roosevelt's message in May led to acute chest and intestinal complications by the end of the month. A medical specialist, called from Dublin, could do nothing but confirm that his condition was critical. News that he was ill was carried by the press. On 7 June Wolseley, in one of his infrequent periods of lucidity, wrote to him:

> My dear Butler. Today's papers state that you are unwell. I earnestly pray that this note may reach you in the enjoyment of rapid recovery and that I may soon hear of you being the strong merry comrade you always were to me. I always looked upon you as a host in yourself, ready to undertake any difficult job, and the more dangerous it was the more you enjoyed it. May God in his mercy soon restore you to your family and all your friends, of whom none have ever valued your friendship more than your very attached friend and old comrade.[13]

Butler never saw that letter. He died that very morning in Bansha. The cause of death would be registered as 'Acute Intestinal Infection 7 days. Cardiac Failure'. After he had passed away Elizabeth said of him: 'he taught me how to live, and now he has taught me how to die'.[4] Among the many letters of sympathy which were sent to Bansha Castle was one from Queen Alexandra, who had lost Edward VII the previous month.

Butler's will, unaltered since he had made it on his return from South Africa in 1899, left all his possessions to Elizabeth, except for a bequest of £100 to his unmarried sister Frances, who had nursed him at Netley after the Asante war. His total estate was valued at just over £9000. Small bills outstanding included £2.4s.0 due to a Clonmel vinter, £3.10s.0 due to a Dublin tailor and a £5 annual subscription to the Catholic Truth Society.

The funeral service, presided over by Archbishop Fennelly of Cashel, was held in the village church of Bansha on 10 June 1910. Mass was celebrated by the parish priest of Tipperary, Canon Arthur Ryan. During the service Butler's coffin, covered by a white pall, rested on a small catafalque. On the pall lay his ceremonial sword, his plumed dress hat and his military decorations. The piled wreaths included one from the viceroy, Lord Aberdeen, and several from old army comrades such as Brackenbury and Kelly-Kenny. Among the mourners were Butler's son-in-law, Randolph Kingscote, and Laurence Waldron who had secured the nationalist seat in the 1904 by-election for the St Stephen's Green Division of Dublin.

The funeral procession, a mile of mourners in carriages and on foot, wound its way from Bansha to the graveyard at Killardrigh where Butler's own father had been buried among his ancestors thirty years before. The coffin was borne on a gun carriage drawn by eight black horses. The white pall had been removed as the coffin was carried from the church, and replaced by the Union Jack. To the beat of muffled drums, the band of the Royal Irish Regiment, Clonmel, led the cortege. The graveyard and its environs were quietly thronged for the last rites before, in the light of a high summer afternoon, Butler's remains were slowly lowered into Irish earth in the valley of the Suir.

Elizabeth Butler lived on at Bansha Castle for the next twelve years. In 1922, during the Irish civil war, her home was commandeered first by republican and then by state forces. Elizabeth, seventy-five years old, moved to Gormanston Castle, County Meath, to live with her daughter Eileen. She died in Gormanston in 1932 and was buried just down the road from the castle at Stamullen Cemetery.

EPILOGUE

Paying tribute to Butler at a meeting of Tipperary Executive Council just after his death, Canon Arthur Ryan, parish priest of Tipperary town, spoke of Butler as 'a member of an alien army and so in a sense an alien to the governed people of Ireland'. He was reflecting a common, if incorrect, view in Tipperary of Butler, for Butler as a nationalist and a Home Ruler was typical of the majority of his countrymen in 1910. However, Ryan was right about Butler being an alien, although it was in a manner other than which he meant. Butler was essentially an outsider. The breadth and independence of his views, coupled with his emphatic expression of them, made him, throughout his life and no matter where he was, something of a solitary. It is this trait of Butler's that has been responsible for his near eradication from the historical memory of Britain and Ireland. To both countries he was something of an embarrassment. If Butler was too much of an imperialist for nationalist Ireland, he was also too nationalist for imperialist Britain. In the Irish Free State of the 1920s he could be publicly described as having been 'an Orange Catholic', yet the strongly unionist *Irish Times* had said at the time of his death that 'with Sir William's political opinions Irish Unionists could have little sympathy'.

In public life Butler's Irishness was subsumed by his Britishness, no less than if he had been English, Scots or Welsh. In *The Great Lone Land*, when discussing what he saw as an English tendency to denigrate all those outside a narrow cultural ambit, Butler refered to himself as Anglo-Saxon. Whether this was an *ad hoc* reference for the purpose of the argument, or an exercise in self-definition by a young man, by Butler's middle years Ireland and the 'Celtic race' were central strands of his identity, a development strongly supported by his wife, whose natural sympathies for the oppressed and marginalized were focused to telling effect in 'Evicted'.

Butler should be seen in the context of his own time. His military career was shaped by the unprecedented imperial expansion of Great Britain, in which many Irish of his generation, nationalist and unionist, played a significant part. The Irish were to be found in the imperial public service; in administration, law, medicine, the army and the police. In the private sector they worked in commerce, finance, farming and industry throughout the empire. Irish missioners – British subjects – followed and sometimes preceded the Union Jack around the globe. During the 1880s nationalist MPs in the imperial parliament in London argued that Home Rule would ensure Ireland's loyalty to the empire. Butler was drawn to the Home Rule movement both as a sympathizer and, in his later years, as a minor activist. In the five years left to him in his retirement he was active in Irish public life, but his outspokenness and his lifelong tendency to stand with one foot out of the circle of conformity made him occasionally an awkward ally and a captious colleague – as it had done throughout his career. However, his warm candour drew others to him at a visceral level, though they might not agree with either his views or his forceful expression of them. Further, his outspokenness can be overstressed. Few observers would have predicted in the late 1880s that it would be Redvers Buller and Garnet Wolseley who would end their military careers in discredit and indignity respectively, while Butler would end his own career entrusted by the Secretary of State for War with the investigation of a major army scandal, and nominated to contest a seat for the Liberal Party in the General Election of 1906.

Butler drew much of his emotional and intellectual strength from deep internal reserves. He possessed a self-reliance and independence which can be seen not only in his official dealings with others and the views he propounded, but also in many of the enterprises he undertook throughout his life. On the Red River Expedition his commission was a solo one; his two Canadian treks were planned as lone ventures; in the Asante War he was the only officer of the Ring to live alone with the Akim; his responsibilities for the boats on the Gordon Relief Expedition kept him as senior officer on the Nile while his colleagues went upriver with the expedition; his command at Wadi Halfa was at the outer limit of Egyptian control of the Nile Valley.

As an author, Butler's *oeuvre* was considerable: fourteen publications, which included collections of eclectic essays, two travel books, accounts of his military campaigns, three biographies, a novel and an unfinished auto-biography. Much of his writing has dated, but at his best, and this encom-passes a considerable variety and quantity, he is a writer of wit and of marked descriptive and persuasive power – as many of the excerpts quot-ed in the preceding pages show. Three of his works, *Charles George Gordon*, *The Great Lone Land* and *Red Cloud*, have secure niches in the pantheon of nineteenth century biography, travel and juvenile fiction.

In *The Great Lone Land*, already referred to at the end of Chapter Three, William Francis Butler stands at the source of the Rainy River in August 1870, solidly and solitary between two worlds. His right arm is out-stretched in greeting towards the approaching flotilla, while three Ojibwa canoeists kneel below and behind him. The image captures the alien in this generous-spirited man, who throughout his life may have smiled at the world he lived in and served, but who, in words quoted by his brother-in-law Wilfred Meynell after his death, smiled in a manner 'that hurt half of his mouth'.

NOTES AND REFERENCES

All brief, unattributed quotations are from Butler's writings.

Abbreviations

MP Meynell Papers. Private collection of Catherine Eden, Hermia Eden, Elizabeth Hawkins

NLI National Library of Ireland

PRO Public Record Office, Kew

RCWISA Royal Commission into the War in South Africa. Parliamentary Papers 1904, vols. 40–2

WP Wolseley Papers. Hove Central Library

CHAPTER 1: ROOTS

1 William F. Butler, *An Autobiography* (London 1911), pp. 11–12.
2 Martin Ryan, 'Sir William Francis Butler: The eviction scene of his childhood', *Tipperary Historical Journal* (1999), pp. 38–42. This monograph examines a famine diary of Richard Butler and a Land Commission archive.
3 Lord Dunboyne believes that Butler's patrilineal lineage is as follows: s/o Richard of Ballyslatteen (d.1870), s/o John of Ballycarron (d.1801), s/o Thomas of Ballycarron (d.1767), s/o Toby of Grange (d.1725), s/o John of Garranlea (d.1694), s/o John of Derryclooney (d.1642), s/o Thomas of Derrycloney (d. after 17 March 1592), s/o Theobald of Derryluskan (d.1610), s/o John of Derryluskan (d. by Feb 1551/2), younger s/o James 9th Lord Dunboyne (d.1508).
4 Butler, *ibid*, pp. 1–2.
5 Clongowes Wood College Archive.
6 *Ibid.*
7 Butler, *ibid.* p. 4. Butler's etymology is faulty here. *Tula* is Irish for a hill.

CHAPTER 2: GONE FOR A SOLDIER

1 Butler, *Autobiography*, p. 40.

2 *Ibid.* The original source is untraceable. Butler quotes from the diary in his autobiography.

3 *Ibid.* pp. 36–7.

4 *Ibid.* pp. 49–50.

5 *Ibid.* p. 349.

6 *Ibid.* p. 65.

CHAPTER 3: CANADA AND THE RED RIVER

1 Butler, *Autobiography*, p. 92.

2 *Ibid.* p. 90.

3 *Ibid.* pp. 93–4.

4 William F. Butler, *The Great Lone Land*, (London 1872), p. 320. In 1872 Butler did kill buffalo again, but for survival.

5 Wolseley to Frances Wolseley. 6 Oct 1890. Quoted in Joseph Lehmann, *All Sir Garnet: A Life of Field Marshal Lord Wolseley*, (London 1964), p. 24.

6 Field Marshal Viscount Wolseley, *A Story of a Soldier's Life*, (London 1903), vol. 2, p. 200.

7 Butler, *Autobiography*, pp. 107–8.

8 The Ballyslatteen estate had been made over to Thomas Butler on the occasion of his marriage in 1867. William inherited a 78-acre farm from his father which yielded him a yearly rental of between £60 and £50. He sold the farm shortly before his own death in 1910.

9 Louis Riel (1844–85). Of mixed French, Irish and Native American ancestry. Executed for treason against the Dominion of Canada. Riel has left a complex legacy. Largely ignored in the decades immediately after his death, he has become a symbol of the fractures in Canadian national identity. He is seen variously as a proto-French-Canadian separatist, a champion of the rights of the First Nations, a strong proof for the Métis of historic nationhood, and an early examplar of western Canada's resistance to control by the east.

10 Butler, *The Great Lone Land*, p. 8.

11 Wolseley, *ibid.* pp. 201–2.

12 Butler, *Autobiography*, p. 119.

13 Butler, *The Great Lone Land*, p. 113.

14 *Ibid.* p. 118.

15 *Ibid.* p. 121.

16 J. Dennis Duffy, *Mapping the Great Lone Land: How the Butlers Did It* (University College Dublin 1995). Inaugural lecture, Craig Dobbin Chair of Canadian Studies. A lucid exposition of the imperial assumptions behind the artistic endeavours of *The Great Lone Land* and *Evicted*.

17 Butler, *ibid.* p. 135.

18 *Ibid.* pp. 139–40.

19 *Ibid.* p. 189.

CHAPTER 4: SEARCHING FOR A ROAD

1 Butler, *The Great Lone Land*, p. 197.

2 *Ibid.* p. 243.

3. Hamilton, *These are the Prairies* (Saskatchewan 1848), pp. 87–9. Quoted in Edward McCourt, *Remember Butler* (London 1967), p. 69.

4 Butler, *ibid.* p. 336.

5 *Ibid.* p. 306.

6 *Ibid.* Appendix. pp. 353–86.

7 S.W. Horral, 'Sir John A. Macdonald and the Mounted Police Force for the Northwest Territories', *Canadian Historical Review*, vol. LIII, no. 2 (1972).

8 Butler, *Autobiography*, pp. 122–3.

9 *Ibid.* pp. 128–9.

10 *Ibid.* pp. 133–4.

11 *Ibid.*

12 William F. Butler, *The Wild North Land* (London 1874), pp. 11–12.

13 *Ibid.* pp. 260–1.

14 *Ibid.* p. 79.

15 *Ibid.* pp. 301–2.

16 *Ibid.* p. 358.

17 *Ibid.* p. 338. Red Cloud (1822–1909). Between 1866 and 1868 he successfully resisted U.S. encroachment on ancestral Sioux lands. Captain William Fetterman led an 81-man force out of Fort Phil Kearny on the Powder River in December 1866. Against orders, he pursued what he thought were ten frightened Indians. They led him into a 2000-man ambush prepared by Red Cloud. Lester Wallick was an American actor manager, with his own Broadway theatre a premier venue for popular drama.

CHAPTER 5: THE WHITE MAN'S GRAVE

1 Butler, *The Wild North Land*, pp. v-vi.

2 Stanley (1841-1904) has been the subject of more biographies than any other nineteenth-century British explorer. He was born in Denbigh in North Wales to Elizabeth Parry, an unmarried domestic servant, and given the name of his father, John Rowlands. At the age of seventeen, he had shipped as a cabin boy from Liverpool to New Orleans where he had been befriended by a childless couple named Stanley whose name he took. In 1873 Stanley's achievements were still as nothing to what he would go on to do in the following seventeen years as the foremost explorer and empire builder in Central Africa.

3 H.M. Stanley, *Coomassie and Magdala* (London 1874), p. 154.

4 William F. Butler, *Akim Foo: The Story of a Failure*, Appendix 1 (London 1876), pp. 253-4.

5 *Ibid.* p. 23.

6 *Ibid.* p. 192.

7 *Ibid.* p. 110.

8 *Ibid.* p. 212.

9 *The Times*, 9 Mar. 1874.

10 Stanley, *ibid.* pp. 243-4.

11 *The Times*, 16 Apr. 1874.

12 Butler, *Autobiography*, pp. 169-70.

CHAPTER 6: SOUTHERN AFRICA

1 John Robinson, *A Lifetime in South Africa* (London 1900), p. 36.

2 *Ibid.*

3 *Ibid.* p. 38.

4 William F. Butler, *Far Out: Rovings Re-told* (London 1880), pp. 278-9.

5 *Ibid.* p. 269.

6 Butler, *Autobiography*, p. 183-4.

7 H. Rider Haggard, *The Days of My Life* (London 1926), vol. 1, pp. 50-1.

8 Butler, *Autobiography*, pp. 188-9.

9 Butler, *Far Out*, pp. 158-74.

10 *Annual Register* (1879), p. 13.

11 Butler, *Autobiography*, p. 198.

12 Viscount Gormanston, private papers.

13 Butler, *ibid.*, p. 204.

14 Wolseley to Louisa Wolseley, 13 Aug. 1879, in Sir George Arthur, ed., *The Letters of Lord and Lady Wolseley*, 1870-1911 (London 1922), p. 43.

15 Butler, *ibid.* p. 213.

16 Butler, *Far Out*, p. 190.

CHAPTER 7: 'YOUR LIFE IS STILL BEFORE YOU'

1 Butler, *Autobiography*, p. 215.

2 Elizabeth Butler, *Autobiography* (Kent 1993), p. 134.

3 Viola Meynell, *Alice Meynell* (New York 1929), p. 2.

4 G. Storey, K. Tillotson, A. Easson (eds), *The Letters of Charles Dickens* (Oxford 1993), vol. 7, p. 178.

5 Elizabeth Butler, *Autobiography*, p. 37.

6 Alice Meynell. Quoted in J.G. Snead-Cox, *Life of Cardinal Vaughan* (London 1910), vol. 1, p. 262.

7 Elizabeth Butler, *ibid.* p. 88.

8 At the height of her popularity in the 1870s Elizabeth Thompson's earnings were

substantial. Where possible she worked to commissions.

The Roll Call was commissioned for £126. Its success allowed her to sell the commission of two earlier paintings for £1200. Her next commission, *Quatre Bras*, paid her £1126. 'Balaclava' had originally been an untitled commission, for which she had agreed in 1873 to accept £80. In 1876 she negotiated a price in three figures for it. For *Inkermann*, exhibited at the time of her marriage, she was paid £3000.

While these earnings were high, they were less than one-tenth of the profits earned by The Fine Arts Society from engravings of the paintings. Sales of the engravings netted the society over £51,000 during the years 1874-7. See Paul Usherwood, and Jenny Spencer-Smith, *Lady Butler: Battle Artist* (Gloucester 1987), pp. 41–3 & p. 67. Also, Elizabeth Butler, *Autobiography*, pp. 89–91.

9 MP, Elizabeth Butler to Christiana Thompson, June 1877.

10 Elizabeth Butler, *Autobiography*, p. 144.

11 *Contemporary Review*, Feb. 1881, pp. 230–1.

12 Haggard, *The Days of My Life*, vol. 1, pp. 186–7.

13 *Contemporary Revie,. ibid.* p. 221.

14 *Ibid.*, July 1881, pp. 104–5.

15 WP, Butler file/3, Butler to Wolseley, 21 Nov. 1881.

16 Butler, *Red Cloud: The Solitary Sioux* (London 1882), pp. 326–7. The editing of *Red Cloud*, before it was used as a school text in the Irish Free State in the 1930s and 1940s, is an interesting example of expurgation. One of Butler's enduring memories of his Suir Valley boyhood was of listening to fireside tales from old Irish soldiers who had followed the British flag in Europe and farther afield. He drew on these memories for the opening chapter of *Red Cloud* which deals with the Kerry boyhood of the narrator.

Butler gives the boy a soldier-father who had been wounded fighting in India. One of the neighbours is a pensioner from Her Majesty's 40th Regiment who in his youth had followed the Duke of Wellington 'from the Tagus to Toulouse'. Killarney, the nearest large town, 'boasts' three heroes of the Peninsular War. These and similiar references were expunged from the school edition of *Red Cloud* by the book's editor the Reverend Timothy Corcoran, S.J., Professor of Education at University College Dublin, 1909–42.

Corcoran (1872–1943) was, like Butler, a Tipperary man, but unlike Butler was noted for his republican views and anglo-phobia. The deletions in *Red Cloud* cannot be explained away as the expression of an anti-military philosophy by the moral guardians of Irish youth, for what is not expunged is an old Catholic priest who feeds the boy's imagination with stories of France and the campaigns of Napoleon.

Britain, unlike France, was clearly not on the side of the angels for the new Ireland. 'History', wrote Butler in his autobiography, 'loves its lies and carries them into a green old age; they sell better than truth.'

CHAPTER 8: THE EGYPTIAN CAMPAIGN AND ITS AFTERMATH

1 *The Times*, 21 Feb. 1876.
2 Wilfrid Scawen Blunt (1840–1922). Landed Conservative background. A strong critic of imperial expansion. He spent ten years as a diplomat before an inheritance allowed him to pursue political issues untrammelled by the need to hold his tongue. He first came to Egypt in 1875, and bought a house and estate there, taking to wearing Arab dress and indulging a passion for horses. He became friendly with Urabi and promoted the native Egyptian cause. He was Urabi's most vocal defender in England.

A man of wide sympathies, he spent two months in jail in Galway in 1887 for trying to address a proscribed Home Rule meeting. His social circle in England was linked to Butler's through Cardinal Manning, a family friend. He wrote *The Secret History of the English Occupation of Egypt*, which exposed the involvement of European bankers in the 1882 invasion.

3 Butler, *Autobiography*, p. 222.
4 *Ibid*. p. 240.
5 *Ibid*. p. 243.
6 In 1880, in a speech in the House of Lords, Dunraven suggested that the solution to Ireland's land hunger and poverty lay in a planned emigration policy that would settle an Irish colony in Manitoba. He was distrustful of Parnell. In 1879, when Parnell went on a successful tour of the United States, Dunraven had written an article for the *New York Herald* criticizing him as an irresponsible rabble rouser: 'Of all the quack cures for hard times the Parnell pill is the simplest and the most deleterious. It consists of the maxim "when hard up don't pay your bills".' NLI, Ir94108/19.
7 Butler, *Autobiography*, p. 256.
8 Butler, *Autobiography*, p. 191.

CHAPTER 9: THE GORDON RELIEF EXPEDITION

1 WP, Butler file/4, Butler to Wolseley, 28 Feb. 1884. Colonel Valentine Baker was a British officer in Egyptian service. He had been sent in December 1883 to re-assert Egyptian authority in the Eastern Sudan where his force was routed on 5 Feb 1884.
2 Hansard, *Parliamentary Debates*, 3rd series, vol. 288, 12 May 1884, col. 55.
3 William F. Butler, *The Campaign of the Cataracts* (London 1887), pp. 41–2.
4 Ian Hamilton. Quoted in Gwynn Harries-Jenkins, *The Army in Victorian Society* (Toronto 1977), p. 198.
5 Butler, *ibid*. pp. 141–2.
6 Butler, *Autobiography*, pp. 285–6.
7 Adrian Preston (ed), *In Relief of Gordon* (London 1967), pp. 75–6.
8 *The Tablet*, 25 Dec. 1886.

9 *Daily Telegraph*, 31 Dec. 1884.

10 Butler, *ibid*. p. 295.

11 *Ibid*. p. 303–4.

12 *Ibid*.

13 Charles Royle, *The Egyptian Campaigns* (London 1900), p. 397.

14 Quoted in Lehmann, *All Sir Garnet*, p. 374.

15 Wolseley to Louisa Wolseley, 18 Mar. 1885, in Preston, ibid. p. 171. On the matter of being Irish, the date of Wolseley's vist to Merowe gives scope for speculation. Wolseley could have come up to Merowe on 17 March when Butler as Officer Commanding would have formally marked Ireland's national day. He chose to come on 18 March. He thus shared with Butler the immediate aftermath of the occasion without compromising his professional distance from drowning the shamrock.

16 Butler, *Autobiography*, pp. 309–10.

17 MP, Elizabeth Butler to Christiana Thompson, 13 Jul. 1885.

CHAPTER 10: ON THE SUDAN FRONTIER

1 Butler, *Autobiography*, p. 319.

2 PRO, WO/32/6139. 24–5 Dec. 1885.

3 Elizabeth Butler, *Autobiography*, p. 153.

4 Butler, *ibid*. p. 327.

5 *The Times*, 2 Jan. 1886.

6 Butler, *ibid*. p. 331.

7 *Ibid*. p. 333.

8 *Ibid*. pp. 337–8.

9 WP, Private Letter Book, /69, Wolseley.

10 Butler, *Autobiography*, p. 345.

11 *Ibid*. p. 348.

CHAPTER 11: THE CAMPBELL DIVORCE CASE

1 Like Wolseley ('the very model of a modern major-general'), Shaw was written into a Gilbert and Sullivan operetta. He attended the opening night of *Iolanthe* in November 1882. Sitting beside Gertrude Campbell who was there as the guest of Arthur Sullivan, he found himself apostrophized by the Queen of the Fairies: 'Oh, Captain Shaw!/ Type of true love kept under!/ Could thy Brigade/ With cold cascade/ Quench my great love, I wonder!'

2 *The Irish Times*, 23 Dec. 1886.

3 *Daily Telegraph*, 4 Dec. 1886.

4 *Ibid*.

5 *Daily Telegraph*, 7 Dec. 1886.

6 *Ibid*.

7 *Daily Telegraph*, 11 Dec. 1886.
8 *Ibid.*
9 *Ibid.*
10 *The Irish Times*, 23 Dec. 1886.
11 *Daily Telegraph*, & *The Times*, 17 Dec. 1886.
12 *The Times*, 18 Dec. 1886.
13 *Daily Telegraph*, 21 Dec. 1886.
14 *Ibid.*
15 *The Times*, 21 Dec. 1886.
16 *The Irish Times*, 23 Dec. 1886.
17 *The Tablet*, 25 Dec. 1886.
18 McCourt, *Remember Butler*, p. 198
19 *Ibid.*
20 MP, Elizabeth Butler to Alice Meynell, 12 Dec. 1884: 'I received a telegram on Monday from Will on receipt of my letter on the subject of the charge. He says "All comes well with God's help" and promises to "cheer up" as I asked him to. Poor fellow. His heart must be full though.'
21 *The Irish Times*, 23 Dec 1886.

CHAPTER 12: RETRENCHMENT AND RENEWAL

1 Butler, Autobiography, p. 349.
2 Gertrude Sweetman, 'Random Recollections of a Great Painter', ts, private collection of Brian Whitlock Blundell.
3 William F. Butler, *Charles George Gordon* (London 1889), p. 188.
4 *Ibid.* p. 109.
5 *Ibid.* pp. 178–9.
6 Arthur, *The Letters of Lord and Lady Wolseley*, pp. 268–9.
7 William F. Butler, *Sir Charles Napier* (London 1890), pp. 127–8.
8 WP, Private Letter Book, /69, Wolseley.
9 MP, Elizabeth Butler to Alice Meynell, 20 Apr. 1888.
10 Butler, *Autobiography*, pp. 351–3.
11 PRO, WO/33/48/A151.
12 Butler, *The Light of The West* (Dublin 1909), pp. 88–9.
13 Usherwood and Spencer-Smith, *ibid.* pp. 94–5.
14 *The Times*, 5 May 1890. Quoted in Usherwood and Spencer-Smith, *ibid.*
15 Elizabeth Butler, *Autobiography*, p. 174.
16 Butler, *Autobiography*, p. 367.
17 *Ibid.* p. 375. The 'three and twenty years' is an example of Butler's punctiliousness – he has allowed for the seven years Jesus spent in Egypt as a child.
18 Wolseley to Louisa Wolseley. 29 Nov. 1890, in Arthur, *ibid.* p. 274.
19 Butler, *Autobiography*, p. 382.
20 Eileen Gormanston, *A Little Kept* (London 1953), pp. 33–5.
21 *The Cornhill Magazine*, May 1912.

22 WP, Butler Letters File, Butler to Louisa Wolseley, 28 Feb. 1898.

23 William F. Butler, *The Life of George Pomeroy Colley* (London 1899), pp. 399–400.

24 NLI, Gormanston Ms. 15,997, Wolseley to Butler, 8 Feb. 1899.

CHAPTER 13: THE NEW SOUTH AFRICA

1 See J.L. Garvin, *Life of Joseph Chamberlain* (London 1934), vol. 3, pp. 364–5. Born in 1868 in England, the son of poor emigrant Irish catholics, Garvin became a journalist with the *Daily Telegraph*. He was a leading conservative socialite and an admirer of Chamberlain. His biography of Chamberlain, unfinished when he died, is partisan. In his account of the South Africa crisis, he is scathing of Butler as Acting High Commissioner referring to him as 'Dear old Butler of Afrikaaner affection' and 'an extraordinary locum tenens ... nothing could abate his quixotic imagination nor rein his tilting pen'.

2 Milner to Chamberlain, 19 Oct. 1899, in Cecil Headlam, ed., *Milner Papers* (London 1931), vol. 1, p. 288.

A Fellow of the Royal Historical Society and the author of several novels, Headlam's few references to Butler are dismissive of him and, in one instance, deliberately misleading. He writes (pp. 291–2): 'In his Autobiography Sir William complained that he was given "no hint that war with the Dutch Republic was a probable contingency", but at the same time affirmed that he knew that "at that time a section of people including several prominent persons at the War Office were at work to bring about that war at an early date". This is in itself something of a contradiction in terms ...'

What Butler actually wrote (*Autobiography*, p. 385) was that he was given 'no hint that war with the Dutch Republic was a probable contingency. Yet I have full reason to think now that even at that time a section of people, including several prominent persons in the War Office, were at work to bring that war about at an early date'. Headlam has taken two consecutive sentences, removed the phrase 'yet I have full reason to think now', and replaced it with his own phrase, 'but at the same time affirmed that he knew'.

3 Butler, *Autobiography*, p. 386.

4 *Ibid.* p. 398.

5 *Ibid.* pp. 409–10.

6 RCWISA, Parliamentary Papers 1904, vol. 40, p. 205.

7 31 Jan. 1899, in Headlam, *ibid.* p. 301.

8 Selborne to Milner, 12 Feb. 1899, Milner Papers, 5f.145 Bodleian Library. Quoted in A.N. Porter, *The Origins of the South African War* (Manchester 1980), p. 184.

9 23 Feb. 1899, in Headlam, *ibid.* p. 303. Walter Hely-Hutchinson was the second son of the 4th Earl of Donoughmore. His childhood home was Knocklofty House, by the river Suir near Clonmel, some twelve miles downriver from Butler's childhood home.

10 RCWISA, vol. 40, p. 201.

CHAPTER 14: 'THE CENTRAL STORM SPOT OF THE WORLD'

1 Butler, *Autobiography,* p. 427.
2 Headlam, *ibid.* pp. 402–3.
3 PRO, WO/32/7850.
4 NLI, Gormanston Ms. 15,997.
5 PRO, *ibid.* Butler to Under Secretary Wyndham, 12 Jun. 1899. Written in red ink across the deciphered cable is the instruction 'Not to be shown to the Cabinet at present'.
6 RCWISA, vol. 41, p. 79.
7 *Ibid.*
8 *Ibid.*
9 Butler, *Autobiography,* p. 452.
10 WP, Wolseley to George Wolseley, 18 Aug. 1899.
11 Butler, *ibid.* p. 454.
12 Richard Rive, *Olive Schreiner: Letters* (Oxford 1988), vol. 1, pp. 381–2.
13 *The Illustrated London News,* 2 Sep. 1899.
14 *Daily Mail,* 20 Dec. 1899. Quoted in McCourt, *Remember Butler,* p. 234.
15 *Daily News,* 6 Nov. 1899.
16 RCWISA, vol. 41, p. 87.
17 Elizabeth Butler, *Autobiography,* p. 218.
18 Thomas Pakenham, *The Boer War* (London 1982), p. xvii.

CHAPTER 15: NEW HORIZONS

1 Esher to HM, 18 Dec. 1899, M.V. Brett (ed.), *The Journals and Letters of Reginald Viscount Esher* (London 1934), vol. 1, p. 251.
2 MP, Butler to Alice Meynell, 13 Jul. 1900.
3 MP, Elizabeth Butler to Alice Meynell, 22 Apr. 1902.
4 *The Times,* 26 Oct. 1901.
5 RCWISA, Butler to WO, 4 Nov. 1901, vol. 41, p. 87.
6 *Ibid.* WO to Butler, 27 Nov. 1901, vol. 41, p. 88.
7 *Ibid.* Butler to WO, 16 Dec. 1901, vol. 41, p. 88.
8 *Ibid.* WO to Butler, 18 Feb. 1902, vol. 41, p. 92.
9 Gormanston, *A Little Kept,* p. 20.
10 Elizabeth Butler, *Autobiography,* p. 230.
11 Stephen Gwynn, *Experiences of a Literary Man* (London 1926), pp. 210–11.
12 R. Barry O'Brien, *Studies in Irish History* (Dublin 1903), pp. 1–65. The volume consists of six essays. Butler's stands apart from the other five. It is the transcript of a performance, not a work of scholarship. Butler's view of Cromwell was the majority view in Ireland, and was a view understood and sympathised with in England. Unveiling a statue to Cromwell outside the Houses of Parliament in 1899 Earl Rosebery, the Liberal Unionist and former Prime Minister,

had remarked: 'I am one of those who were I an Irishman would not be contributing to a statue of Oliver Cromwell'. *Daily News*, 15 Nov. 1899.

13 NLI, Ms. 15,069, Butler to Alice Stopford Green, 28 Aug. 1904.

14 RCWISA, vol. 41, p. 80.

15 Esher to HM, 11 Feb. 1903, in Brett, Reginald Viscount Esher, p. 374–5.

16 Esher to HM, 12 Feb. 1903, ibid.

CHAPTER 16: HOME

1 NLI, Ms. 15,069, Butler to Alice Stopford Green, 21 Mar. 1903.

2 Courtesy of Viscount Gormanston. A revised version of the verses titled 'A Request' is in Gormanston's *A Little Kept*, pp. 37–8.

3 PRO, WO/32/9221.

4 Elizabeth Butler, *Autobiography*, p. 240.

5 NLI, Ms. 15,069, Butler to ASG, 10 Aug. 1905.

6 *Irish Independent*, 10 Oct. 1907.

7 *Ibid.*

8 Gormanston, *A Little Kept*, p. 56.

9 NLI, W.T. Perkins, *Channel Tunnel* (Channel Tunnel Company 1907).

10 NLI, Ms. 15,069, Butler to ASG, 13 Oct. 1909.

11 Butler, *Autobiography*, p. 141.

12 *The Irish Times*, 8 Jun. 1910.

13 *Irish Independent*, 11 Jun. 1910.

14 Butler. *ibid.* Afterword, p. 459.

SOURCES

UNPUBLISHED

Public Archives:

Central Library, Hove. Wolseley Papers.

National Library of Ireland, Dublin. Mss., Butler; Gormanston; Redmond; Stopford Green.

Public Record Office, Kew. Colonial Office Series CO/48 and War Office Series WO/32; WO/33; WO/132.

Private Collections:

Dom Urban Butler, private correspondence, Downside Abbey.

Clongowes Wood College Archives.

Gormanston family archive.

Meynell Papers.

Gertrude Sweetman, ts.

PUBLISHED

Periodicals

Army and Navy Gazette, Canadian Historical Review, Catholic Herald (London), The Cornhill Magazine, The Contemporary Review, Daily Mail, Daily News, Daily Telegraph, Freeman's Journal, The Graphic, The Illustrated London News, Irish Independent, The Irish Times, Leinster Express, Macmillan, The Nineteenth Century, Pall Mall Gazette, The Tablet, The Times, Tipperary Free Press, Tipperary Historical Journal

Reference

Annual Register, Army Lists, 1858–1910, Burke's Irish Family Records, Dictionary of National Biography, Dod's Parliamentary Companion, Hansard Parliamentary Debates, 3rd & 4th series, *Parliamentary Papers*, vols 40-2, *Who Was Who*

SELECT BIBLIOGRAPHY

Affrifah, Kofi, *The Akyem Factor in Ghana's History 1700–1875* (Ghana Universities Press, Accra 2000)

Arthur, Sir George (ed.), *The Letters of Lord and Lady Wolseley, 1870–1911* (Heinemann, London 1922)

Beckett, J.C., *The Making of Modern Ireland 1603–1923* (Faber, London 1966)

Best, Geoffrey, *Mid-Victorian Britain 1851–1875* (Weidenfeld and Nicolson, London 1971)

Blunt, Wilfrid Scawen, *My Diaries.* (Martin Secker, London 1921)

— *The Secret History of the English Occupation of Egypt* (Fisher Unwin, London 1907)

Boyce, D. George, *Nineteenth Century Ireland* (Gill and Macmillan, Dublin 1990)

Brackenbury, Major Sir Henry, *The Ashanti War*, 2 vols (Blackwood, London 1874)

— *The River Column* (Blackwood, London 1885)

Brady, Ciaran, and Edward Gillespie (eds), *Natives and Newcomers* (Irish Academic Press, Dublin 1986)

Brett, M.V. (ed.), *The Journals and Letters of Reginald Viscount Esher* (Ivor Nicholson and Watson, London 1934)

Brogan, Hugh, *Longman History of the United States* (Longman Group, London 1985)

Brown, Dee, *Bury My Heart at Wounded Knee* (Barrie and Jenkins, London 1971)

Bryan, Liz, *The Buffalo People* (University of Alberta Press 1991)

Butler, Lady Elizabeth, *Autobiography* (Fisher Press, Kent 1922)

— *From Sketch Book and Diary* (Constable, London 1909)

Butler, William F., *Akim Foo: The Story of a Failure* (Sampson Low, London 1875)

— *An Autobiography* (Constable, London 1911)

— *The Campaign of the Cataracts* (Sampson Low, London 1887)

— *Charles George Gordon* (Macmillan, London 1889)

— *Far Out: Rovings Re-told* (Isbister, London 1880)

— *From Naboth's Vineyard* (Chapman and Hall, London 1906)

— *The Great Lone Land* (Sampson Low, London 1872)

— *The Invasion of England* (Sampson Low, London 1882)
— *The Life of George Pomeroy Colley* (John Murray, London 1899)
— *The Light of the West* (Gill, London 1909)
— *A Narrative of Historical Events Connected with the Sixty-Ninth Regiment* (Mitchell, London 1870)
— *Red Cloud* (Sampson Low, London 1882)
— *Sir Charles Napier* (Macmillan, London 1890)
— *The Wild North Land* (Sampson Low, London 1874)
Cosgrove, Art (ed.), *A New History of Ireland*, vol. II (Clarendon Press, Oxford 1987)
Daly, M.W., (ed) *The Cambridge History of Egypt*, vol. II (Cambridge University Press 1998)
Davenport, T.R.H., *South Africa: A Modern History*, 3rd edn (Macmillan, London 1987)
Duffy, J. Dennis, 'Mapping the Great Lone Land: How the Butlers Did It' (University College Dublin 1995), Inaugural lecture, Craig Dobbin Chair of Canadian Studies.
Fitzpatrick, J. Perc., *The Transvaal from Within* (Heinemann, London 1900)
— *South African Memories* (Cassell and Company, London 1932)
Flanagan, T., *Louis 'David' Riel; Prophet of the New World* (University of Toronto Press 1979)
Fleming, G.H., *Lady Colin Campbell: Victorian 'Sex Goddess'* (The Windrush Press, Gloucesterhire 1989)
Flint, John E. (ed.), *The Cambridge History of Modern Africa*, vol. 5 (Cambridge University Press 1976)
— *Cecil Rhodes* (Hutchinson, London 1976)
Forde, Daryll and P.M. Carberry (eds), *West African Kingdoms in the Nineteenth Century* (Oxford University Press 1967)
Foster, R.F., *Modern Ireland 1600–1972* (Allen Lane, London 1988)
Friesen, G., *The Canadian Prairies: A History* (University of Toronto Press 1984)
Garvin, J.L., *Life of Joseph Chamberlain*, vols 2 & 3 (Macmillan, London 1933/34)
Gormanston, Lady Eileen, *A Little Kept* (Sheed and Ward, London 1953)
Green, Stopford Alice, *Irish Nationality* (Williams and Northgate, London 1911)
— *The Making of Ireland and Its Undoing* (Macmillan, London 1908)
Gwynn, Stephen, *Experiences of a Literary Man* (Thornton Butterworth, London 1926)
Hake, A. Egmont, *The Journals of Major-General Gordon at Khartoum* (Kegan Paul Trench, London 1885)
Haggard, H. Rider, *The Days of My Life*, 2 vols (Longmans, London 1926)
Hall, R., *Stanley: An Adventurer Explored* (Collins, London 1974)
Hancock, W.K., *The Sanguine Years*, 2 vols (Cambridge University Press 1962)
Hamilton, Albina, *These Are The Prairies* (Regina Press, Saskatchewan 1948)
Hardy, W.G., *From Sea unto Sea* (Doubleday, New York 1970)
Harries-Jenkins, Gwynn, *The Army in Victorian Society* (Routledge Kegan Paul, London 1977)

Harris, Christina Phelps, *Nationalism and Revolution in Egypt: The Role of the Muslim Brotherhood* (Hoover Institution on War, Revolution and Peace, The Hague 1964)

Headlam, Cecil (ed.), *Milner Papers*, 2 vols (Cassells, London 1931 & 1933)

Hill, Douglas, *The Opening of the Canadian West* (Heinemann, London 1967)

Hobsbawm, E.J., *The Age of Empire* (Weidenfeld and Nicolson, London 1987

— *Industry and Empire: An Economic History of Britain since 1750* (Weidenfeld and Nicolson, London 1968))

Horral, S.W., 'Sir John A. Macdonald and the Mounted Police Force for the Northwest Territories.' *Canadian Historical Review*, vol. LIII, no. 2 (1972)

Hutchins, Francis G., *The Illusion of Permanence: British Imperialism in India* (Princeton University Press 1967)

Judd, Denis, *Radical Joe. A Life of Joseph Chamberlain* (Hamish Hamilton, London 1977)

Kiernan, V.G., *The Lords of Human Kind* (Weidenfeld and Nicolson, London 1969)

Lehmann, Joseph, *All Sir Garnet: A Life of Field Marshal Lord Wolseley* (Jonathan Cape, London 1964)

— *The First Boer War* (Jonathan Cape, London 1972)

Leslie, Shane, *Salutation to Five* (Hollis and Carter, London 1951)

Lichthein, George, *Imperialism* (Allen Lane, London 1971)

Lyons, F.S., *Ireland Since the Famine* (Weidenfeld and Nicolson, London 1971)

McCarthy, Justin, *A History of Our Own Times* (Chatto & Windus, London 1880)

McCartney, Donal, *UCD: A National Idea* (Gill and Macmillan, Dublin 1999)

McCourt, Edward, *Remember Butler* (Routledge & Kegan Paul, London 1967)

McMillan, Alan D., *Native Peoples and Cultures of Canada* (Douglas and McIntyre, Vancouver 1988)

McNaught, Kenneth, *The Pelican History of Canada*, 2nd edn (Penguin, Harmondsworth 1988)

Marlowe, John, *John Cecil Rhodes: The Anatomy of Empire* (Paul Elek, London 1972)

Maxwell, Leigh, *The Ashanti Ring* (Leo Cooper, London 1985)

Melville, C.H., *Life of General the Rt. Hon. Sir Redvers Buller*, 2 vols (Arnold, London 1923)

Meynell, Alice, *John Ruskin* (Blackwood, London 1900)

Meynell, Viola, *Alice Meynell* (Scribners, London 1929)

Miller, J.R., 'From Riel to the Métis'. *Canadian Historical Review*, vol. LXIX, no. 1 (1988)

Milner, Sir Alfred, *England in Egypt* (Arnold, London 1902)

Morris, Donald R., *The Washing of The Spears* (Jonathan Cape, London 1966)

Morrissey, Thomas S.J., *Towards a National University: William Delany S.J. 1835–1924* (Wolfhound Press, Dublin 1983)

Neidhardt, W.S., *Fenianism in North America* (Pennsylvania State University Press 1975)

O'Brien, R. Barry, *Studies in Irish History* (Browne and Nolan, London 1903)

O'Connor, T.P., (ed) *Cabinet of Irish Literature*, vol. 4 (Blackie and Son, London 1880)

O'Meara, Barry E., *Napoleon in Exile: or, A Voice from St. Helena*, 2 vols (Simpkin and Marshall, London 1822)

Oliver, R. and T.D. Fage, *A Short History of Africa*, 6th edn (Penguin Books, London 1988)

Oliver, Roland, and G.N. Sanderson (eds), *The Cambridge History of Africa*, vol. 6 (Cambridge University Press 1985)

Owram, Douglas, 'The Myth of Louis Riel', *Canadian Historical Review*, vol. LXIII, no. 3 (1982)

Pakenham, Thomas, *The Boer War* (Futura, London 1982)

— *The Scramble for Africa* (Weidenfeld and Nicolson, London 1991)

Perkins, W.T., (ed) *Channel Tunnel* (Channel Tunnel Company, London 1907)

Porter, A. N., *The Origins of the South African War: Joseph Chamberlain and the Diplomacy of Imperialism* (Manchester University Press 1980)

Porter, Andrew, (ed) *The Oxford History of the British Empire*, vol III (Oxford University Press 1999)

Powell, Geoffrey, *Buller: A Scapegoat?* (Leo Cooper, London 1994)

Preston, Adrian, (ed) *In Relief of Gordon* (Hutchinson, London 1967)

Reade, Winwood, *The Story of The Ashanti Campaign* (Smith Elder, London 1874)

Richardson, Joanna, *Victor Hugo* (Weidenfeld and Nicolson, London 1976)

Rive, Richard, *Olive Schreiner: Letters*, 2 vols (Oxford University Press 1988)

Robinson, John, *A Lifetime in South Africa* (Smith Elder & Co, London 1900)

Robinson, Ronald, *Africa and The Victorians; the Official Mind of Imperialism* (Macmillan, London 1981)

Royle, Charles, *The Egyptian Campaigns* (Hurst and Blackett, London 1900)

Ruskin, John, *The Bible of Amiens* (George Allen, London 1908)

Seeley, J.R., *The Expansion of England* (Macmillan, London 1884)

Senior, Hereward, *The Fenians and Canada* (Macmillan of Canada, Toronto 1978)

Smith, Iain R., *The Origins of the South African War* (Longman, London 1996)

Snead-Cox, J.G., *Life of Cardinal Vaughan*, 2 vols (Burnes and Oates, London 1910)

Spear, Percival, *The Oxford History of Modern India, 1740–1975*, 2nd edn (Oxford University Press 1978)

Stanley, George F.G., *Louis Riel* (The Ryerson Press, Toronto 1963)

Stanley, Henry Morton, *Coomassie and Magdala* (Sampson Low, London 1874)

Stead, W.T., (ed) *Coming Men on Coming Matters XI* (Whitefriars Street, London 1905)

Stone, Laurence, *Road to Divorce: England 1530–1987* (Oxford University Press 1990)

Stone, Norman, *Europe Transformed* (Fontana, London 1983)

Storey, Graham, Kathleen Tillotson, Angus Easson, (eds) *The Letters of Charles Dickens*, vol. 7 (Clarendon Press, Oxford 1993)

Surridge, Keith T., *Managing the South African War 1899–1902* (The Boydell Press, Woodbridge 1998)

Symons, Julian, *England's Pride: The Story of the Gordon Relief Expedition* (Hamish Hamilton, London 1965)

Tignour, Robert L., *Modernisation and British Colonial Rule in Egypt, 1882–1914* (Princeton University Press 1966)

Trigger, Bruce G., and Wilcomb E. Washburn (eds), *The Cambridge History of the Native Peoples of the Americas*, vol. I, part 2 (Cambridge University Press 1996)

Underhill, Ruth M., *Red Man's America* (University of Chicago Press 1971)

Usherwood, Paul, and Jenny Spencer-Smith, *Lady Butler: Battle Artist* (Alan Sutton, Gloucester 1987)

Vatikiotis, P.J., *The History of Modern Egypt: from Muhammad Ali to Mubarak,* 4th edn (Weidenfeld & Nicholson, London 1969)

Vaughan, W.E., (ed) *A New History of Ireland*, vols V & VI (Clarendon Press, Oxford 1989 & 1996)

Wolseley, Field Marshall Viscount, *The Soldier's Pocketbook*. 3rd edn (Macmillan, London 1874)

—A *Story of a Soldier's Life*, 2 vols (Constable, London 1903)

Wood, Field Marshall Sir Evelyn, *Winnowed Memories* (Cassell, London 1918)

WILLIAM FRANCIS BUTLER: A CHRONOLOGY

1838 31 October, born Ballyslatteen, Co. Tipperary.
1858 17 September, gazetted Ensign without Purchase, 69th Regiment of Foot.
1860 November, Madras, India.
1863 November, Lieutenant by Purchase.
1864 May, return to United Kingdom.
1867 March, the Curragh; September, Canada.
1870 *History of The Sixty-Ninth Regiment* published; The Red River Expedition.
1870–1 Commission to the Saskatchewan.
1871 May, Fellow of the Royal Geographical Society.
1872 Promoted to Captain; *The Great Lone Land* published.
1872–3 Winter on the Saskatchewan; trek across the Rockies.
1873–4 The Gold Coast and the Ashanti War.
1874 *The Wild North Land* published; promoted to Major, order of Companion of the Bath.
1875 April-August, Natal; *Akim Foo* published.
1876 April, introduction to Elizabeth Thompson.
1877 11 June, marriage to Elizabeth Thompson.
1879 March, Natal and the Zulu War.
1880 Promoted Lieutenant-Colonel; assigned Assistant Adjutant General, Western District, Devonport; *Far Out: Rovings Retold* published.
1882 *Red Cloud* published; Egypt, Tel-El-Kebir; aide-de-camp to Queen Victoria.
1884–5 The Gordon Relief Expedition.
1885–6 Officer Commanding, Wadi Halfa; Brigadier-General.
1886 December, the Campbell divorce case.
1887 April, invested as Knight Commander of the Bath; *Campaign of the Cataracts* published.
1888 April, moved to Delgany, Co. Wicklow.
1888 December, Assistant Adjutant General, War Office.

1889 Parnell and the Pigott forgeries; *Charles Gordon* published.

1890 March, Officer Commanding, Alexandria; *Sir Charles Napier* published.

1892 December, promoted Major-General.

1893 November, Officer Commanding, 2nd Infantry Brigade, Aldershot.

1896 February, Officer Commanding, South-Eastern District, Dover.

1898 November, Officer Commanding, HMF South Africa, Acting High Commissioner, South Africa, and Acting Governor Cape Colony.

1899 *Sir George Pomeroy Colley* published; August, leaves South Africa after resigning his post; appointed Officer Commanding, Western District, Devonport.

1901 Membership of the Irish Literary Society, London.

1902 Promoted Lieutenant-General.

1905 June, *The Butler Report* published; purchase of Bansha Castle, Co. Tipperary, and retirement to Ireland.

1906 Tour of South Africa; invested as Knight Grand Cross of the Bath; *From Naboth's Vineyard* published.

1908 Senator, National University of Ireland.

1909 Privy Councillor, Ireland; *The Light of the West* published.

1910 7 June, died at Bansha Castle.

INDEX

Abu Klea, 114

Accra, 55, 56, 60

Act of Union, 70, *see also* United Kingdom of Great Britain and Ireland

Adye, General Sir John, 95, 99-100

Afghanistan, 72, 86

Afrikaaners, 169, 170, 182, 187

Aldershot, 16, 162, 193

Alexandria, 94, 106, 159, 161

Akim, 55-62 *passim*

Amoaful, battle of, 60

Archibald, Adam, 35, 36, 91

Asante, 50-65 *passim* 150

Baker, Colonel Valentine, 105, 226n

Balkans, 72, 104

Ballycarron, Co. Tipperary, 2, 3, 209

Ballyslatteen, Co. Tipperary, 2, 4, 5, 9, 25, 85

Ballyslatteen House, 4, 209

Bansha, Co. Tipperary, 209, 210, 213, 216

Bansha Castle, 209, 210, 211, 214, 216

Baring, Evelyn, Lord Cromer, 103, 159, 161

Basutoland, 70

Bird, Thomas, 136, 138-44 *passim*

Blandford, Marquess of, George Spencer Churchill, 112, 134-38 *passim*

Blood, Gertrude, *see* Campbell, Lady Colin

Bloomfontein, 69, 182, 183

Blunt, Wilfrid Scawen, 94, 199, 226n

Boers, 67, 69, 87-8, 166-81 *passim*

Brackenbury, Lt. General Sir Henry, 52, 67, 72, 79, 108-18 *passim*, 188, 216

Brand, President Jan Hendrik, 69

Brantford, 20, 22

British army, 8-9, 10, 23, 42, 71, 79, 87, 157, 165, 179

Brodrick, St John, 193, 195, 196, 203

Buller, General Sir Redvers, 22, 52, 72-9 *passim*, 108, 157, 188, 189, 191, 194, 195

Burma, 11, 23

Butler Report, 207-8

Butler, Lady Elizabeth, *née* Thompson,
64, 81-6, 113, 119, 122, 124, 128, 148-52, 158-61, 162, 163, 172, 178, 187, 190-1, 198-9, 204, 206, 207, 209, 211, 212-13, 216

PAINTINGS
After the Battle, 98; *Balaclava*, 83; *Evicted*, 158-9; *Missing*, 82; '*Listed for The Connaught Rangers*', 85; *The Remnants of an Army*, 86; *Return from Inkeremann*, 84; *The Roll Call*, 64, 81, 82, 83; *Rorke's Drift*, 86

Butler, Ellen, *née* Dillon, 3, 5, 6

Butler, Henry, 9

Butler, Martin, 120, 199

Butler, Mary Patricia, 85

Butler, Patrick, 86, 122, 128, 199, 205

Butler, Richard, 90, 198

Butler, Richard (father of W.F.), 1, 3, 4, 7, 9, 25

Butler, Thomas, 25, 222n

Butler, Lt-General Sir William Francis, KGCB

ACTIVITIES AND INTERESTS
athletics, 9; buffalo hunting, 21-2; canoeing, 31-2, 47, 215; dogs, 28-30, 39, 45, 46-7, 162; history, 200; horse riding, 10, 11, 28, 70, 161, 162; literature, 7, 20, 86; military history, 14-15, 17, 83; Napoleon, 14-16, 129, 162-3, 211, 213; trekking, 37-9 ,41, 46-8; walking, 17; wildfowl shooting, 10, 28, 35

BELIEFS AND ATTITUDES
ideal of service, 184, 189; imperialism, 10-11, 37, 39-40, 51-2, 68, 83-4, 87-8, 91, 94, 152, 199; Irish nationality/nationalism 5, 18, 19, 70, 89-90, 120, 152-5, 156, 157-8, 186, 199-201, 205, 211-12, *see also* Home Rule/Home Rule Party; religion, 18, 63, 80, 84, 162, 163, 204

BOOKS
Akim Foo, 55, 65; *An Autobiography*, 1, 214-5; *The Campaign of the Cataracts*,

118; *Sir George Pomeroy Colley*, 116-17; *Far Out : Rovings Retold*, 86; *The Great Lone Land*, 36-9, 44, 46, 49, 54, 91, 215; *Charles George Gordon*, 152-3; *The Invasion of England*, 87; *The Light of the West*, 214; *From Naboth's Vineyard*, 211; *Sir Charles Napier*, 153-4; *A Narrative of the 69th Regiment*, 17, 22; *Red Cloud*, 49, 90-92, 225n; *The Wild North Land*, 46, 47, 49, 214

CHARACTER TRAITS

considerate, 78, 124, 128, 129, 187, 193; energetic, 9-10, 22, 28, 54, 74, 90, *see also* TRAVELS; impetuous, 99-100, 110; intelligent, 23, 38, 115, 157, 177, 202, 207; money-conscious, 7, 13, 113; organizational ability, 11, 59, 74, 95, 96, 99, 106, 112, 117, 119, 122, 125, 162, 193; outspoken, 72, 75, 76, 77, 88, 99-100, 126, 154, 172, 179, 185, 195-6, 202; painstaking, 125, 157, 166, 209; reflective, 10-11, 44, 50, 64, 68-9, 91, 154, 187, 206; restrained, 189-90, 192; self-reliant, 28-32, 38, 46-8, 118; witty, 12-13, 20, 28, 70, 74, 112, 126, 160-61, 165, 202, 208

CONTEMPORARY ASSESSMENTS OF

Sir Charles Parker Butt, 144; Duke of Cambridge, 63-4; Edward VII, 198; Viscount Esher, 192-3, 202-3; Eileen Gormanston, 164; Stephen Gwynn, 200; H. Rider Haggard, 70-71; Victor Hugo, 18; Cardinal Logue, 211-12; Viscount Milner, 170, 176, 181; Winwood Reade, 62; Henry Morton Stanley, 54, 62; Lt-General Stephenson, 124, 130; Viscount Wolseley, 23-4, 55, 111, 118, 186, 215

MILITARY LIFE AND CAREER

ensign, 9; Fermoy, 9; training, 9; India, 10-14; Burma, 11; lieutenant, 13; England, 16; Aldershot, 16-17, 162, 193; Guernsey, 17; the Curragh, 19; Canada, 19-24; battle of Trout River, 27; Red River Expedition, 28-33; Saskatchewan Expedition, 35-41; captain, 44; Asante Expedition, 51-65; major, 63; Companion of the Bath, 63; Natal, 66-70, 74-8, 176-7; Orange Free State, 69; War Office, 71-2, 157; lieutenant-colonel, 80; Devonport, 80, 86, 93, 101, 103, 146, 186-208 *passim*; Egyptian campaign, 95-101; river column on

Gordon Relief Expedition, 107-12; battle of Kerbekan, 115-16; Merowe, 118-9; Wadi Halfa, 122, 127-31; battle of Ginnis, 125-6; sick leave, 131; Knight Commander of the Bath, 152; army ordnance report, 157; colonel, 157; OC, Alexandria, 159-61; OC, Dover, 163; GOC, South Africa, 171-87; acting high commissioner to South Africa, 171-6; lieutenant-general, 198; Army Remount enquiry, 194-5; commission into the war in South Africa, 201-3; *The Butler Report*, 207-8; retirement, 210; Knight Grand Cross of the Bath, 211

PERSONAL AND FAMILY

ancestry, 2; appearance, 9; attraction to women, 13, 38, 67, 83, 136, 141; baptism, 2; bereavements, 6, 7, 25, 85; birth, 2; children, 85, 86, 90, 102, 120, 128, 151, 172, 198-9; courtship and marriage, 81, 83-4, 150; death, 215; fatherhood, 84, 151, 162, 163-4; funeral, 216; honeymoon, 84-5; parents, 3, 6-7; schooling, 5-6, 7; siblings, 4, 25, 63, 81, 163, 216

TRAVELS *see also* MILITARY LIFE AND CAREER

Belgium, 17; Canada, 20, 22, 28-41, 45-8, 102; Cyprus, 73; Napoleonic battlefields, 17, 160; Palestine, 161; Paris, 25, 42-3; Rome, 163; St Helena, 14-16, 80, 211; southern India, 13; South Africa, 210-11; United States, 20-22, 28, 45, 48

VIEWS ON

Africans, 50, 55-6, 67, 79; Arabs, 98, 119; army, 10, 16, 87, 111; army bureaucracy, 71, 157; army contractors, 71-2, 207-8; Boers, 69-70, 166-7; Burmese, 11; Christian missioners, 46; civilization, 10-11, 44, 45, 102; Cromwell, 200; democracy, 90; denominational education, 201; Gaelic League, 214; Germany, 42, 85; Home Rule, 155; international finance, 94, 172, 175, 185; Irish national education system, 20; Métis, 25-6, 39; military conscription, 86; modern Irishmen, 211-12; Napoleon, 14-15, 163; Native Americans, 36-7, 39, 49, 91; War Office, 72, 207; West Africa, 65

Cahir, 2, 4

Cambridge, Duke of, 63, 71, 87, 157

Campbell, Lady Colin, née Blood, 101, 133-49 *passim*

Campbell, Lord Colin, 111, 134-45 *passim*

Canada, 19-20, 25-6, 90 *see also* Butler, W.F., MILITARY LIFE AND CAREER/TRAVELS

Cape Coast Castle, 52, 53, 54

Cape Colony, 168-86 *passim*, 210

Capetown, 78, 172-86 *passim*

Cardwell, Edward, 42, 52, 71

Case, Horatio Nelson, 22, 24, 41

Cashel, 4

Catholic Truth Society, 204, 211-12

Celtic Revival, 199

Cerf Volant, 39, 41, 45, 47, 48, 86

Ceteswayo, King, 73-8 *passim*

Chamberlain, Joseph, 169-82 *passim*, 195-8, 201

Channel Tunnel, 213

Chelmsford, Lt-General Lord, 74, 75, 77

Churchill, Winston, 114, 209

Clongowes Wood, Co. Kildare, 205, 213

Colley, Edith, née Hamilton, 67, 87, 166

Colley, Major-General Sir George Pomeroy, 53, 67-9, 75, 79, 87-8, 166-7

commando, 69, 167

Connaught, Duke of, 95, 101, 162, 182, 190

Cooper, James Fenimore, 20

Corcoran, Timothy, S.J., 225n

Cree, 36, 39, 40, 45

Crimea, 7, 8, 9

Croagh Patrick, 204

Cromwell, Oliver, 4, 200, 230n

Curragh military camp, 19

Delany, William S.J., 214

Delgany, 155-6, 157, 158

Devonport, 80, 86, 93, 101, 103, 105, 146, 187-208 *passim, see also* Plymouth

Dickens, Charles, 81, 82, 102

Dickens, Frank, 102

Dinan, 132, 151, 152

Disraeli, Benjamin, Beaconsfield, Earl of, 72, 93

Doherty, Richard, 9

Dongola, 106, 107-19 *passim*

Dover Castle, 163, 165, 166

Downside Abbey, 199, 204

Drury Lowe, General, 95, 99

Dunboyne, James, 9th Earl, 2

Dunboyne, Lord, 221n

Dunraven, Earl of, 101, 102

Durban, 67, 74-8 *passim*

Earle, Major-General William, 113, 115, 116

Edgar, Thomas, 174

Edmonton, 38, 102

Edward VII, King, 101, 194, 198, 202-3, 211, 216

Egypt, 93-101 *passim*, 103-06 *passim*, 159

Elgin, Earl of, 201

Esher, Viscount, 192, 201-3

Fenianism/Fenians, 19, 20, 27, 89

Fermoy, Co. Cork, 9, 24

First Nations of Canada, 36-7, 39, 45-6, 49, 90-91

Ford, Henry, 161

Fort Garry, 25-36 *passim*, 41, 45

Fort Kearney, 21

Fort Phil Kearney, 223n

Fort Pitt, 38, 102

Foster, Arnold, 207

French, Lt-Colonel George Arthur, 41

Frere, Sir Bartle, 73, 180

Froude, James Anthony, 70

Gaelic League, 214

Galtee Mountains, 4, 19, 209, 213

Garvin, J.L., 229n

Gemai, 109

Gifford, Captain Lord Ederic, 67, 72, 79

Ginnis, battle of, 124-5

Gladstone, Sir William Ewart, 42, 80, 87, 99, 100, 103, 106, 153, 162, 192

Glencar, 85, 121, 131, 171

Glover, Captain John, 53-62 *passim*

Gold Coast, 50-51, 66

Gordon, General Charles, 80, 100, 104-19 *passim*, 152-4

Gormanston, Co. Meath, 216

Gormanston, Eileen, née Butler, 102, 151, 163-4, 199, 212

Gormanston, Jenico Edward Preston, 15th Viscount, 213

Great Famine, 2, 5, 89

Green, Alice Stopford, 200, 210, 214

Gregory, Lady Augusta, 100

Grenfell, Major General, 121-29 *passim*

Guernsey, 17, 18

Gwynn, Stephen, 200

Haggard, H. Rider, 70, 88
Hamilton, General Sir Ian, 108
Headlam, Cecil, 229n
Hely-Hutchinson, Walter, 176, 229n
Hicks, William, 103
Home Rule, 155-62
Home Rule Party, 89, 121, 155, 162, 205
Hugo, Victor, 17-18
Hythe, Hampshire, 16, 163

Iolanthe, 227n
Irish Literary Society, 199-200
Irish nationalist MPs, 156, 157, 158, 199
Irish Parliamentary Party, *see* Home Rule Party
Isandhlwana, 73, 74

Jameson, Leander Starr, 169
Jameson Raid, 169, 184
jingoism, 72

Kelly-Kenny, General Sir Thomas, 197, 216
Kerbekan, battle of, 115-6
Kerry, County, 65, 85, 91
Khartoum, 103-17 *passim*
Killadrigh, Co. Tipperary, 25, 216
Kimberley, 69, 168, 180, 191
Kingscote, Elizabeth 'Coos', *née* Butler, 86, 122, 128, 151, 198, 204
Kingscote, Randolf, 198, 204, 216
Kitchener, General Lord Herbert Horatio, 193-4
Kofi, Kari Kari, King, 51-61 *passim*
Korti, 112-18 *passim*
Kosheh, 122-25 *passim*
Kruger, President Paul, 168-82 *passim*
Kumasi, Ghana, 51-61 *passim*

Lake of the Woods, Ontario, 32
Land League, 89
Land War, 89
Lansdowne, Marquis of, 171, 184-8 *passim*
Leeds, 208
Leo XIII, Pope, 163, 204
Liberal Party, 80, 155, 192, 193, 208-9
Lloyd George, David, 193
Lockwood, Frank, 139
Logue, Cardinal, 211

MacCalmont, Lt Hugh, 79
McCann, James, 200, 205

McCourt, Edward, 146
Macdonald, Sir John A., 41
Mackenzie River, 90, 150
Madeira, 63, 70, 175
Madras, 11, 12, 13
Majuba, 88, 166, 177, 188
Malabar Coast, 13
Manning, Cardinal Henry, 83, 84, 145
Mansfield, Jim, 13, 20, 45
Maurice, Frederick, 79
Merowe, 118-9
Métis, peoples, 25, 26, 36, 39
Meyer, Kuno, 200
Meynell, Alice, *née* Thompson, 81-85 *passim*, 193
Meynell, Wilfrid, 84, 85, 146, 201
Milner, Alfred, Viscount, 170-85 *passim*, 201, 210
Montreal, 23, 24, 27
Morley, John, 155
Muhammad Ahmad, the 'Mahdi', 103, 106, 121
Mulrany, Co. Mayo, 204, 206
Murphy, John Patrick, 139

Napier, General Sir Charles, 153-4
Napoleon Bonaparte, 14-16, 37, 129, 162-3, 213
Napoleon, Eugene Louis, 76-7, 80, 86
Napoleon, Empress Eugenie, 76, 80, 162, 193
Napoleon III, Louis Bonaparte, 17, 42, 76
Natal, 65-71 *passim*, 168, 176-7
National University of Ireland, 214
Nazareth, 161
Netley, Royal Victoria Hospital, 63, 81
New Inn, 2
Niagara Falls, 20
North-West Mounted Police, 41

O'Connell, Daniel, 5
Ojibwa, 31, 32, 34
Omaha, Nebraska, 20
O'Meara, Barry, 15, 129
Orange Free State, 68, 69, 168, 210
O'Shea, Katherine, *née* Wood, 52, 139, 158, 162
Ottawa, 27, 41, 105, 106

Paris, 25, 42-4
Parnell, Charles Stewart, 89, 121, 155, 156, 158, 186

Peace River, 47
Pembina, United States, 26, 28
Penal Laws, 3
Petrolia, Ontario, 22, 24
Phoenix Park murders, 156
Pietermaritzburg, 67, 70
Pirates of Penzance, The, 75
Pius IX, Pope, 18
Plains Indians, 36, 91 *see also* First Nations
    of Canada
Plunkett, Sir Horace, 200
Plymouth, 80, 86, 90, 101, 106 *see also* De-
    vonport
Prince, William, 109
Purchase system, 8, 13, 42, 87

Rainy River, Ontario, 32, 34, 219
Reade, Winwood, 53, 62, 63
Red Cloud (Mahpiua Luta), 49, 223n
Red River, 26, 28-35 *passim*
Redmond, John, 199, 201, 205
Remount Department, 194-5, 198, 203
Repeal Movement, 5
Rhodes, Cecil, 168-75 *passim*
Richmond Gaol, 5
Riel, Louis, 25-6, 29-33 *passim*, 222n
Ripon, Marquess of, 80
Roberts, Field Marshal Lord, 79, 188, 194,
    203
Robertson-Ross, Colonel, 41
Robinson, John, 67
Roosevelt, Theodore, 215
Rorke's Drift, Natal, 74
Rosebery, Lord, 162, 230n
Royal Commission into the War in South
    Africa, 201-3
Royal Geographical Society, 42,44
Royal Hibernian Military Academy, 211
Royal Hospital, Kilmainham, 162
Ruskin, John, 83, 86, 193
Russell, Brevet-Major Baker, 52
Russell, Sir Charles, 139, 158
Ryan, Canon Arthur, 216, 217

St Helena, island of, 14-16, 80, 211
St Laurence O'Toole, Academy of, 7
Salisbury, Lord, 156, 159
Schreiner, Olive, 172, 187
Schreiner, W. P., 172, 182, 187
Selborne, Earl, 176, 181, 184
Shaw, Eyre Massey, 112, 135, 144
Sinclair, Mary, 38, 102

Smith, Donald, 201
Smuts, Jan, 179
South African League (SAL), 171-84, 202
South African War (Great Boer War), 188,
    191
Stanley, Henry Morton, 54, 107 223n
Stephenson, Lt-General Sir Frederick,
    106, 122-30 *passim*
Stewart, Major-General Sir Herbert, 79,
    95, 102-14 *passim*
Sudan, 108-29 *passim*
Suez Canal, 92-6 *passim*
Sweetman, Captain Michael, 163

Tawfiq, Khedive, 93-4, 99, 103, 159
Tel-el-Kebir, battle of, 96-8
Tennyson, Alfred Lord, 7, 49, 83
Thompson, Christiana, *née* Weller, 81-2, 83
Thompson, Thomas, 81-2
Toronto, 26
Transvaal, 68, 73, 78, 87-8, 168-89 *passim*,
    210
Tullabeg College, Co. Offaly, 6-7, 214

uitlanders, 168-79 *passim*
Ulundi, Zululand, 77
United Kingdom of Great Britain and
    Ireland, 5, 152, 155
Urabi, Ahmad, 94, 98-101 *passim*, 186, 199

Victoria, Queen, 64, 86, 101, 106, 152, 162,
    165, 189, 194

Wadi Halfa, 108-9, 119-30 *passim*, 177
Waldron, Laurence, 205, 216
Waterloo, battle of, 17
Whitford, Lt John, 13
Wodehouse, Ensign, 24, 44
Wolseley, Field Marshal Lord, 7, 23-35, 42,
    51-80, 87, 90, 95-119, 153, 155, 161-2, 165,
    167, 171, 179-91, 193-5, 213, 215, 227n
Wolseley, George, 186
Wolseley, Louisa (*née* Erskine), 24, 67, 104,
    165
Wolseley Ring, 51-3, 79, 95, 107-17 *passim*,
    188, 203
Wood, General Sir Evelyn, 52, 74, 75, 79,
    88, 95, 108, 188, 197
Wyndham, George, 183, 201

Yeats, William Butler, 199

Zulus, 73-8 *passim*